PSYCHOBABBLE

PEARSON

At Pearson, we believe in learning – all kinds of learning for all kinds of people. Whether it's at home, in the classroom or in the workplace, learning is the key to improving our life chances.

That's why we're working with leading authors to bring you the latest thinking and the best practices, so you can get better at the things that are important to you. You can learn on the page or on the move, and with content that's always crafted to help you understand quickly and apply what you've learned.

If you want to upgrade your personal skills or accelerate your career, become a more effective leader or more powerful communicator, discover new opportunities or simply find more inspiration, we can help you make progress in your work and life.

Pearson is the world's leading learning company. Our portfolio includes the Financial Times, Penguin, Dorling Kindersley, and our educational business, Pearson International.

Every day our work helps learning flourish, and wherever learning flourishes, so do people.

To learn more please visit us at: www.pearson.com/uk

PSYCHOBABBLE

EXPLODING THE MYTHS OF THE SELF-HELP GENERATION

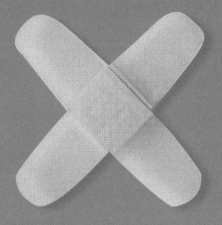

DR STEPHEN BRIERS

PEARSON

Harlow, England • London • New York • Boston • San Francisco • Toronto • Sydney
Auckland • Singapore • Hong Kong • Tokyo • Seoul • Taipei • New Delhi
Cape Town • São Paulo • Mexico City • Madrid • Amsterdam • Munich • Paris • Milan

PEARSON EDUCATION LIMITED

Edinburgh Gate
Harlow CM20 2JE
Tel: +44 (0)1279 623623
Fax: +44 (0)1279 431059
Website: www.pearson.com/uk

First published in Great Britain in 2012

ISBN: 978-0-273-77239-2

British Library Cataloguing-in-Publication Data
A catalogue record for the print edition is available from the British Library

Library of Congress Cataloging-in-Publication Data
Briers, Stephen, 1965-
  Psychobabble : exploding the myths of the self help generation / Stephen Briers.
    p. cm
  Includes bibliographical references.
  ISBN 978-0-273-77239-2 (pbk.)
  1. Self-help techniques--Evaluation. 2. Psychology, Applied. 3. Psychology--Popular works. I. Title
  BF632.B657 2012
  158--dc23
                                        2012029772

10 9 8 7 6 5 4 3 2 1
16 15 14 13 12

Print edition typeset in 11pt Sabon by 3
Printed in Great Britain by Henry Ling Ltd., at the Dorset Press, Dorchester, Dorset

NOTE THAT ANY PAGE CROSS REFERENCES REFER TO THE PRINT EDITION

Contents

Acknowledgements

To my very dear wife and long-suffering sons: thank you for all your patience and support. I promise I won't write anything else for a while. Many thanks also to the team at Pearson, especially Paul East and Elie Williams for all their hard work behind the scenes. This book also owes much to the academics, bloggers and journalists who kindly furnished me with so much stimulating material, and also to Drew and Natalie Dee, creators of *Married To The Sea*. Their genius cartoons made me laugh out loud during a particularly gruelling phase of the writing. Most of all, thank you to my magnificent editor, Rachael Stock, who went way beyond the call of duty and generously offered to edit this book whilst technically on leave. I'm not sure about the wisdom of sawing through the branch you're sitting on (or even helping someone else do so) but you have selflessly steadied my hand and I'm truly grateful. Finally, I want to acknowledge the contribution of my faithful hound, Lola, who has stayed glued to my side throughout the whole process, even though I suspect her devotion may have had something to do with her ability to persuade me to keep on putting my hand in the biscuit tin and turn a blind eye whenever she snuck up on the sofa in my office. I have only two words to say to her: GET DOWN!

PUBLISHER'S ACKNOWLEDGEMENTS

Cartoons from the strip, Married To The Sea (marriedtothesea. com).

'Men willingly believe what they wish.'

JULIUS CAESAR

'I believe in an open mind,
but not so open that your brains fall out.'

ARTHUR HAYS SULZBERGER

'Man is what he believes.'

ANTON CHEKHOV

Introduction

WHAT'S SO WRONG WITH POPULAR PSYCHOLOGY ANYWAY?

We live in the age of self-improvement. As we go about our daily lives we are subjected to a million messages – some subtle, and some less so – intimating that a happier, richer, more successful life is just around the corner. With the immediate survival needs of food and shelter taken care of for the majority, western civilisation has now turned its attention to how much better it could all be. And this in turn has spawned a prolific, multi-million dollar industry of stadium-filling gurus, bestselling books, magazines and websites telling us how to be happier, thinner, richer, and all round better people. But is our culture of self-help really helping? Or is it just creating expectations that none of us can live up to? Has the casual psychologising of everyday life enlightened us, or are we just making a rod for own backs?

These are questions we all need to be grappling with. This book is an invitation to pause, take stock, and maybe start weeding out some of the more insidious modern myths that have taken root in our collective psyche. I'm not simply trying to be a killjoy or score cheap points at other people's expense. I fully appreciate that many contributors to the burgeoning self-help industry are sincere, well-intentioned individuals who genuinely want others to benefit from their wisdom and experience. The majority are not charlatans out to make a quick buck from our credulity. Some are well-informed and well-qualified to offer advice, and such people absolutely deserve to be listened to. However, insofar as this does feel like a grumpy tirade, it's because I am increasingly concerned that something significant is happening within our society to which we continue to turn a naively blind eye.

It's too easy to dismiss the world of self-help as an amusing diversion, a quick read on the plane or a pleasant escapist fantasy of a life reinvented and transformed. Maybe we might even pick up a few handy tips or a couple of insights along the way. What's the harm? After all, nobody takes these things that seriously, do they? But the truth is that secretly many of us do. Increasing numbers of us are turning to the pages of self-help books in search of answers to lives that feel in need of fixing. The phenomenal growth of the self-help sector in the last century is a testament not only to our rising levels of insecurity and self-doubt, but to the stealthy psychologising of our culture as a whole.

The ideas and values associated with popular psychology have infiltrated our culture so deeply that we now take them largely for granted. Even for those of us who regard ourselves as fairly knowing, they form part of that framework of assumptions that constitutes the invisible scaffolding for the way we approach our lives. They shape our evaluations of other people and ourselves. They subtly colour the tone of everyday experience, bringing with them an agenda that radically affects the kinds of decisions and choices we make both as individuals and as a society. Rather alarmingly, much of this has taken place without us ever having paused to examine these precepts, or to question whether we can afford to follow where they lead. Whilst we may like to think that popular psychology holds up a mirror that allows us to understand ourselves, it is also a distorting mirror that remakes us in its own image. In *The Selfish Gene*, Richard Dawkins introduced us to the *meme*, defined as 'an idea, behaviour or style that spreads from person to person within a culture'. Thanks to the powerful engine of the self-help industry, the memes of popular psychology are busy replicating themselves so effectively that they have become an integral part of the fabric of our lives and thought processes.

Consider, by way of illustration, the popularity of talent shows like *The X Factor*. The format dictates that every contestant must undergo a journey of personal transformation. Their motivations are accounted for in terms of an emotive back story that usually implies some cod-psychological rationale for their decision to audition while the audience is invited to nod (and vote) approvingly as contestants 'grow' as artists and people over the ensuing weeks. Shania is a natural talent but 'just needs to believe in herself more'. Ricky could be world-class but needs to get in touch with who he really is inside if he is ever to give a truly 'authentic' winning performance. And Cassie could be great if she ever manages to let go of those emotional demons from her past.

Under the guidance of mentors whose assertive sound bites would make many motivational speakers blush, the contestants are prompted to change their lives and take charge of their fates. If they can just believe hard enough, give it 110 per cent, focus on their goals and 'stay in the zone', then maybe that elusive recording contract will be theirs. However, all the while the pseudo-psychological lore of such shows whispers in our ear that the true prize on offer is not the record contract but the personal fulfilment awaiting anyone brave enough to try and 'live their dream'.

You can dismiss this all as good storytelling by the production company but these format points are also an indication of the extent to which popular psychology and popular culture have become intimately fused. Psychobabble is a language that, like it or not, we are all learning to speak fluently, and elements of those Saturday night prime-time shows could have been lifted straight from the pages of the countless self-help books that line the shelves of your local bookstore, not to mention the CDs purchased and training courses attended by millions of us every year.

The most successful self-help books have a long reach:

classics like *How to Win Friends and Influence People* and *I'm OK, You're OK* are said to have sold 15 million copies worldwide. *You Can Heal Your Life* by Louise Hay has sold over 35 million, while *Men are from Mars, Women are from Venus* and the *Chicken Soup for the Soul* series claim over 50 million and 100 million sales respectively. These are big numbers in the publishing world. If you are reading this you will almost certainly have heard of these books and probably have a fair idea of what is in them. But even if you haven't, you will still have been affected by them.

The congregational minister Edwin Paxton Hood once admonished: 'Be as careful of the books you read, as of the company you keep; for your habits and character will be influenced as much by the latter as by the former.' Perhaps we should be taking his advice to heart. The values and preoccupations of popular psychology are already profoundly influencing the nature of the stories we tell ourselves about who we are and who we can become. The question we need to ask is, when we take a cold hard look at the outcome, do we really like what we see?

KEEPING IT SIMPLE

One of the major selling points of any good self-help book is actually one of the most misleading, namely the promise that it will distil a potentially complex situation or life challenge into a manageable and readily digestible form. This would be great if it were remotely possible. As you may have noticed as you have fumbled along through the years, human beings are complex, their lives are complex, and the social environment they are trying to navigate is complex. There are innumerable variables involved in even the most simple of human activities. As the new branch of science known as 'chaos theory' has been amply demonstrating over recent years, even small local variations can produce a truly bewildering variety of outcomes – so great in fact as to render prediction virtually impossible, even in a closed, deterministic system.

The virtue of parsimony enshrined in Occam's razor – the principle that a simple explanation or theory is usually preferable to a complex one – is all very well, but as our understanding of the world grows more sophisticated we are being forced to acknowledge that even the most economical explanations at our disposal are not necessarily straightforward. It turns out Oscar Wilde was right when he wrote: 'The truth is rarely pure and never simple.' For example, in the mysterious world of particle physics, Superstring Theory remains the most promising candidate to provide us with a workable 'Theory of Everything'. This is the Grail of modern physics, the theoretical framework that will finally allow physicists to reconcile the uneasy bedfellows of quantum physics and general relativity. However, as Brian Greene points out in *The Elegant Universe*, although the theory looks sound, the maths involved is proving so complex that even the best mathematical brains in the world are currently struggling to make the highly convoluted sums add up.

Understanding the way inert matter behaves is hard enough, but when we start trying to understand ourselves we have a truly momentous task on our hands. As David Rogers explains: 'The most extensive computation known has been conducted over the last billion years on a planet-wide scale: it is the evolution of life. The power of this computation is illustrated by the complexity and beauty of its crowning achievement, the human brain.' If, as Rogers claims, we are sitting at the apex of some notional pyramid of complexity, the chances that we will ever understand ourselves in any depth are pretty remote. After all, it is not even as if every human brain is identical or even running the same software. I would furthermore suggest that the chances that *any* significant aspect of our multifaceted, multidimensional and highly idiosyncratic lives (especially those murky unresolved zones we tend to demarcate as 'problems') can ever be covered adequately by a brace of simple rules, five key principles or seven effective habits, are practically next to zero.

Yet this is precisely what the bulk of self-help books offer. Many popular-psychology authors and publishers even exalt in the fact. Take Norman Vincent Peale for example, the father of positive thinking, who berates us for 'struggling with the complexities and avoiding the simplicities'. This would be all very well if life *were* simple, but if the maps we are using to guide us aren't sufficiently detailed to do justice to the terrain we are traversing we shouldn't be surprised if we go astray. The American editor and social commentator H. L. Mencken pointed out the dangers inherent in oversimplification when he quipped sarcastically that 'For every problem there is a solution which is simple, clean and wrong'. Popular-psychology authors take note! The subtle eddies of the mind and heart are not some pan of stock that can be reduced to its concentrated essence – at least not without leaving a pretty bitter taste in our mouths.

Ironically, of course, the appetite for these absurdly simplified models of our complex lives is greatly enhanced by the fact that modern life is becoming increasingly hard for us to get our heads around. We move constantly between different contexts; in turns we play the roles of parent, partner, colleague, friend, carer, leader, member of the community, to name but a few. The rampaging growth of information technology now means that we are bombarded with more information and more competing demands on our attention than ever before. We are drowning in choice.

The need to organise this chaotic flow of experience, to impose some kind of order on unruly chaos, is thus a universal and pressing one. We all need concepts that allow us to carve reality up into manageable chunks and impose a framework of understanding and predictability on our experience, but we need to choose the right ones. As the mythologist Joseph Campbell pointed out (and it is to Campbell, ironically, we owe that ultimate self-help maxim: 'Follow your bliss'), every society needs its myths to stabilise the treacherous, swirling vortex of reality. In our modern world, successful self-help books are almost certainly filling the gap left by the ebbing tide of religious faith.

However, a major drawback of the world of Psychobabble is that the categories on offer are usually a good deal less sophisticated or flexible than your average zodiac sign. Our craving for order is so urgent that we cheerfully embrace two-dimensional classifications that leave us constantly trying to jam round pegs into square holes. We eagerly latch onto those features of our partner that just go to prove they are indeed from Mars or Venus or wherever, while mentally binning aspects of their behaviour that don't fit the stereotype. Are you an extrovert or an introvert, a thinker or a feeler, a type A or a type B, a permissive parent or an authoritarian one? How many of us have completed a personality questionnaire which required us to choose between discrete alternatives, all the while thinking, 'But *sometimes* I'm like this, while on other occasions I am more like this...'? There is little room for such fuzziness or ambivalence in Psychobabble's brave new world.

While claiming to educate and enlighten us, Psychobabble continually dumbs us down. Rather than attending to the exceptions and contradictions that might indicate the need to review our assumptions (which is how real science generally proceeds), we satisfy ourselves with a blinkered vision of reality because it feels safer. As George Orwell warned us in his novel *1984*, overly rigid systems of thought or 'restricted codes' are the best way to shut down new possibilities of thought and self-awareness. How ironic then that an industry devoted to helping people grow and explore human potential actually offers a conceptual vocabulary so limited that it effectively restricts opportunities for self-discovery and the articulation of our individuality. If we become too fluent in Psychobabble we risk losing the ability to express or maintain contact with what makes each life truly unique.

WHY DON'T WE FEEL BETTER YET?

As Mencken points out, the trouble with overly simple solutions is that they often don't work too well in the real world. Whilst our psychological mythologies may provide us with a welcome emotional security blanket in the short term, as technologies for producing any kind of sustained change in the long term the techniques recommended in so many self-help books are likely to come up empty. How many of our lives have been truly transformed by what we have read or heard? You may have felt inspired at the time but how many of us are now slimmer, sexier, richer, more confident or successful than we were before we shelled out our hard-earned cash on the latest book or course that was going to revolutionise our lives?

I'm not saying that all self-help books are a waste of time – I think some are genuinely helpful – but in my experience their long-term impact tends to be directly proportional to the extent to which their insights and recommendations are based on valid research. Science certainly isn't without its limitations and experiments are only as good as their design, but when it comes to knowing things about the world, scientific enquiry is probably the best way of proceeding that's currently available.

Psychology has always posed a particular challenge for science since it has to concern itself with slippery concepts like meaning and value as well as more readily measurable commodities like behaviour or brain activity. Formal psychology is also a mere babe amongst the sciences: not even 150 years have passed since Wilhelm Wundt first set up his laboratory in Leipzig to try and investigate consciousness in a systematic fashion. It's therefore hardly surprising we still don't know that much about the mysterious workings of the mind; considerably less, in fact, than the applied disciplines of clinical psychology and psychiatry would have you believe. What we do know inevitably coincides with the areas of mental activity most accessible to testing and observation: domains like memory, perception, and reasoning. Once we get into the stuff that preoccupies most of us on a daily basis (i.c. how to navigate our relationships, further our careers, manage our moods, raise our kids and so forth) we drift ever further into the woods of speculation. We also need to recognise that many of these key aspects of our lives are socially constructed. They are matters of preference and societal value, simply the way we do things around here rather than anything written into our DNA. When it comes to understanding the human mind, sometimes there are questions to which there are no right and wrong answers. Nevertheless, we are getting better at testing out and measuring what people perceive to be working for them and what actually improves their quality of life.

We should therefore not be too surprised when we discover that the helpful techniques and well-meaning advice don't necessarily deliver the changes they promise. The bottom line is that often the techniques don't work simply because there is no reason (apart from the enduring power of placebo) why they should. There is precious little quality control in the world of self-help, where conviction is all too often a willing stand-in for reasonable proof. The biologist Thomas Huxley once opined gravely that 'The deepest sin against the human mind is to believe things without evidence.' If he is right, then the self-help section of your local bookstore is a veritable den of iniquity.

We may roll our eyes at the medical practices of times gone by, when drilling holes in people's heads was seen as the best way of letting out the demons, cupping could rebalance the humours, or rubbing the corpse of a bisected puppy into the skin of a victim was the state-of-the-art cure for bubonic plague. But while contemporary remedies for the mental and emotional ills of our age may be less dramatic, many of our own psychological cures and theories boast scarcely more respectable scientific credentials.

Perhaps the deal is that in order to remain accessible to a broad audience, 'popular' psychology has to restrict itself to ideas that not only capture the public imagination, but also avoid placing an excessive burden on the public

Should all self-help books carry a health warning?

understanding. The technicalities of research methodology, the mysteries of multiple regression and double-blind trials, the difficulty of evaluating the significance of results which may vary from study to study; none of this is exactly sexy. And at the end of it all, of course, your best outcome is only a tentative balance of probability, another provisional hypothesis waiting to be disproved. Perhaps we can excuse ourselves for wanting to scroll down to the punch-line, however ill-informed, caveat-ridden and ineffectual it may turn out to be.

The danger is that it is consequently very easy for popular-psychology authors to blur the boundaries between opinion, ideology and reputable fact. It is increasingly in vogue for self-help authors to enlist the backing of scientific studies to support their views, but while the results may look like science and sound like science, because popular psychology is effectively 'science lite' the quality of the studies cited is seldom evaluated and contradictory evidence rarely considered.

In the Melanesian archipelagos of the southwest Pacific, shortly after WWII, anthropologists became aware of a strange phenomenon taking place amongst the indigenous islanders. In Papua New Guinea, for example, natives were found clustered in the forest around a roughly hewn model of an airplane complete with its own airstrip, gazing expectantly at the skies and waiting devoutly for deliverance. These islanders were members of what became known as a 'cargo cult', a religious movement in which less technologically developed societies integrate the products and processes of more 'advanced' industrialised cultures into their religious rituals and beliefs. This often resulted in tribes imitating the procedures and processes associated with this benevolent technology, but without real understanding of the function of the behaviour they were copying.

It was with reference to such practices that in his address to the Californian Institute of Technology in 1974, the Nobel Prize-winning physicist Richard Feynman warned against the dangers of 'cargo cult science', in other words, behaviour that looks scientific on the surface but doesn't actually follow the stringent protocols of proper scientific method. Popular psychology, it seems to me, is particularly vulnerable to such a charge, since

The danger is that it is very easy for popular-psychology authors to blur the boundaries between opinion, ideology and reputable fact.

scientific theories and precepts are often twisted to serve the purposes and fit the belief systems and values of the self-help gurus. Let's just say that if I have to read one more vague allusion to Heisenberg's uncertainty principle to justify the idea that the mind can directly influence events in the material world, I may not be responsible for my actions ...

The enterprise of Psychology is challenging enough but, given how difficult it is for us to know *anything* about ourselves, it seems particularly important that we don't start building our house on sand. There are many ways of knowing, and science is only one of them, but when it comes to establishing what will work reliably in the real world it is often hard to beat. Psychobabble may sound rational enough but often it is the discourse of superstition as much as it is of sense. It creates unrealistic expectations that ultimately lead to disappointment and disillusionment. Life is hard enough without chasing empty promises or kidding ourselves to expect the impossible. Perhaps we owe it to ourselves to try and evaluate systematically what's on offer, and what it can do for us, rather than grabbing at false hope because it temporarily alleviates our pain.

IT'S ALL ABOUT YOU!

We do ourselves no favours when we start mistaking theories as facts or confuse wishful thinking with reality. However, perhaps the most compelling objections to the world of popular psychology lie not with its truth claims but with its morals. Psychobabble seems to pander to some fairly ignoble aspects of ourselves, or at least to the most regressed. Not only is its worldview childlike in favouring simplistic, black and white solutions to complex problems, but its core values are too. When it boils down to it, most self-help books address fairly rudimentary drives: stop it hurting; give me what I want; make me more powerful. While there is nothing inherently wrong with these instincts, I would politely venture to suggest that they don't really amount to a manifesto for a grown-up life.

Copernicus may have successfully booted Earth from the heart of the cosmos but Psychobabble places each of us back at the very centre of the world. Just as we may go to the gym to sculpt our bodies, Psychobabble offers us tools to primp and preen our lives, to edit our personal biographies into something more pleasing. It encourages us to become self-absorbed narcissists, perennial teenagers for whom the world barely exists beyond themselves. If, as conventional therapeutic wisdom insists, we have to 'learn to love ourselves first', is it any wonder we are not always that aware of anyone else around us? There are plenty of titles showing us how to develop the social skills to attract friends or influence people, but where are the equivalent books showing us how to *be* a good friend, or develop the skills and attitudes that might enable us to become more altruistic or serve our communities better? With our focus fixed eternally on our own personal development, self-enhancement, and the constant upgrading of our own lives, we are condemned to an eternal childhood of self-absorption.

While Psychobabble stokes our society's overbearing sense of entitlement, it also places us under increasing pressure. It encourages us to reference unrealistic baselines by insisting, for instance, that happiness is the normal state of human existence. Consequently, if we do find ourselves feeling unhappy or shy or frightened, our response is to feel that something is badly wrong that must be fixed as soon as possible. There is little room for the notion that these experiences might be legitimate, or ordinary, or have something important to teach us. We end up pathologising routine aspects of everyday life.

The self-help section of your local bookstore is actually a Bill of Rights in disguise, and it sets the bar pretty high. Let's not forget, you *deserve* to be happy, accomplished and beloved – just like everyone else. After all, you're worth it! With such messages beamed at us every day in subtle and not-so-subtle forms, is it any wonder that people feel angry or ashamed when their lives don't measure up, or that they can get so preoccupied with trying to get things back on course?

The underlying imperative behind so much popular psychology is the need for constant change. By teaching us to structure our experience exclusively in terms of problems (or 'challenges') and solutions, the self-help industry keeps us on a never-ending treadmill. There is no sense that you can relax, that things might actually be good enough as they are, or that even if they aren't so great right now, this might be something to be tolerated and endured rather than fixed. Although I suspect he was referring to the problems of the Middle East (in which case, depending on your political persuasions, you might view this as something of a cop-out), the Israeli politician Shimon Peres once said something profoundly true: 'If a problem has no solution, it may not be a problem, but a fact – not to be solved, but to be coped with over time.' However, popular psychology is having none of that. Instead it feeds off our dissatisfaction with ourselves and our lot. It tells us not only that things can be improved, but that it is our responsibility to improve them.

This is a lot of pressure for any normal, flawed human being to accommodate. I remember browsing the self-help section of my local bookstore one sunny afternoon and rapidly feeling overwhelmed. There was just so much to do; so many areas of my life apparently in need of urgent attention. If I were to awaken the giant within, familiarise myself with the rules of life, become highly effective, lose 40 pounds and embrace a more confident, happier, assertive, creative, focused, flowing and decisive version of myself I clearly had my work cut out. Where was I going to find the time for all this? Perhaps what I needed was a book that would teach me to speed-read or give me some top tips on managing my time more effectively?

There is no sense that you can relax, that things might actually be good enough as they are, or that even if they aren't so great right now, this might be something to be tolerated and endured rather than fixed.

Surveying the vast amount of help out there it's easy to feel like a gardener who returns from a long vacation to discover that their whole plot is completely overrun by weeds. We all like to pretend that we are wise to the game, that being sophisticated souls we are immune from the grandiose claims of the popular-psychology market but, come January, how many of us will be sneaking out with the latest fad diet book under our arm, even if it is discreetly shrouded in a suitable bag? The trouble is that it is only human nature to turn the enticing notion that we *could* be better into the nagging conviction that we *should* be better. All these books to which we turn in order to feel good about ourselves can very easily end up making us feel worse. A faint whiff of the Aryan suffuses the whole enterprise. Our weakness and vulnerability must be expunged; only a pristine or radically revised version of ourselves is ultimately acceptable. Self-improvement is a duty. Don't you dare let me catch you being less than the Best Possible You! No wonder we feel tired. Isn't it about time we stopped allowing ourselves to be bullied by those who say they are trying to help us?

I will admit upfront that I am about to start lobbing stones from the glassiest of houses. As a practising clinical psychologist I am a fully paid-up member of the change industry and painfully conscious that over the years my clients have heard a constant stream of Psychobabble issue from my own lips. Even worse, I have written self-help books myself. While I hope they are not the worst examples of their kind, I am sure I have taken liberties with the science and will probably do so again in the pages that follow, so you had better keep your wits about you.

I am inviting these accusations of hypocrisy because I really do believe this is important. I am increasingly weary of some of the nonsense that is put about in the name of psychology and the subtly debasing effect it has on us and our culture. It's about time we all adopted a much more robust and critical attitude towards the whole business. Myths of all kinds certainly have their place in our society and I personally believe they are sometimes vehicles for deep truths that cannot be expressed adequately in other forms. However, in the spirit of calling a spade a spade, let's be clear about what we are dealing with: Psychobabble isn't the language of a rich mythic tradition that can unify us within the enclave of a common sacred story; it is often lazy pseudoscience that ought to be robustly interrogated so we can see what's real, solid and potentially useful to us, and what is just smoke and mirrors.

In a culture that has fallen a little too much in love with the voices of experts it's all too easy to submit ourselves to their confident pronouncements and stop reflecting upon and weighing what we are hearing. The premise of this book is that we may not know that much about the human mind yet, but since we all have one we should probably do our best to use it. Berne's most famous patent clerk urged us to remember that 'the important thing is not to stop questioning', but that can be especially hard when we are being told what we badly want to hear. Nevertheless, it's time to be firm with ourselves, take back some responsibility for our own lives, and wean ourselves off the easy panaceas the world of Psychobabble is all too eager to flog us.

I hope this doesn't read like one of those smart-alecky 'Everything You Think You Know is Wrong' books. I am not trying to be argumentative for the sake of it. I am not even claiming that the views and positions expressed in these pages are necessarily right. My hope is merely that they stimulate your own thinking, and give you the confidence to start drawing your own conclusions. If you disagree with me, that's completely fine. As Caroline Aherne's great comic creation Mrs Merton used to enjoin her audience: 'Let's have a heated debate ...'

In medicine, doctors sometimes talk about *iatrogenesis*, which is a fancy way of describing those unfortunate occasions when the interventions designed to cure us have the unfortunate side-effect of making us worse. I have a strong suspicion that this may be exactly what is happening in the case of popular psychology. Whether by the end of this book you agree with me, I hope that what follows will provide some entertaining food for thought, ease the heavy burden of unrealistic expectation, and discourage any of us from ever taking the received wisdom of our times at face value.

A BRIEF WORD ON REFERENCING

Whenever a study, quotation or reference of any kind is mentioned in the text, look up the original page number in the References at the end of the book and you will find the relevant lines from the main text reprinted in italics with a brief reference underneath e.g. Rogers (1990). This will then give you sufficient information to find the full reference in the Bibliography, on p.237 or, where a web reference is cited, online.

Referencing has been done this way in order to avoid cluttering the main text with numbering, while still allowing the reader to locate the relevant sources more easily than if they had just been listed at the end of each chapter. Have a quick look at the reference section and you should find the system fairly self-explanatory.

MYTH 1

The root of all your problems is low self-esteem

'High self-esteem isn't a luxury', insists Jack Canfield, author of popular-psychology classic *Chicken Soup for the Soul*, 'It's a necessity for anyone who has important goals to achieve.' These days Canfield is preaching to the converted. The catalogue of personal and societal ills now laid at the door of low self-esteem is extensive. Over the years, poor self-esteem has been implicated in aggressive behaviour, underachievement in the classroom and workplace, teenage pregnancy and obesity – in fact, almost every undesirable or pathological behaviour you may care to think of.

In therapy, it is now taken as read by clients and therapists alike that issues of self-esteem underlie many patients' difficulties. Widely accepted theoretical models maintain that even narcissistic patients, defined as they are by their wildly inflated and grandiose self-images, are only overcompensating for an inner lack of self-worth. In all schools of psychotherapy, improvements in self-esteem are regarded as a valid yardstick of therapeutic progress. After all, we all have the right to feel good about ourselves, don't we?

At the risk of being dragged to the marketplace and stoned, I would have to question whether we always do. I know this sounds harsh, but if your opinion of yourself is so painfully low you might want to ask yourself why and indeed whether there is anything you should be doing to rectify the situation?

There is a certain overlooked wisdom in the words of American mystery writer Jane Haddam, who observed sardonically: 'In my day we didn't have self-esteem, we had self respect – and no more of it than we had earned.' Has optimal self-esteem become yet another construct in that free-floating pantheon of psychological 'rights' to which we are now automatically entitled, irrespective of our actions and choices?

In saying this, I do fully acknowledge the painful plight of the many people out there who have been programmed to believe that they are worthless by the neglectful or sadistic way they have been treated. If you have been significantly abused or belittled in the course of your life, there is a significant risk that you will have drawn mistaken conclusions about yourself from those experiences: 'People treat me badly and tell me I'm rubbish, so it must be true …' Under such circumstances, anyone's self-concept can be seriously damaged and their self-confidence shaken. Children are especially vulnerable to such interpretations, and clinically it's heartbreaking to discover how difficult it can be to help such individuals appreciate that any 'badness' is a property of their abusers rather than themselves.

However, the number of people who regard themselves as suffering from low self-esteem far exceeds those who have been through such experiences. It is hard to escape the nagging suspicion that in our culture low self-esteem is too frequently wheeled out as justification for passivity, reluctance to change or even a bid for sympathy, when the individuals concerned would do better to engage with the fact that our emotions (especially negative ones) are often a rallying call to action. Courage, persistence and timely apologies are often far better

Has optimal self-esteem become yet another construct in that free-floating pantheon of psychological 'rights' to which we are now automatically entitled, irrespective of our actions and choices?

antidotes to low self-esteem than endless positive affirmations or lavish, undeserved praise.

But however it is obtained, we can surely all agree that high self-esteem is worth having, can't we? Well, that may depend upon what you are prepared to sacrifice for it. While the evidence is that increased self-love certainly does make us *feel* better, just like romantic love it can also make us blind, or at the very least a bit short-sighted. Not only is the dividing line between high self-esteem (supposedly good) and narcissism (clearly bad) a pretty fine one, but the research suggests that the high self-esteem crowd are somewhat prone to Emperor's New Clothes syndrome.

In various studies, people with high self-esteem scores consistently rate themselves as more attractive, popular, socially skilled and intelligent than average. However, other people don't necessarily agree with them. Their self-ratings simply

Young lady! Can you find another place to have bad self-esteem?

In the modern world, low self-esteem is seldom regarded as a virtue ...

aren't upheld by the independent evaluations of their peers or by objective tests of their attributes and abilities. In other words (shocking news, I know), simply believing something doesn't necessarily make it true. The science suggests that if our self-esteem is riding high, we might feel great, but we are probably also slightly delusional.

When unpacking the evidence regarding the benefits of self-esteem we also need to be careful not to put the cart before the horse. Yes, there are indeed reasonable correlations between higher self-esteem and academic performance. However, this doesn't mean that feeling better about yourself necessarily makes you a better student. Perhaps the academic high achievers feel better about themselves simply *because* they have performed well rather than the other way round? Certainly the many well-meaning initiatives that have attempted to improve pupils' performance by targeting the self-esteem of low achievers have unfortunately yet to yield any notable successes to date.

The stark conclusion of the most comprehensive objective review of the self-esteem literature so far conducted is that we need to be extremely cautious about affording self-esteem too much causal power. Contrary to popular belief, research suggests that most bullies are *not* secretly suffering from poor self-esteem – quite the opposite in fact. Dan Olweus, who has spent many years researching childhood bullying in Norway, claims that he could find no evidence that male playground bullies were particularly anxious or insecure. In an article entitled *Violent Pride*, Roy Baumeister reports on experiments demonstrating that it was the most highly egotistical individuals in his sample who responded aggressively when threatened rather than those with low self-regard. He explains:

> 'A crucial influence on our thinking was the seemingly lofty self-regard of prominent violent people. Saddam Hussein is not known as a modest, cautious, self-doubting individual. Adolf Hitler's exaltation of the 'master race' was hardly a slogan of low self-esteem. These examples suggest that

high self-esteem, not low, is indeed an important cause of aggression.'

Your self-esteem rating does *not* predict the quality of your relationships or how long they will last. And high self-esteem won't necessarily stop your children smoking, drinking, taking drugs or becoming sexually active at an early age. In laboratory tasks, people with high self-esteem don't outperform their self-deprecating peers (even if they assume they will) and even the contribution that low-self esteem makes to delinquency is negligible once you start controlling for other factors. On the basis of the hard evidence we have collected, it looks like initiatives to improve levels of self-esteem within the population are highly unlikely to prove the cure-all for society's ills. It seems the $245,000 annual budget ploughed into the Task Force on Self-esteem and Personal and Social Responsibility by the State of California since 1986 could have been better spent elsewhere.

While bestselling author Louise Hay assures us that 'If we really love ourselves, everything in our lives works ...', it is worth pointing out that almost every great religious and moral tradition throughout history has regarded any significant degree of self-love with grave suspicion. St Augustine of Hippo, for example, takes almost the diametrically opposite position to Hay:

'Do you desire to construct a vast and lofty fabric? Think first about the foundations of humility. The higher your structure is to be, the deeper must be its foundation.'

Meanwhile, the Buddha warns us that: 'Self-love for ever creeps out, like a snake, to sting anything which happens to stumble upon it.' What passes today as a virtue to be fostered would

Almost every great religious and moral tradition throughout history has regarded any significant degree of self-love with grave suspicion.

have been considered a sin or shortcoming to be abjured in ages past. A voice of contemporary concern, however, has been raised by the psychologist Professor Jean Twenge, who fears that narcissism and overpowering levels of entitlement are rapidly becoming a destructive cultural norm in the West.

Twenge and co-author Professor Keith Campbell are also sceptical of the widespread belief that narcissism is actually a compensation strategy developed by people who deep down don't feel that good about themselves. They argue this has real implications for the way we respond to what they describe as the 'narcissism epidemic' they fear is currently sweeping America:

'In many cases, the suggested cure for narcissistic behaviour is "feeling good about yourself." After all, the thinking goes, fourteen-year-old Megan wouldn't post revealing pictures of herself on MySpace if she had higher self-esteem. So parents redouble their efforts, telling Megan she's special, beautiful, and great. This is like suggesting that an obese person would feel much better if she just ate more doughnuts ...'

Being able to accept yourself, warts and all, with some measure of compassion is psychologically healthy, but that's not where most self-esteem gurus are setting the bar. As inspirational author Alan Cohen insists: 'Wouldn't it be powerful if you fell in love with yourself so deeply that you would do just about anything if you knew it would make you happy?' Powerful perhaps. Desirable? I'm not so sure. It sounds as if this kind of self-love might be capable of justifying some pretty selfish and ruthless behaviour.

Cultivating the belief that we are just the most adorable guys and gals who fully deserve only very the best life can offer may be seductive, but it hardly reflects the reality of the situation. We all stuff up, compromise ourselves, and do innumerable dumb things we end up regretting. That's being human. And feeling bad about ourselves is often life's way of letting us know we could do better. Interviewed by *O Magazine* in 2003, comedian

Jay Leno made precisely this point when he observed: 'A little low self-esteem is actually quite good. Maybe you're not the best so you should work a little harder …' I certainly agree that if life hasn't taught you a bit of humility by the time you reach adulthood, you probably haven't been paying enough attention. Either that or you need to be getting out there and making a few more mistakes.

Perhaps our biggest mistake is in thinking that self-esteem is something we have to have before we can hope to achieve anything useful or worthwhile, like some kind of fuel tank that must be kept topped up if we are to stand any realistic chance of getting to our destination. Isn't it ultimately more helpful to us as a barometer of our progress, an essential, ongoing source of feedback about the wisdom of our choices and the validity of our actions? It's not supposed to be a constant, a permanent property of a person like the colour of our eyes or the shape of our fingerprints: it would actually be less helpful to us if it was.

A value defended, a job well done, a skill mastered or an obstacle overcome – these we should welcome as legitimate sources of satisfaction and grounds for some measure of personal pride. However, to expect someone to feel good about themselves without having put in the work, in the way Psychobabble's doctrine of self-esteem promotes, is like awarding someone a medal before they have even run the race. It's meaningless. Popular psychology does anyone few favours pretending otherwise.

We all stuff up, compromise ourselves, and do innumerable dumb things we end up regretting. That's being human. And feeling bad about ourselves is often life's way of letting us know we could do better.

Let your feelings out!

If one had to pinpoint the most significant developments that have taken place in society over the last 50 years, an obvious candidate would be our radically revised position regarding the expression of our feelings. Prior to the 1960s the infamous British 'stiff upper lip' was universally regarded as a virtue, but these days the repression of emotion is seen as the root of a host of psychological and physical problems.

The growing consensus that repressing your feelings is a bad thing has only been reinforced by reality TV's love affair with characters whose appeal to the public lies not only in their larger-than-life personalities but their apparent lack of any kind of emotional filter. Jade Goody, who sadly died in 2009, was a prime example. Her utter emotional transparency in the *Big Brother* house assured her celebrity status. Every fleeting emotion, every high and low was writ large for all to see. Although she was sometimes treated as a figure of fun because of her poor general knowledge ('Has Greece got its own moon?') and some fairly spectacular malapropisms ('They were trying to use me as an escape goat ...'), Jade Goody achieved cult hero status. Whatever her educational shortcomings, there was an emerging consensus that her unparalleled degree of emotional directness and expressivity was admirable, while it also made her highly watchable. What previous generations would have considered childlike or undisciplined was construed as a positive: it made Jade 'authentic', someone who was always truly and fully herself. Jade Goody's fame was a product of a culture that views emotional repression as self-denial, surely the most heinous of modern sins.

And yet the story of Jade Goody is also a cautionary one for all advocates of wearing your heart on your sleeve. The Greek Orthodox church has a saying, 'the greatest virtues cast the longest shadows', and, ultimately, Jade's lack of emotional restraint caused her downfall. Her inability to 'bite her tongue' and moderate an outpouring of frustration and resentment towards Bollywood actress Shilpa Shetty in a later series of *Big Brother* caused an international outcry. On this occasion it appeared that Jade's unmediated emotions had unfortunately found expression in an outpouring of racist abuse, although Goody herself always denied that Shetty's ethnicity had ever been either a cause or focus of those feelings. However, the overnight transformation of Jade Goody from popular folk hero to *cause célèbre* in the wake of *Celebrity Big Brother* in 2007 should have been a wake-up call to the potential hazards of giving such free range to the expression of one's emotions.

So how have we all been sold this idea that we should be wearing our insides on the outside at all times? Once again the finger points accusingly at Dr Freud, whose hydraulic model of the mind constructed it as a closed system of opposing forces and pressures. In this model, buried emotions caused dangerous build-ups of pressure, producing leaks and ruptures between the different layers of the psyche that manifested themselves on the surface in the form of neurotic symptoms. Freud's talking cure aimed to achieve *catharsis*, the release of pent-up emotional blockages by bringing repressed conflicts into conscious awareness. It is Freud we ultimately have to thank for phrases like 'letting off steam'. Given this kind of analogy, it is easy to appreciate why the repression of emotion seemed like such a bad idea.

As we have begun to unpick the relationship between physical and emotional health, and especially the effects of chronic stress on the immune system, there is a growing body of research data indicating that the repression of emotion could indeed be a fairly dangerous pastime. Dr George Solomon from the University of California is only one of a number of medical academics citing convincing research showing that people who repress their feelings are more at risk of rheumatoid arthritis, infections and certain types of cancer. Yet it's not that clear-cut. How do we explain the fact that Japan, a collectivist culture in which the suppression of certain emotions is actively encouraged, is also one of the most physically healthy countries in the world? In Japan there is an important crucial distinction between *hon-ne*, which roughly translated means 'honest feeling', and *tatemae*, which means 'polite face'. One Japanese blogger, reflecting on the origins of this distinction, speculates that in a nation 70 per cent covered by mountainous terrain, agricultural workers had to cooperate in order to produce sufficient food from very limited fertile land. Strong self-expression or self-assertion would have been counter-productive to survival. Yet despite this distrust of unguarded emotional display, citizens of Japan can expect on average to live up to the age of 75 in full health according to the World Health Organisation. Perhaps other factors are muddying the picture, but we should reflect on how this fits with the apparently strong connection between emotional repression and systemic illness in the West.

And even here in the Western world there is emerging evidence that letting it all out isn't necessarily the best strategy for everyone. After the tragic destruction of the World Trade Center on 11 September 2001, a team from the University of Buffalo emailed over 2,000 people that same day, asking them to share their thoughts in writing about the events of 9/11. Three-quarters of the people surveyed wrote a response, while the remaining quarter ignored the request. Over the next two years the Buffalo team regularly contacted everyone in the sample, screening them for signs of emotional distress and physical problems. What they discovered ran counter to what we are conditioned to expect. Those who had not responded to the initial request to share their feelings actually did *better* than those who had written their emotions down, and in fact those who wrote the most also proved to be the most vulnerable to unwanted psychological and physical symptoms.

Now there are many caveats to be applied before jumping to conclusions. We don't know, for example, that those who chose not to write anything down made that decision because the disaster made less impression on them: maybe there was less of an emotional response in the first place amongst this group, whereas those who wrote the most may simply have been the most powerfully affected by what had occurred. In other words it may not be the case that the key distinguishing factor between the two groups is necessarily their capacity to express their feelings, but the intensity with which they experience them in the first place. However, these findings do correspond with a study of heart attack survivors conducted by Dr Karni Ginzburg and colleagues. They found that 'repressors' were much *less* likely to suffer from post-traumatic stress disorder than those who dwelt on their brush with death. Some people, Dr Ginzburg concluded, naturally tend to repress their negative emotions, and for these individuals a repressive style enables them to cope better than their more emotive peers. Letting it all out may not be for everyone.

But surely we all know that anger is one emotion that it is better not to bury? In San Diego one businesswoman has even opened up a store in which her customers pay to go and smash plates in order to get things off their chest, but again several decades of research casts doubt on whether the theory that it is always a better idea to vent your fury is actually a very sound one. According to Professor Jeffrey Lohr, who has reviewed over 40 years of work addressing the issue, 'In study after study the conclusion was the same: Expressing anger does not reduce aggressive tendencies and likely makes it worse'. Lohr argues that while indulging your angry feelings may be a briefly enjoyable thing to do, this kind of venting doesn't even ultimately reduce the feelings of anger.

Perhaps before jumping on the bandwagon of free expression, we should remind ourselves of an observation made by Charles Darwin back in 1872 that 'the free expression by outward signs of an emotion intensifies it'. In other words, by allowing what we feel to show through our behaviour we actually make the underlying feeling stronger. If the emotion you are expressing is joy or love then that wouldn't necessarily be a bad thing, but if the emotions you are experiencing are less desirable ones (anger, jealousy, contempt) then reinforcing them through your behaviour might not be such a smart move.

Some backing for this was recently provided by a study in which moderately painful heat was applied to the forearms of subjects who had previously been instructed to assume either relaxed, neutral or negative expressions while the procedure was carried out. Those who adopted negative expressions reported higher levels of pain than the other two groups. Again this suggests that the very expression of emotion to some extent conditions our experience of emotion and that there is a feedback loop between the two domains. Maybe cultures like Japan, where people will sometimes default to a smile that may appear incongruent with their underlying emotions, or Thailand where complaining is considered uncouth and the expression of anger positively barbaric, have simply grasped this principle better than we have in the West?

The modern maxim that we must be true to our feelings at all times is based on an assumption that our feelings arise spontaneously within us, and that they are therefore more likely to represent the truth about us and our reactions. Seen in this light, expressing your feelings – whatever they may be – becomes an issue of personal integrity. What we forget though, is the extent to which we actively manipulate our own emotional lives and indeed have them manipulated for us by society. Arlie Hochschild, a Professor of Sociology at Berkeley, claims that the spontaneity of our feelings is often an illusion:

If the emotions you are experiencing are less desirable ones then reinforcing them through your behaviour might not be such a smart move.

she argues that whether we are aware of them or not, we tend to regulate our emotions according to implicit 'feeling rules' that tell us what to feel in a given situation, for how long and at what level of intensity. Thus in the United States the normal duration of grief after a bereavement is assumed to last between 18 and 24 months, after which you may find yourself being referred for treatment for an emotional state that starts to be considered pathological.

The outpouring of public grief following the death of Diana, Princess of Wales in 1997, is a more local example of how even authentic emotion can be cued, summoned and coordinated through cultural processes. We don't normally have such a powerful response to the death of a relative stranger, after all. At such points it is as if normal people become accomplished method actors, self-inducing feeling so effectively that it is experienced as entirely genuine. And in a sense it is, although one suspects that people were drawing on other sources of more personal loss to cue the relevant emotions. However, without our ability to read and respond to expectations and permissions generated by society, one can't help but wonder if the levels of grief expressed would have been quite so intense or universal?

We may therefore select the feelings we experience more than we think. If this is so, then a harmonious and civilised way of life requires us individually and collectively to choose wisely which feelings we encourage. I am not saying that the repression of feeling is a good thing, or that feelings we deny, bury or disavow don't sometimes prove enormously damaging for our well-being. However, as a society what we do seem to have lost sight of is that there is a huge difference between owning and acknowledging the full range of our feelings and letting them all

What we forget though, is the extent to which we actively manipulate our own emotional lives and indeed have them manipulated for us by society.

spill out at the drop of a hat. You can acknowledge your *hon-ne* while still preserving your *tatemae*.

The word *catharsis* originally comes from Greek tragedy, where Aristotle used it to refer to a purging of emotion to the end of restoring harmonious balance. The point is that in Greek drama this was a carefully orchestrated group experience conducted within a highly structured, ritualised setting. Similarly, in the therapist's office the unmediated expression of emotion is sometimes encouraged because the therapist (rightly or wrongly!) believes that they can help contain those feelings and channel them in the interests of fostering your insight or healing. Both contexts are specialised arenas set apart from everyday life, and it is a mistake to assume that behaviour appropriate in your therapist's office is necessarily the way to go in the high street.

Of course we must be prepared to acknowledge our feelings, and not only the positive, more palatable ones. It can be especially important to own the emotions that make us feel downright uncomfortable such as fear, disgust, anger and guilt. Repressed feelings can indeed do us a lot of damage, and I would be an irresponsible psychologist to suggest otherwise. However, precisely because emotions are not just harmless, affective froth, we need to treat them with a greater degree of respect and care. Like the infamous Brazilian butterfly whose beating wings ultimately cause a tornado in Texas, our feelings can be powerful forces that bring about unintended consequences, as poor Jade Goody discovered. When we put them out there we therefore need to be conscious of the potential impact that they can have. Our emotions would appear to well up from the most primitive and oldest parts of our brains, but let's bear in mind that evolution has kindly given us a higher cortex so we don't have to be at their mercy the whole time. There is a thin line between emotional expressivity and emotional incontinence. Let's try not to confuse one with the other.

Emotional intelligence is what really counts

Over the last 17 years Daniel Goleman has done a remarkable job of selling emotional intelligence to the world. Many of us are familiar with his claim that, 'What really matters for success, character, happiness and life long achievements is a definite set of emotional skills – your EQ – not just purely cognitive abilities that are measured by conventional IQ tests.' However, as the popularity of emotional intelligence has gathered pace, psychologists Peter Salovey and John Mayer's original concept has mutated into something scarcely recognisable. Emotional intelligence has since become a patchwork of many disparate parts, some of which don't necessarily belong together and which are in constant danger of unravelling.

This hasn't stopped the Psychobabble generation falling more than a little bit in love with emotional intelligence. The theory sits well with its sentimental vision of the heart as ultimately wiser than the head and panders to its egalitarian sentiments. Emotional intelligence is seductive because at the very moment it promises to give you a leg-up in life, it potentially also levels the playing field. The strapline on the cover of Goleman's most famous book reassures us that emotional intelligence 'can matter more than IQ' and, even if your EQ is a little sluggish right now, the good news is that your emotional competencies can always be developed, refined and expanded.

In business circles emotional intelligence has become a truly aspirational science. With all its talk of self-awareness, authentic values and interpersonal sensitivity, modern emotional intelligence may sound rooted squarely in humanistic ideals of self-actualisation and personal growth. However, reading Goleman, you may conclude that honing your emotional skills could be the key to fast-tracking your professional advancement. After all, Goleman reports that when he commissioned researchers from the management consultancy firm Hay/McBer to examine the competencies underlying the talents of 'star performers' from over forty different corporations, emotional competencies were found to be twice as important as conventional intellect or expertise.

However, other research has sadly found no convincing evidence that emotional intelligence confers any significant advantage in terms of getting on in the world. One of the most authoritative reviews of the evidence to date, conducted in 2004 by social scientists David Van Rooy and Chockalingam Viswesvaran, discovered that there seemed to be only a very marginal correlation between high EQ scores and professional attainment. In fact, while conventional IQ ratings may indeed prove a pretty poor predictive indicator of success in the workplace, it turned out (for their sample at least) that they still proved more reliable than emotional intelligence scores.

Yet the notion of emotional intelligence has become so embedded in commercial culture and the lexicon of management consultancy that even findings like these have done little to slow its momentum. Despite these contradictory results, Goleman suggests that if you start considering the very top ten per cent of leaders then you *definitely* start to see the difference that their elevated emotional intelligence is making. Having had Lyle and Signe Spencer's original competence framework

> **While conventional IQ ratings may indeed prove a pretty poor predictive indicator of success in the workplace, it turned out that they proved more reliable than emotional intelligence scores.**

studies reanalysed, Goleman reports that among the star leaders reviewed, 'On average close to 90 percent of their success in leadership was attributable to emotional intelligence', while at the most senior levels 'emotional competence accounts for virtually the entire advantage'. These are important and potentially significant findings, so I was disappointed not to be able to examine the details of the methodology and data from either of the studies for myself. Although the brief summaries offered in Goleman's book *Working with Emotional Intelligence* are intriguing, my search for a full account of this research in any peer-reviewed, academic journal has so far come up empty-handed.

Nevertheless the agenda seems clear: however smart you may or may not be, you will definitely need to be cultivating the heightened emotional awareness of Bill Gates or the late departed Steve Jobs to ensure success. But hold on a minute: in interviews both Gates and Jobs have freely admitted to a pretty 'robust' and confrontational management style that makes neither of them the obvious standard bearer for warm, fuzzy people skills. But neither, by all accounts, were Winston Churchill, Catherine II of Russia, Attila the Hun, Boudica or Mao Zedong – all of whom have been considered to be highly successful leaders in their time. When I think of such historical figures, they don't immediately strike me as typical exemplars of the emotionally intelligent individual portrayed by Goleman:

> '... poised and outgoing, committed to people and causes, sympathetic and caring, with a rich appropriate emotional life ... comfortable with themselves and the universe they live in.'

I am not saying that there aren't leaders out there whose social skills and emotional acumen haven't helped them reach the top. However, I have a horrible suspicion that, more often than not, one of the key attributes of many high-achieving leaders is their ability to make the hard decisions and sacrifices that their more empathic, sensitive peers would balk at. They often seem to possess a single-minded focus that allows them to steam-roller all opposition to their plans. Far from being sensitively attuned to all incoming social and interpersonal data coming from the environment, their real skill is sometimes being able to prioritise ruthlessly and screen out such extraneous factors. These men and women can't afford to get distracted by images of the grieving relatives of the foot soldiers they are about to send to the front. Like doctors who must administer a painful cure, such men and women have to train themselves to ignore the patient's screams of agony and possibly sometimes even the plaintive whispers of their own conscience.

So what's going on here? Is emotional intelligence the indispensable asset it is alleged to be or is it largely irrelevant? Could it even be a handicap in some contexts? I guess it all rather depends upon how emotional intelligence is to be defined, and this is where things start getting really messy.

I am not going to bore you with the immense difficulties psychologists have encountered in trying to agree how to measure people's EQ, but suffice it to say that when Salovey and Mayer originally coined the term 'emotional intelligence' in the 1990s they used it in a very specific and circumspect way. Their 'ability' model focused exclusively upon mental processes involved in perceiving and then reasoning with information derived from emotions. Emotional intelligence therefore resembled other forms of intelligence, and was distinguished chiefly by the specific type of data upon which it operated – in much the same way as some people reason better with words and some people display a particular aptitude for processing

More often than not, one of the key attributes of many high-achieving leaders is their ability to make the hard decisions and sacrifices that their more empathic, sensitive peers would balk at.

visual imagery. Emotionally smart people were, quite simply, good at identifying, and manipulating emotional information.

However, these days emotional intelligence has become a nebulous hybrid of abilities, personality traits, values and interpersonal skills. While supporters of EQ will be quick to tell you that traditional IQ accounts at best for only 25 per cent of the variance between successful people and lower achievers, it doesn't therefore follow that emotional intelligence can automatically claim the remaining 75 per cent (although this is often implied by people who cite this particular statistic). This tendency to treat emotional intelligence as 'everything else' not accounted for by conventional intelligence is partly why the concept has ended up as such a ragbag. Critics have been left despairing of ever being able to identify a coherent common factor or unifying principle. This is one of the primary objections raised by the well-known psychologist Hans Eysenck who complains that Goleman, 'exemplifies more clearly than most the fundamental absurdity of the tendency to class almost any type of behaviour as an "intelligence"'.

Professor Eysenck has a point. Just because something works or proves adaptive in a particular environment doesn't necessarily mean it is the product of intelligent behaviour. When a hedgehog rolls itself into a ball to protect itself from predators, the behaviour achieves a good outcome for the hedgehog, but not because the hedgehog has consciously (or even unconsciously) evaluated the situation and decided that the whole curling-up strategy presents the best chance of survival. The behaviour is adaptive, certainly, but is driven by instinct rather than insight. When we say it's a 'smart' thing for the hedgehog to do, we are using a metaphor. The successful outcome creates the illusion or assumption that some kind of intelligent process was involved, because not unreasonably we tend to equate good outcomes with intelligent problem-solving strategies.

While Goleman's four dimensions ('self-awareness', 'self-management', 'social awareness' and 'relationship management') may look like an approximate fit with Salovey and Mayer's original categories, closer inspection reveals what a very different beast we are dealing with. How does self-confidence relate to reasoning with emotion? Attributes such as self-confidence, 'achievement drive' and superior self-control undoubtedly confer significant benefits in life, but are they really demonstrations of emotional *intelligence*? Several researchers have also criticised the degree to which facets of emotional intelligence overlap with established personality traits like agreeableness and extroversion. Sure, these traits may sometimes predispose their owners towards useful types of social behaviour – just like the hedgehog's instincts – but how they relate to some underlying mental faculty or skill is less clear. Regarding the five abilities that Goleman originally identified, Hans Eysenck observed:

> 'If these five "abilities" define "emotional intelligence", we would expect some evidence that they are highly correlated; Goleman admits that they might be quite uncorrelated, and in any case if we cannot measure them, how do we know they are related? So the whole theory is built on quicksand; there is no sound scientific basis.'

In most settings high levels of intelligence often reveal themselves in a capacity to think 'outside the box' in ways that generate challenges to social orthodoxy. Great thinkers are often eccentrics. By contrast, developing your emotional intelligence (Goleman's version of it anyway) seems destined to turn you into your boss's vision of a model employee. The cynic in me wonders whether the emotional intelligence movement is actually geared towards cultivating compliant citizens for large corporations? When you unpack Daniel Goleman's expanded

Developing your emotional intelligence seems destined to turn you into your boss's vision of a model employee.

categories you uncover various 'emotional competencies' that, to my mind, read like a small ad for employee of the month: 'Trustworthy, achievement and service-oriented individual seeks kindly industrialist to help him rise through the ranks ...' My outsider's impression is that some of the values commended in the emotional intelligence literature don't always characterise those at the very top of the corporate tree. I'm not sure that 'transparency' would always be regarded as a particular asset in the boardroom.

Working towards developing a high EQ may make you a much nicer, more considerate and affable person to be around. It probably will endear you to your manager, but there is a suspicious goodness of fit between the values of emotional intelligence and ones that serve the vested interests of large corporations. In the same way that the German sociologist Max Weber famously identified a convenient overlap between *The Protestant Ethic and the Spirit of Capitalism*, emotional intelligence appears to create people likely to slot meekly into corporate culture rather than set it alight. We need to question whether this version of 'emotional intelligence' is ultimately more about socialization than empowerment.

Personally, like Daniel Goleman, I am all in favour of ethical, empathic leadership. In fact I would far rather live in a world in which companies looked after their employees' emotional wellbeing and developed heightened people skills, even at the cost of reduced profitability. I'd certainly rather work in one. However, while I can believe that some of the competencies shoehorned into the concept of emotional intelligence would make for a better world, I am not buying the notion that what commonly passes for emotional intelligence is the golden ticket to meteoric professional advancement. There are leaders, thankfully, who do embody some of the characteristics associated with a high EQ, but there is definitely more than one way to skin a cat, and it is just nonsense to insist that these qualities are a prerequisite for success.

The emotional intelligence industry panders to a pleasant fantasy that the nice guys and gals not only can finish first, but are in fact more likely to do so. Hopefully this is sometimes true, but I think a moment's honest reflection would confirm that it's hardly the norm. Wanting to believe that success arises naturally from pro-social attitudes and warm interpersonal skills is akin to the popular but misguided belief, routinely reinforced by Hollywood, that the good and the brave will also be beautiful or handsome.

A lot of the values and behaviours that supposedly indicate the operation of emotional intelligence might be deemed morally admirable, but true intelligence of any kind sometimes requires a capacity to stand back and take a long, cool look at the way things actually are, setting aside our fantasies of how we might wish them to be. Readers still determined to get to the top of the pile would be well-advised to swap their copy of Goleman for an edition of *The Prince*. Even in the fifteenth century Niccolo Machiavelli understood the psychology of power. He wrote:

> 'How we live is so different from how we ought to live that he who studies what ought to be done rather than what is done will learn the way to his downfall rather than to his preservation.'

Take Machiavelli's advice. Read the biographies of outstanding high achievers throughout history or those of our contemporary Captains of Industry and ask yourself honestly: 'What is it that enabled these men and women to get to the top?' If you discover a significant and consistent overlap with the assorted

True intelligence of any kind sometimes requires a capacity to stand back and take a long, cool look at the way things actually are, setting aside our fantasies of how we might wish them to be.

traits and characteristics cobbled together under the heading of 'emotional intelligence' I, for one, will be most surprised. There may be many valid reasons to try and become a more empathic, sensitive, and likeable person but, regrettably, I strongly suspect that getting ahead of the pack isn't necessarily one of them.

Let your goals power you towards success!

I must have read Michael Rosen and Helen Oxenbury's classic tale to my children a hundred times when they were little and yet they never seemed to tire of it: 'We're going on a bear hunt ... We're going to catch a big one ...'. If ever there was a celebration of the motivational power of a clear-cut objective this story is it. No matter how big the obstacles they encounter, the fictional family's clarity of purpose drives them relentlessly forwards towards the fulfilment of their quest. Can't go over it? Can't go under it? No matter: they'll just go through it. Until, that is, they encounter the bear they have been searching for. Suddenly, catching the bear no longer seems quite as desirable as they had formerly imagined; the story ends with the family dashing pell-mell for the safety of home, pursued by one very angry animal.

It is now widely accepted that setting goals is essential if we are to achieve anything in almost any field of activity. Self-help books invariably tell us that our aims have to be specific, and our objectives broken down into a series of manageable and measurable sub-goals. Psychologically there are various problems with this approach as we shall see, but Rosen and Oxenbury's tale highlights one of the most overlooked issues: goal setting is only helpful if the goals that we have set ourselves are actually the right ones in the first place.

Underlying most of our goal-setting activities is the natural belief that achieving those goals will in some way make us happier. Regrettably, according to Harvard psychologist Daniel

Gilbert, we are often very poor at knowing what we want or, to be more precise, predicting accurately the true value of the things we think we want. We may secretly anticipate that the new house we have set our heart on will make us feel great once we have the keys in our hand. Fired up by this vision of our future pleasure, we set the appropriate financial targets, make the necessary sacrifices and watch with excitement as our overtime hours bring the cherished goal ever closer to fruition.

Unfortunately, all the hard evidence of several decades of research suggests that your new purchase (a) is highly unlikely to make you as happy as you think it will and (b) any pleasure that may come as a result will be more short-lived than you had imagined. This doesn't just apply to material goals, alas, but all manner of things that we think will improve our quality of life. The truth is that when we make these judgments about what will make us happy we get it wrong all the time.

If it's any consolation, our feebleness at effective forecasting can sometimes work in our favour when it comes to the impact of significant negative events. Gilbert believes that when the big disasters occur – say we tragically lose a spouse or find ourselves unemployed – we often cope better than we had anticipated because we steel ourselves to cope with the crisis and our defences are activated. However, we are left relatively undefended against chronic or petty insults to our well-being, with the net effect that these can actually have a more detrimental cumulative effect on us than life's bigger challenges. The old adage that we 'shouldn't sweat the small stuff' may actually be rather misguided. It may be exactly the small stuff that we should be paying most attention to.

If Gilbert's work tells us we should be careful what we wish for, we also need to make sure our goals are realistic ones. Otherwise the very targets that are supposed to be motivating

We are often very poor at predicting accurately the true value of the things we think we want.

end up de-motivating us. So many self-help writers and coaches encourage us to 'reach for the stars' but this may be bad advice unless we are already on a roll.

Research demonstrates that while so-called 'stretch goals' may be stimulating and motivating for people who have already enjoyed the reinforcement of recent successes, they can be crushing and disheartening for those with a weaker track record of accomplishment. In other words, reaching for the stars only makes any kind of sense if the stars lie within your reach already. You also need to have available resources for such goals to be useful to you. If you have used everything you've got to get where you are or are battling to maintain the status quo then a stretch goal will simply stretch you to breaking point and ping you back towards burnout. Please note that people apparently only achieve stretch goals about ten per cent of the time, and that successively failing to achieve goals creates a downward spiral in which performance becomes ever more impaired as motivation and confidence declines. Most of us should probably aim lower and build from there.

There are recent neurological studies that back this up. The brain, it turns out, is quite a conservative and vulnerable organ, primed to resist any activity that requires any radical reformulation of its patterns of activity. Push too far and your higher centres will shut off. Your grey matter will rebel by seeking to pull you back towards the comfort of the familiar. This process is analogous to what happens in muscles that are overstretched. The myotatic or 'stretch' reflex automatically causes muscle fibres to contract and resist the process of stretching, which is why, as any fitness coach will tell you, effective physical stretching has to be done gently and in incremental stages.

Another problem with our goals is that they can also unhelpfully narrow our attention as all our resources are funnelled

Reaching for the stars only makes any kind of sense if the stars lie within your reach already.

towards our target objectives. Under such circumstances we can very easily lose sight of the bigger picture and our lives can get hopelessly out of balance. Writing this I am reminded of one of my clients who worked as a bodyguard to A-list celebrities. He was explaining how when involved in a fight every ounce of his attention is concentrated on removing the obstacle (in this case his opponent) from in front of him. This ability to produce a laser-sharp, focused beam of aggression has proved an invaluable and highly effective technique for him in his work. There is absolutely no question in his mind that the object in front of him *will* yield and, invariably, it does. He's a burly chap. However, there is a downside, he tells me. In this state of pure focus on what lies in front of him, he is actually quite vulnerable. There are no spare attentional resources to devote to what might be going on behind him. For this reason, he tells me, bodyguards often have to have 'wing men' who, quite literally, watch their backs.

Similarly, some of you may have encountered the well-known selective attention task devised by Daniel Simons and Christopher Chabris. If you don't know this one already then do take a moment to log on to YouTube at www.youtube.com/watch?v=vJG698U2Mvo before you read any further.

By introducing a simple goal of counting how many times the players in white shirts pass a basketball between them, most observers watching the video completely fail to notice the presence of someone dressed in a gorilla suit walking in plain sight across the field of view. When we create goals for ourselves we stop attending to supposedly 'irrelevant' information that may not actually be irrelevant at all. In an article entitled 'Goals Gone Wild: The Systematic Effects of Over-prescribing Goal-Setting', the authors point out that losing touch with the context can encourage risky and unethical behaviour and the neglect of equally important objectives and relationships. The prescriptive nature of goals can also lull us into a kind of mental laziness, even downright stupidity: the goals provide us with a simplified agenda and one in which we no longer have to look to the way different elements of the task interact.

Sometimes goals create a sense of false priority so that people end up making sacrifices that, with the benefit of hindsight, seem hardly worthwhile. How many businesspeople have woken up to find themselves at the top of their organisations but feeling like empty shells, abandoned or ignored by the family and friends whose needs they have repeatedly set aside in order to achieve their 'dreams'?

Perhaps the most toxic thing about our obsession with goal-setting is the implication that we always have to get somewhere else, become more, do more. Where we find ourselves now, the ethos of goal setting whispers insistently, is never quite enough. By implication, who we *are* is never quite enough either. And yet all the Positive Psychology research tells us that supposedly high achievers are on the whole no happier with their lives than their lower achieving counterparts. I guess it all comes down to what achievements really count.

Whilst our goals may all too often induce the kind of tunnel vision demonstrated so elegantly in the Simons-Chabris task, by contrast contentment is one of a group of positive emotions that the cognitive psychologist Barbara Fredrickson believes actively expands our field of attention and the range of thoughts and actions that lie open to us. As a relatively stable mental disposition, contentment is not quite the same thing as happiness, which tends to be a transient emotion. However, it certainly seems to be largely independent of achievement. The yogi T. K. V. Desikachar says that contentment ('santosa') is 'the accepting of what has happened ... what we have and what we've been gifted with.' Goal setting, which ultimately is

> **Goal setting, which ultimately is about wanting more rather than being satisfied with the riches we already have, is the enemy of gratitude.**

about wanting more rather than being satisfied with the riches we already have, is the enemy of gratitude. Yet happiness researcher Dr Robert Emmons is only one of several scientists to have discovered experimentally that people encouraged to cultivate gratitude were up to 25 per cent happier on average after just ten weeks than people in the control condition. Interestingly, the sorts of things that the 'gratitude group' identified as their sources of gratitude were fairly simple and readily available to most of us. Brace yourself for a special Disney moment, but they listed things like 'sunset through the clouds', 'the generosity of friends' and even just 'the chance to be alive'. And if this stuff just makes you cringe then you *really* need to take a leaf out of Emmons' book: that kind of cynicism won't keep you warm at night, you know...

Goal setting is a statement that you will only be satisfied when you get what you want. Perhaps we need to be thinking more about how we can escape the trap of our own desires in the first place? This is of course the central idea in many Eastern philosophies including Buddhism and Taoism. We should also acknowledge that the practice of mindfulness, which encourages people to be fully present in the moment without concern for past or future, is also proving highly effective in outcome studies as a treatment for depression in the West and in producing stable improvements in people's quality of life.

Student Luo Lu, in a doctoral examination of Chinese folk psychology, summarises the Taoist position on happiness in a way that seems diametrically opposed to all our frantic goal-setting strategies. Lu explains:

> 'Happiness in Taoism is the personal liberation from all human desires, through following the Natural force, not doing anything, accepting fate calmly, and facing life with a peaceful mind. In so doing, one may reach the ultimate happiness of merging with the universe, termed "tian ren he yi". Happiness in Taoism, therefore, is not an

emotional feeling of joy, rather, it is a cognitive insight and transcendence. Taoists practice a life style of withdrawal, isolation and quietness. The ultimate goal is to achieve anonymity, vanishing into the Nature, transcending the Nature, and merging with the Nature.'

So, 'vanishing into the Nature' is the key, is it? Now there's an item you won't be finding on many Westerners' 'To Do' lists. Goal setting has a place in our lives: we all need to get things done and occasionally challenge ourselves. However, we also need to be careful that our goals don't cause us to lose sight of what really matters to us. In all our striving towards happiness and achievement we don't want to end up developing a mindset that effectively keeps it forever at arm's length.

No one can *make* you feel anything

The belief that we have total control over our responses to other people and can determine entirely the impact they have on us is surprisingly widespread. Dr Kate Wachs summarises the position as follows:

'Just as money can't make you happy, other people can't make you happy either. No one can make anyone think or feel or do anything. The only person who has that distinction is the person who owns the thoughts, feelings, and behaviour. When you accept this truth, then and only then can you be truly happy.'

The view expressed here is no longer the preserve of wibbly self-help books – now it's commonplace in management development coaching. Nearly all of us must have had the startling revelation that 'no one can actually *make* you feel anything' bestowed upon us, often in tones of eye-watering sincerity, by well-meaning friends, partners or the latest self-help blockbuster.

This has surely got to be one of the most ludicrous propositions in the whole of popular psychology. To add insult to injury, this absurd gobbet of enlightenment is invariably delivered up in such sanctimonious tones that it makes me, for one, feel all kinds of things – the uppermost of which is a desire to grab the collar of the person dispensing it and scream: 'Have you actually spent *any* time in the company of real people?'

Of course people make us feel things: I challenge you to name one significant emotional peak or trough in your life that does not have something to do with your reactions to a fellow human being. The entire history of our species is a millennia-spanning testimony to the profound impact we have on one another at all kinds of levels, many of which we have precious little conscious control over. The degree to which we are affected and influenced by other people is actually quite terrifying, but equally disquieting is our collusion with the rather smug fantasy that we are fundamentally untouchable, and that we are capable of orchestrating our own reactions to every encounter.

Okay, so I am being slightly unfair. Cognitive Behavioural Therapy (CBT) has successfully demonstrated over numerous clinical trials that teaching people to reinterpret their experiences can indeed have a beneficial knock-on effect on their emotions, and this is precisely the point that Dr Wachs is trying to make. If I believe my boss has it in for me I am likely to perceive her performance review as overly critical and nit-picking; if, on the other hand, I believe she likes me and is genuinely trying to help, I will respond to her advice as constructive criticism and leave the room with a smile on my face instead of elevated blood pressure. As thinking creatures we do have some choice about how we frame events, and of course this does influence how we subsequently feel about them.

In fact there is evidence that just the very process of thinking things through can turn down the intensity of our emotional responses. In California at the turn of the century Ahmad Hariri and colleagues found that when people were simply asked to label the expressions on faces (in other words engage in some intellectual processing of what they were seeing) their MRI scans showed reduced blood flow in the fear centres of the brain and a corresponding increase in the prefrontal cortex, the area

The degree to which we are affected and influenced by other people is actually quite terrifying.

Okay, Mrs. Philips... You'll be in the machine for the next four hours. We'll be monitoring your vitals to find out how annoyed you get during the experiment.

Remember: no one can make you feel anything ...

that helps us regulate our emotional reactions. Keeping a cool head, thinking things through, trying to be objective – all of these things can genuinely help us to some degree.

However, while the techniques of CBT have undeniably helped countless thousands of people, we are usually talking about damage limitation *after* the event. In the moment, our reactions tend to be instantaneous, unbidden and emotionally charged. It takes time and a great deal of dedicated practice to reprogramme our automatic responses to certain stimuli. The prospect that our rationality is a fire extinguisher capable of dampening down every unwanted emotion may be comforting, but it is largely a fantasy.

Reason can only help us so far because so much of what is transacted between human beings affects us at an entirely unconscious or instinctual level. For example, say you have done your grocery shop and are just about to leave the car park when you see someone else waiting for your space. Being the kind, helpful person you are you would naturally be as quick as you can to vacate the space so the next customer can occupy it. This is certainly what most people *say* they would do. However, the reality is that people who are conscious of someone waiting to take their space actually take slightly longer to leave than when no one else is around. We know this because Barry Ruback and Daniel Juieng conducted a series of experiments demonstrating precisely this phenomenon in 1997. Similarly, in another of Ruback's experiments men were found to linger longer in library aisles when joined by a male confederate. Even as supposedly civilised people we are still in thrall to ancient territorial instincts that continue to determine our behaviour, even though we may be completely oblivious to them.

Moreover, while we may think we are in control of our responses, it appears that we are very easily cued into behaving in ways that conform to other people's expectations of us without even realising it. In 1977 at the University of Minnesota Dr Mark Snyder and colleagues conducted an ingenious experiment that showed just how powerful this effect can be. A group of men were asked to hold phone conversations with women after they had been given a photo of a woman who had been judged either highly attractive or frankly rather plain by independent raters. The study set out to explore the impact of the stereotype that physical attractiveness is associated with other positive qualities such as intelligence, kindness, sociability and so on. What was fascinating was that the women, irrespective of how attractive they actually were, responded in keeping with the expectations of the man they were talking to: the men who thought they were talking to an attractive woman ended up having conversations with women who were independently rated as being far more sociable, poised, sexually warm and outgoing. As the authors of the research concluded: 'What had initially been reality in the minds of the men had now become reality in the behaviour of the women with whom they had interacted – a behavioural reality discernible even by naive observer judges, who had access *only* to tape recordings of the women's contributions to the conversations.'

An even more graphic example of our tendency to conform instinctively to the roles that others create for us is the behaviour of the subjects in Stanley Milgram's experiments who administered what they believed to be dangerously high levels of electric shocks to other people just because a man in a white coat told them to. Or what about the behaviour of the students randomly allocated to play the role of guards in the infamous Stanford prison experiment conducted in the seventies? These young men, all of whom had been psychologically evaluated as well-balanced and intelligent beforehand, obligingly fell into role and produced some truly sadistic behaviour, punishing their pretend prisoners in ways strongly reminiscent of more recent images from Abu Ghraib. We may think we would be immune, but as one of the student guards retaliated to a hostile audience during questions at the end of a lecture about Zimbardo's experiment: 'Can you say for sure that you would have done any different?' We may like to think we can control our actions and reactions in the way popular psychology assures us we can, but as Yale psychologist John Bargh reminds us, people are reluctant to recognise how much of their everyday experience 'is determined not by their conscious intentions and deliberate choices, but by mental processes put into motion by their environment'. In other words, we may think we're calling the shots, but most of the time we are not even aware of the extent to which we are being unconsciously cued into particular roles by the actions and behaviour of those around us. How we

We may think we're calling the shots, but most of the time we are not even aware of the extent to which we are being unconsciously cued into particular roles by the actions and behaviour of those around us.

experience the world, and even how we experience ourselves, is largely determined by others.

On a more upbeat note, these invisible tendrils of social influence can produce positive effects too. Dr Robert Rosenthal reports on an experiment in which students were allocated to two classes. The teacher of one was told that the children in that class were gifted and exceptionally able, while the other was informed that her class was made up of children who were underachievers and likely to need extra help. In fact at this point there was no difference in the average ability of either class. However, lo and behold, by the end of the year the students in the 'gifted' class were indeed outperforming their peers while the underachievers became precisely that.

Further evidence of the way other people automatically condition our responses to them has come from Alex Pentland's 'reality mining' studies at Massachusetts Institute of Technology (MIT). By equipping subjects with modified smart phones which recorded data regarding aspects of their non-verbal communications (including proximity, tone and posture), the MIT team have demonstrated a subliminal level of interaction taking place between people that turns out to be a far more reliable index of what's really going on between them than the superficial content of their conversation. We are not only highly attuned to these 'honest signals' but they powerfully influence our behaviour and mood, again without us even being aware of it. As Pentland explains, 'honest cues are also unusual because they trigger changes in people receiving the signals, changes that are advantageous to the people who send them.' So potent is this second channel of communication that by observing the first five minutes of a mock salary negotiation, judges on the lookout for the relevant subliminal behaviours were able to predict with an 87 per cent accuracy who would come out on top.

One aspect of non-verbal communication that Pentland's team have focused upon is the non-conscious mimicry that tends to occur automatically when people spend time in each

Be on the lookout for those subtle body-language clues ...

other's company. Various studies have confirmed that people tend to copy each other's body language, facial expressions, speech patterns and vocal tones. The reason this automatic mimicry is crucial in understanding social influence is because psychologists believe it may be one of the mechanisms that underlie emotional contagion, i.e. the ability of one person to transfer emotions to another. What we do with our bodies has a direct impact on the emotions we experience. Smile (even though your heart is breaking) and science suggests you will indeed feel better. Slump in your seat and your mood is more likely to become listless and despondent. In fact this feedback mechanism is so effective that researchers from the University of Cardiff found that women whose ability to frown was inhibited after receiving botox injections reported feeling much happier and less anxious – even though they believed the procedure hadn't significantly improved their appearance!

It seems likely that by unconsciously copying the behaviour and micro-expressions of people around us we consequently end up replicating their emotions. In fact, research has established that even feelings like loneliness can be catching. A careful investigation conducted in Framingham, Massachusetts found that if even one person in a neighbourhood felt lonely for one day a week, the level of perceived loneliness across the neighbourhood also rose. More dramatic examples of contagion would be the kind of mass hysteria you see sweep across crowds, or the tragic events that took place in another Massachusetts town, Salem, in 1662 when a number of teenage girls were tried as witches after replicating each other's screaming and convulsions so closely that a local minister decided they were 'beyond the power of epileptic fits or natural disease to effect'.

It is not only through the subconscious power of imitation that we are exposed to the emotions of those around us. It turns out that we are neurologically configured to connect up with what others around us are experiencing. In recent years scientists have discovered specialised mirror neurones in the brain that effectively put us into the other person's shoes. Simply watching someone kicking a ball fires up the motor centres of our own brains that would be involved if we were the ones doing the kicking. But it also appears to be true of emotions as well. When we see someone upset, mirror neurones trigger a sympathetic activation of our own emotional processing centres. Far from other people not being able to make us feel anything, we are in fact hard-wired in ways that predispose us to feel their pain or share their joy.

Mirror neurone research suggests there is substantial psychological mileage in the old adage that 'we become like the company we keep'. Whether this is pleasurable, enlightening, soothing or discordant depends on a host of interpersonal variables. Other people can expose us to the best and the worst in ourselves. They can transport us to delirious emotional heights but, as Sartre pointed out, they can also take us straight to hell. However, it is certainly naive to assume that we are in full control of the emotional impact of such encounters.

Far from relying upon the dodgy adage that no one can make us feel anything we don't allow, instead we should recognise just how vulnerable and open we are to the invisible and unconscious influence of those around us. We would be well advised, therefore, to make thoughtful choices about the company we keep or, as the silent movie star Louise Beal astutely put it: 'Love thy neighbour as yourself, but choose your neighbourhood.'

We should also be mindful of our own impact on others. We've seen that other people can't necessarily choose how to respond to us. So how we are around other people really matters – yet this is rarely, if ever, the subject of any self-help guru. They and we naturally attend to the way other people leave us feeling, but how much do we reflect upon the way we can change the atmosphere in a room or how our manner affects other people? In years to come I suspect we will no longer think about pollution as merely what happens when you pump toxic fumes into the atmosphere or fail to recycle domestic waste. While physical waste is obvious to us all, 'emotional pollution' is no less of a real issue. Its cumulative effects can be significant. As the eco-campaigners would say: we all need to take responsibility for ensuring we are part of the solution and not part of the problem.

Of course, you might also want to question whether you might not *want* to allow other people to make you feel things from time to time. Rumour has it that other people can sometimes make you feel pretty good. Even when they don't,

> **We should recognise just how vulnerable and open we are to the invisible and unconscious influence of those around us.**

while it might be prudent to keep those feelings to yourself sometimes, our spontaneous internal reactions to the people around us and the things that happen to us are an important part of being fully alive. Surely we're not now aspiring to be emotionally vacant Stepford Wives who sail through life's twists and turns completely unruffled, with never a hair out of place? Other people will always have the capacity to make us laugh and cry. They can light us up with joy one moment and cast us into despair the next. That's just how it is. And to be honest, would we really want it any other way?

MYTH 6

Think positive and be a winner!

'When life hands you lemons, make lemonade ...'[1] famously advised Norman Vincent Peale, a Reformed Church minister and founding father of the Positive Thinking movement. If you ever needed a demonstration of the power of positive thinking, then the way the ideology of 'accentuating the positive' has infiltrated every level of Western culture since the 1950s might well clinch the argument.

Of course the policy of always insisting on a glass half full has also had its detractors. Writer and journalist Barbara Ehrenreich is the latest champion in a valiant tradition of hardcore dissenters and her acerbic commentary *Smile or Die* is well worth a read. However, it is fair to say that such conscientious objectors are very much in the minority. Increasingly they cut Canute-like figures railing against an unstoppable cultural tide. Most of us now take it for granted that a positive mental attitude is very much an asset in life and should be nurtured whenever possible.

Positive thinking can now be found in a myriad of forms, ranging from confidence-building affirmations to visualisations for combating illness or losing weight, but here I want to focus on the least fanciful tip of the iceberg: the idea that a positive mental attitude is the key to generally getting on in life, as well as providing a reliable foundation for your mental health.

---

[1] Or as some wag once said: 'When life hands you *melons*, it's probably also handed you dyslexia ...'

While Peale's legacy has left a great deal of blatant quackery in its wake, the rise of Cognitive Behavioural Therapy (CBT) has given positive thinking a new gloss of scientific respectability. Of course, CBT has tended to avoid phrases like 'positive thinking' (probably precisely because of their somewhat dubious heritage), but certainly makes no bones about the destructive impact of 'negative' thoughts upon people's mood and state of mind. And of course you don't need to be a rocket scientist, or even a psychologist, to appreciate how a more positive attitude can lift your mood or have beneficial knock-on effects upon your behaviour.

Professor Martin Seligman, who is interested in what helps some people cope better than others, has done a great deal of methodical research demonstrating how important an optimistic explanatory style may be in warding off depression. He notes that depressed people tend to blame themselves for their misfortunes rather than find mitigating circumstances as their more optimistic counterparts tend to do. They tend to see setbacks as permanent rather than temporary and generalise from specific incidents to reach bleak conclusions about themselves and their lot in life. If negative thinking predisposes you to some forms of mental illness, then surely it stands to reason that positive thinking has to be the most appropriate antidote, doesn't it?

Well, Canadian researchers Joanne Wood, John Lee and Elaine Perunovic wouldn't necessarily agree. They found that while repeating positive affirmations (e.g. 'I am a lovable person') can provide an emotional boost for some people, if you suffer from low self-esteem then these affirmations can actually make you feel worse, not better. The reason for this appears to

If you suffer from low self-esteem then these affirmations can actually make you feel worse, not better.

be that for someone who feels truly wretched, parroting positive sentiments opens up a credibility gap so wide that it cannot be bridged. Instead of using such affirmations as stepping-stones to a more upbeat reality, depressed people just become more painfully conscious of the discrepancy between where they find themselves and where they would like to be. One individual, after attempting to cure himself of depression using positive self-affirmations, described how they merely became 'slogans of self-loathing'.

Similarly, independent studies have shown that while for non-depressed people positive affirmations do appear to dampen down levels of responsiveness in the amygdala (effectively the 'fear centre' of the brain), for depressed people the opposite effect is produced: the amygdala becomes *more* rather than less active while the affirmations are being rehearsed.

This is not the only context in which positive thinking can be counter-productive. It would also appear that sometimes people who are especially good at visualising their preferred future (as self-help books often encourage you to do) may unwittingly trigger a relaxation response usually only activated once goals have been successfully achieved. Perversely, this could make it harder for people who successfully picture their desired future to marshal the energy, focus or discipline they may require to make it a reality. The poet and novelist Anatole France once pointed out that 'To accomplish great things we must dream as well as act', but of course the opposite is equally true. Dreaming without action doesn't usually accomplish too much.

Not only can too much positive thinking rob you of your motivation to act, but it can also handicap you psychologically in other ways. Joseph Forgas, a professor of social psychology, reports that 'Whereas positive mood seems to promote creativity, flexibility, cooperation and reliance on mental shortcuts, negative moods trigger more attentive, careful thinking, paying greater attention to the external world'. Positive thinking, just as surely as negative thinking, can blinker us to important aspects of reality. Barbara Ehrenreich believes that the blind optimism that positive thinking fosters induced the kind of recklessness that ran rife on the trading floors in the 80s and 90s and helped drag the world towards global financial meltdown.

In 2011, Bettina von Helverson and colleagues conducted a research study that indicates depressed people are also better at sequential decision-making. She reported that '... depressed participants accepted options less readily, which led to longer search and better choices' and concluded that '[t]hese results suggest that depression, by fostering greater persistence, may improve performance in certain tasks.' Maybe cloud nine isn't always the best place to sit when you're at work? Ronda Muir, who runs a consultancy firm to the legal profession, speculates that an intuitive grasp of this principle may explain why generations of Swiss watchmakers have traditionally piped downbeat music into their workshops in order to hone their concentration and accuracy.

In fact, the assumption that positive feelings are incompatible with stress and depression may also reflect a peculiarly Western take on happiness. Research conducted at the University of Seattle found that while a lack of positive emotions coincided with stress and depression symptoms in European Americans, amongst immigrant Asian participants no such association could be detected. Commentators trying to make sense of these findings believe the most likely explanation is that in Asian cultures suffering is regarded as a precondition of growth. Consequently a perpetually positive person might also be thought of as spiritually weak or immature. Within Eastern cultures both positive and negative feelings are to be accepted on the basis that everything is in constant flux. Received wisdom is that all feelings, whether positive or negative, will ultimately pass and both must therefore be accommodated. The idea of trying to replace one type of feeling with another is quite alien to the Eastern mind.

So how do you tell if a thought is positive or not? The

"Just keep kicking and you'll stay afloat!"

"Okay... like this?"

"Yes! Isn't that fun?"

"No."

Nobody feels positive all of the time ...

simple rule of thumb here in the Western hemisphere is that a positive thought is one that makes us feel good, while a negative one makes us feel bad. At least that is often what CBT seems to be telling us. The trouble is that what makes us 'feel good' is not necessarily good *for* us. The 'feel-good factor' can prove a pretty flaky criteria for deciding on the value of many things, especially what we choose to fill our minds with. By this kind of reckoning heroin could be seen as a very 'positive' drug, but that doesn't mean I want to start taking it.

A commitment to unrelenting positivity can not only make us quite irritating to be with, it can also make us rather selfish and narrow-minded. If I repeatedly tell myself that I should be striving to feel good at all times and avoiding or disavowing any thought pattern that makes me uncomfortable or sad, I inevitably have to focus on a fairly narrow repertoire of thoughts and beliefs. Sooner or later I will also need to start disconnecting myself from other people and their concerns. Too much empathy becomes a threat to my ability to maintain my positive state of mind which is, after all, the main priority. Not only do I need to focus exclusively on thoughts that keep me feeing good, but I have a duty to insulate myself against other people's pain and negativity.

The latent dangers of unbridled positivity are nicely illustrated by the resonance between aspects of a positive mental attitude as commended to us by the self-help industry and the thought patterns characteristic of hardened criminals. I don't want to overplay this, but it is interesting that criminologists agree that one of the dominant features of the criminal mindset is a pervasive sense of entitlement. As Yochelson and Samenow explain: 'The main cognitive distortion leading to offending is thought by some to be the over-valuing of self-centred attitudes and thoughts that entitle an offender to behave in a deviant manner'. Of course, much positive-thinking teaching deliberately encourages us to think in terms of our rights and dues and exhorts us to 'name it and claim it'. Most positive affirmations are about the self: I challenge you to find one that focuses on the needs or rights of others.

The Psychological Inventory of Criminal Thinking Styles (PICTS) contains eight sub-scales designed to pick up thought patterns commonly found in repeat offenders. One of these addresses the tendency of criminals to cut off or dissociate from feelings of fear and anxiety when they arise. Positive thinking, with its emphasis on superimposing positive emotions over negative ones is, at one level, a technology for silencing unwanted or distressing emotions, often by denying their very existence.

Offenders are also distinguished by what PICTS describes as their 'Power Orientation' or the need to maintain absolute control over other people and their immediate environment. The most extreme version of positive thinking presented in 'mind over matter' books like Rhonda Byrne's *The Secret* is of course the ultimate fantasy of control. The authors promise that

> **most positive affirmations are about the self: I challenge you to find one that focuses on the needs or rights of others.**

the very fabric of reality can be refashioned any way you like. Positive thinking pursued to extremes allows for no detractors, not even, it would appear, the laws of physics. Aspects of positive thinking could also readily be mistaken for the 'Super-optimism' displayed by criminals. In their case this is usually manifest in an unrealistic confidence in their chances of 'getting away with it', but positive thinking can also generate unwarranted confidence in desired outcomes, regardless of any obstacles that may lie in the way. 'Super-optimism' is also closely related to another PICTS sub-scale, namely 'Cognitive Indolence'. This refers to a generally uncritical attitude to one's thoughts, plans and ideas accompanied by impoverished problem-solving skills. As we have seen, positive thinking, affirmation and visualisation can circumvent the need for more prosaic but effective strategies for achieving your goals. If you can simply dial up a pizza, why trouble yourself with making a shopping list buying the ingredients, kneading the dough and working out the cooking time yourself? On the other hand, ringing a pizza delivery store does *actually* work ...

I am not arguing that positive thinking fosters criminality. But I do think we should be careful about abandoning ourselves wholesale to Vincent Peale's philosophy. Optimistic, life-affirming people can be great company, but like many effective remedies, positive thinking can produce some pretty undesirable side-effects when taken to excess. Denial is never good for the soul, and we need the information provided by the full spectrum of our feelings – not just the more upbeat ones. If we want to live as grown ups then we have to risk confronting reality head-on, however daunting, confusing or disappointing

Is it so far-fetched to imagine a future in which those who prefer to encounter reality in the raw ultimately become marginalised or even persecuted?

that may prove at times, and not become shallow fantasists who just stick our heads in the sand and insist that things are the way we want them to be. Right up to the end, passengers aboard the *Titanic* in 1912 clung stubbornly to the belief that the ship was 'unsinkable'. It still went down.

As you can probably tell, I'm nervous about our headlong rush to embrace the positive. Is it so far-fetched to imagine a future in which those who prefer to encounter reality in the raw ultimately become marginalised or even persecuted? Where 'negative' thinking becomes the new Thought Crime? Call me paranoid, but then I do live in a country where the government is about to conduct a census to check if I'm happy enough.

Let's face it: negative thinking is draining and depressing. No one needs an Eeyore in their life, let alone to become one. However, in my opinion, people who *always* look on the bright side can be pretty annoying too. More often than not they seem – how can I put this politely? – a little bit unbalanced. I invite you to join me in making a brave stand for the middle ground. It may not be particularly glamorous and the terrain can be a little boggy at times, however, ultimately it's also far less likely to give way underneath you.

We need to talk ...

'We need to talk ...' Ouch! If we are totally honest, who amongst us doesn't die inside just a little when we hear our partner utter that ominous invitation, even at those times when we know full well there is an issue between us that has to be addressed? But why does the prospect of a 'talk' make us feel that way? Is it conceivable that the sinking feeling in the pit of our stomach is an inner voice to be heeded rather than to be brushed aside?

The novelist Rose Macaulay once complained that, 'It is a common delusion that you make things better by talking about them.' This seems an extreme position to me: talking things through undoubtedly helps on occasion, and people like me would be out of a job if it didn't. However, I do agree that Psychobabble has promoted the general misconception that the majority of tensions experienced in relationships are the result of communication failure. Surely, the argument runs, if couples could only learn to talk to each other properly, without scrapping, and *really* seek to understand each other's point of view, the large part of their difficulties would be over? This may be so, and couples counselling is founded on this very maxim, but what if talk isn't always the best answer?

First we need to make the crucial distinction between 'talking' and communicating, which is a much larger concept. It's not that most of us are bad at communicating: if anything I would venture to suggest that a lot of difficulties in our relationships occur precisely because of just how well we communicate. It's *what* we communicate that tends to create the problems: most of us can convey our hurt, anger, ridicule, and rejection

This? You want this olive branch? Do you?

You're gonna have to fight me for it.

Make sure you're in the right frame of mind before you talk to your partner...

only too well (if you are seeking independent confirmation, just ask your partner ...). The trouble is that since these emotions are conveyed primarily through non-verbal channels over which we have limited control, we can continue broadcasting them at full volume at the very moment we are ostensibly 'talking' to resolve the issues between us.

We have already seen how influential Alex Pentland's so-called 'second channel' of communication can be. Minute fluctuations in our movements, tone of voice, levels of agitation, our fluency and various other non-verbal markers tend to make our true feelings transparent, even when we seek to mask them. One aspect of non-verbal communication that Pentland's team have focused upon is the non-conscious mimicry that tends to occur automatically when people spend time in each other's company. Various studies have confirmed that people tend to copy each other's body language, facial expressions, speech patterns and vocal tones. These micro-synchronies often take place incredibly fast, much faster than they can be consciously processed. As psychologist Elaine Hatfield points out, it took Muhammad Ali at least 190 milliseconds to even detect a signal light and another 40 milliseconds to respond with a punch. Yet college students have proved capable of synchronising their movements in less than 21 milliseconds, literally less than the blink of an eye. Fans of body-language books should pay attention to this: the speed with which this all happens naturally is so fluid and instantaneous that any attempts to replicate it deliberately are always going to feel clumsy and awkward and are seldom going to be very convincing.

Moreover, the more emotive the situation, the less likely you are to be able to monitor or modify these aspects of your behaviour effectively. Yes, by all means read the body-language books and do your best to adopt a suitably open posture, maintain an appropriate level of eye contact and mirror your partner's gestures. Above all, take especial care not to broadcast the non-verbal signals such as eye-rolling that signal contempt since, as relationship expert John Gottmann has shown in the

While we may choose our words with care, we are much less consciously in control of the subliminal cues we are giving out.

lab, any signs of contempt may well prove fatal to your exchange and possibly to your relationship. However, the chances are your true feelings will still leak out. If you are angry or stressed, your partner will know it. While we may choose our words with care, we are much less consciously in control of the subliminal cues we are giving out. Let's not forget that you are disadvantaged here by the fact the other person knows you a little too well. They have been learning the nuances and subtleties of your non-verbal repertoire for some time. They will instinctively and subliminally detect your clumsy attempts at concealment and the authentic emotions that escape anyway will be highlighted. And, naturally, if your partner rumbles your deliberate use of communication techniques of any kind, they will quite rightly feel manipulated. Needless to say, this will not enhance the quality of your 'talk'.

In a negotiation of any kind, both parties have in mind things that they want from the other. Usually they will be prepared to make concessions in order to achieve them. Even when the currency of exchange are concrete tokens like goods, services, or rates of pay it can be difficult enough for the opposing sides to reach a settlement both can live with. But when a couple 'talks' things are even more complex and the stakes exponentially higher. Neither party is likely to be satisfied with superficial changes in behaviour; what they really want is validation of their point of view. Sara doesn't just want Finn to apologise for his outburst over Christmas; she wants him to agree with her that his actions were completely unacceptable. For his part, Finn needs Sara to recognise that he was being pushed beyond all reasonable limits by her sister's constant carping, that it's crazy that Sara just puts up with it, and that his girlfriend was lucky he didn't do something considerably worse.

For both parties often the only good outcome of the 'talk' is the other person signing up to their particular view of the world. Contrary to common belief, it is often not sufficient for a couple to understand where each other is coming from: these peace talks are often derailed by a covert agenda to achieve consensus, even when perspectives are utterly irreconcilable.

More importantly, validating your partner's worldview under such circumstances invariably involves casting yourself into an undesirable role in that world. It's agreeing to be that 'insensitive brute who can't control his temper' or the 'passive doormat who lets anyone speak to her whichever way they choose'. In these negotiations, concessions come at a heavy price. No one likes to deny their own viewpoint or occupy a devalued position in someone else's meaning system. Unconsciously, participants in such talks are well aware that not only their construction of reality but their very identity is under threat.

Even if, for the sake of restoring the peace, one partner ultimately decides to endorse the other's worldview, the emotional cost can breed underlying resentment that only erupts later in the context of some other issue. If you do go down the talking route, if at all possible, find some re-frame that allows *both* of you to emerge in a positive light with your dignity intact. If you have to, just agree to differ. Author Alexander Penney reminds us: 'The ultimate test of a relationship is to disagree but hold hands.' Do not try and bludgeon your partner into admitting that you are in the right. You may win the battle but you will almost certainly be losing the war.

So if talking is so fraught with hazard, what are the alternatives? Ignoring issues isn't usually advisable (although you'd be surprised how often it seems to work for some couples). To understand another way forward you need to strip things back a little. We often over-complicate things when it comes to our relationships and frequently the issues that preoccupy us and which are the subject of endless debate with our partners are not as pertinent as they feel. We could all do worse than heed this very basic truth: the people we find most attractive and the ones we are closest to are those who consistently make us feel good.

Disappointingly simple, I know, but you would be surprised how often we ignore this at our peril and then end up wondering why we don't feel emotionally connected any more. The people who make us feel good do this in two main ways: first by stimulating positive, enjoyable emotions in us; secondly by validating or affirming us. We naturally seek out the company of people who can trigger a rush of 'feel good' hormones in us, and those who persist in seeing us as a Good Thing, especially when they know about our failings too. As Edna Buchanan put it: 'True friends are those who really know you but love you anyway.' Research into friendship conducted by Carolyn Weisz and Lisa F. Wood from the University of Puget Sound, Washington, also disclosed that even more important than intimacy was the ability of best friends to support and validate people's preferred identities. If these things hadn't taken place at some stage you would never have ended up with your partner in the first place.

If restoring harmony depends upon re-prioritising these objectives, then intense verbal exchanges are not necessarily always the most effective way or direct way of achieving them. Consider the hormone oxytocin, which is a powerful bonding agent. It makes people feel close, warm and secure with each other. It is released by breast-feeding mothers to promote attachment with their babies and also during orgasm. Now if you are hacked off with your partner you may not feel in the mood to proceed straight to the 'make-up sex' (although making love rather than verbal war can be a surprisingly effective way of circumventing emotional distance). However, oxytocin is also released across the full spectrum of physical contact ranging from massage through to sustained eye contact. A reassuring stroke of the shoulder (providing it is meant and received in the right spirit) can be more healing to your relationship than picking over the debris of your last fight, or can at least set the scene for a less fraught exchange between you. Those hormones will help soothe your relational troubles away ... if you let them. Touch is hugely powerful, and if couples could bear to make themselves sit and hold hands for a few minutes before they talked, the conversations they have subsequently might be very different.

Now of course you are probably reading this thinking,

'Physical contact of any kind is the very last thing I want with them right now!' Indeed, you may not be ready or willing to make your partner feel good. If this is the case you have some work to do *before* you talk. You need to focus on the other aspect of the people we like to be around – their ability to hold on to a positive representation of us. Rather than seeking validation *from* your partner, your best chance of success in repairing the emotional breech is simply to put effort into affirming them instead. The theologian Thomas Jay Oord gives us a useful definition of *agape*, one of the Greeks' subcategories of love: 'an intentional response to promote well-being when responding to that which has generated ill-being'. This captures the spirit of what we are aiming for here. However, you will be relieved to hear that I am not advocating that you have to start paying them compliments or telling them how marvellous they are. This is a job best done initially on your own, in private.

In the course of your conflict your internal model of your partner has been damaged. You don't see them as a 'good thing' right now because you are still smarting about what they have just done. But while you see them in a negative light, even if you say nothing at all, your partner will sense it. In this state you are no longer a psychic ally but a threat, and they will protect themselves against you – either by attacking you or withdrawing from you. The internal representations we hold of people are hugely powerful things, influencing both our behaviour and theirs in ways we can scarcely conceive.

I was very struck by the first chapter of Stephen Covey's famous book, *The Seven Habits of Highly Effective People*. What impressed me was not his approach to micromanaging life (which seems to me completely unsustainable for most mere

The internal representations we hold of people are hugely powerful things, influencing both our behaviour and theirs in ways we can scarcely conceive.

mortals), but an anecdote he tells about his son. Covey and his wife had been getting increasingly worried about their child who was struggling academically and apparently came across as emotionally immature and socially awkward. His parents dutifully attempted to boost his self-esteem with a relentless diet of praise and encouragement but nothing seemed to be working. In the end, it dawned on Covey that the real problem was their internal representation of their boy. He explains:

> 'When we honestly examined our deepest feelings, we realised that our perception of him was that he was basically inadequate, somehow "behind". No matter how much we worked on our attitude and behaviour, our efforts were ineffective because, despite our actions and our words, what we really communicated to him was "You aren't capable. You need to be protected"'.

By challenging the inadequate image of their son they carried around with them, Covey and his wife gradually released him to become a confident, self-assured and capable young man. Unfortunately, when couples 'talk' this dynamic is often reversed. If it goes well for you, you successfully wrest from your partner an acknowledgement that your freshly-minted negative image of their inadequacies is actually the more accurate account: the fact they have stuffed up and failed proves it, and they need to accept this. Keep seeing them like that and neither of you are going to be charmed by the ultimate result.

Like it or not, your primary psychological task, for as long as you want to be with the person concerned, is to be the standard-bearer of a positive image of your loved one (even if you do hate their guts right now). Once you achieve this again, being around you will be an enjoyable, affirming experience for your partner, or at least an emotionally safe one, *even if you do nothing else*. I sincerely believe that only under those circumstances can your relationship move forward.

Take yourself away, set aside your hurt for a moment and remind yourself of the qualities you admired in your partner when you first met. Mentally rehearse the good times you had, those occasions when you felt proud to be with them. Internally reassert your faith in them, even if you feel they are challenging that faith to its limits right now.

There is actually good experimental evidence that this works in the form of a study that found levels of marital satisfaction were much higher amongst couples that unrealistically idealised their partners. This was the discovery of Sandra Murray and her colleagues, who followed 222 newlywed couples throughout the first three years of married life. Naturally, when the research was published, there was some scepticism about the wisdom of looking at your partner through such rose-tinted glasses. However, I suspect the study doesn't necessarily reflect the naivety of the couples involved so much as their ongoing commitment to a process of active affirmation and a commendable desire to remain true to the very best image of their chosen Other they could possibly internalise. If love is blind, perhaps that is only because it deliberately chooses to keep staring into the sun. Or maybe Rabbi Julius Gordon hit the nail on the head when he wrote: 'Love is not blind – it sees more, not less. But because it sees more, it is willing to see less.' It is no coincidence that partners viewed in this way felt grateful, appreciative and pleased with their relationships. It's a fundamental and universal need to have someone on our side, to keep faith with the best in us, come what may. This is probably one of the highest services that one human being can perform for another.

Many successful couples swear by the adage of 'never letting the sun go down on your anger'. It's good advice, but it doesn't always have to be achieved through protracted negotiation and 'sorting things out' verbally. Sometimes the best policy is to go back to basics, reset the dynamics of your relationship and leapfrog over the contentious issue for the time being. Go away, lick your wounds and retrieve a less blemished vision of your partner. Thus equipped, then try and ensure that your company is affirming or pleasurable. Do something you both enjoy together. Share a joke. Cultivate a sense of solidarity by gossiping about someone else you both have an issue with. Cook a meal you both really like. I know all these things sound completely counterintuitive when tensions are running high, but if you can manage it you will lay a much stronger foundation for a meaningful reconciliation.

If you can do this, your non-verbal communication will take care of itself. This matters because it is through this channel that we experience emotional attunement with the other: mothers and infants speak volumes to each other in their easy, complementary dance of reciprocal gestures and expressive cues, and often not an intelligible word is uttered by either party.

Of course I'm not saying that you shouldn't talk; there's definitely a time and a place for it. But it isn't always straight away. Bad talk is not necessarily preferable to no talk. And if you are going to have a heart-to-heart, then at least try and make sure that's what it is, rather than a full-frontal assault on your partner's identity. Your conversation needs a context so take care to create the conditions under which it stands the best chance of being fruitful: before the talking can really start there may be other things you need to do first. No one is going to be able to have an effective conversation with you unless they feel safe.

And remember, the time you are most likely to force your point home is the time when you need to tread most carefully. I have always admired the wisdom of the author Marita Bonner when she wrote:

> 'She did not talk to people as if they were strange hard shells she had to crack open to get inside. She talked as if she were already in the shell. In their very shell.'

If talking between couples could only be more like that, I'd be all for it, and Relate would probably be out of business.

Bad talk is not necessarily preferable to no talk.

Whatever your problem, CBT is the answer

If you are reading this, you will almost certainly have heard of it. Cognitive Behavioural Therapy (CBT) is all the rage these days. As a cost-effective, evidence-based treatment for an ever-expanding wide range of conditions it has quite understandably won favour with health-care providers and been widely publicised as a 'magic bullet' for all manner of problems. Fresh with its gleaming seal of approval from the National Institute of Clinical Excellence, CBT is widely perceived as the modern, efficient and scientific cure. CBT is 'therapy à la mode' and its practical, skills-based approach to managing your own mental health sits very comfortably within the expectations, desires and ethos of our busy modern world.

So effective has CBT been at promoting itself that at the practice where I work we regularly get phone calls from clients who specifically request CBT before they have even been assessed or considered other options. This is because they are already persuaded that CBT is the gold standard treatment of choice: in their minds science has proved beyond all doubt that it works and they don't want to be fobbed off with anything else, especially not that drawn-out business with the threadbare couch, those awkward silences, and the murderous rage you feel whenever you think about Daddy 'accidentally' blowing out the candles on your fifth birthday.

The central premise of CBT, that by changing the way we think we can also change the way we feel, is a powerful one and the techniques of CBT have undoubtedly helped a lot of people dig themselves out of some pretty deep holes. I use CBT in my own clinics. I've even written a book about it, so I'd definitely count myself as a believer. However, I am also a believer with reservations. I don't think that Cognitive Behavioural Therapy is necessarily the answer to every contemporary ailment. I believe that there is still a place for other types of therapy and I think there is a risk that CBT may be somewhat overplaying its hand.

Supporters of CBT make a big fanfare about its solid evidence base, but while CBT has certainly been ahead of the game in appreciating that the reputation of the treatment was going to depend on proper outcome studies, so far the results have not been quite as dramatic as people tend to assume. For example, in the spring of 2008 Stefan Hofmann and Jasper Smits performed a meta-analysis of CBT treatment outcomes for anxiety disorders – one of the conditions with which CBT is most closely associated. While many of the studies they looked at failed to satisfy even reasonable standards of rigour, of the ones that remained they calculated that CBT had produced a treatment effect of 0.33 for anxiety symptoms and had notably less of an effect on depressive symptoms. Now that may not mean a lot to you (depending on how much you like to hang out with statisticians), but as a crude rule of thumb you might want to think of 0.2 as small, 0.5 as medium and 0.8 as large effects. By this estimation CBT produced a positive result, albeit a modest one. However, Dr Peter Kramer rather puts this result into perspective by helpfully pointing out that, 'With an effect size of .33, three quarters of treated patients, even if doing somewhat better, would continue to experience symptoms in the range suffered by untreated patients'.

Moreover, while CBT might perform as well, and sometimes better, than certain other types of therapy in the short term, some studies suggest that long-term psychotherapy may actually be a better treatment for chronic depression, or those more complex cases where depression occurs alongside other mental-health problems. In a post on the website for the British

Psychoanalytic Council in 2009, Daniel McQueen accuses the National Institute of Clinical Excellence of choosing to ignore this research because of its own bias towards CBT and cheap, quick treatment protocols. He further claims that evidence for the effectiveness of even shorter-term psychodynamic therapy was binned simply because a larger number of studies existed supporting claims for CBT and Interpersonal Therapy. McQueen protests that 'such vote counting is simply misleading'. The bottom line is that we need to be a bit more sanguine about touting CBT around as some kind of miracle cure. The existing evidence base certainly doesn't suggest that.

In any case, the truth of the matter is that the nature of your relationship with your therapist is far more significant in determining how much benefit you will get from treatment than any particular school of therapy they may belong to. Based on a careful literature review conducted in 1992, M. J. Lambert estimated that while the particular techniques employed account for only approximately 15 per cent of the effectiveness of therapy, the quality of the therapeutic alliance forged between therapist and client contributes a whopping 30 per cent. This is only one in a whole range of studies that would suggest it doesn't matter so much what particular brand of therapy is being used as how you feel about the person doing it. In 2001 Bruce Wampold, a former statistician who examined the outcomes for treatment of depression, supported Lambert's conclusions and reported that no one modality of treatment emerged as significantly better than any other – including CBT. More recently the American Psychological Association sponsored a task force to sort out once and for all what works in the therapy relationship. Once again, the same conclusion emerged: the consensus of several thousand studies was that the nature of the therapeutic relationship had just as much impact on whether clients improved (or failed to improve) as any particular treatment method.

Efficacy apart, it seems to me that there are some fundamental theoretical issues that CBT hasn't really addressed. In founder Aaron Beck's original model, your thoughts, feelings, physiological reactions and behaviour are all connected in a system of mutual influence. If you work with a CBT practitioner, before long you will inevitably find yourself sitting in front of a fetching diagram plastered with two-way arrows illustrating these pathways of mutual cause and effect. However, while the kingdom of the mind thus described may look like a democratic polity in which the wards of thought, sensation, feeling and action all enjoy equal status and influence, when it comes down to the nitty-gritty of actually doing the therapeutic work, you will find that most attention is concentrated on one particular area: your thought life. The mutterings of that critical voice in your head, those unwanted thoughts that pop unbidden into your mind – these are the primary targets of CBT and get the lion's share of its attention. In the realm of CBT, to misquote George Orwell's *Animal Farm*, while all the factors involved are supposedly equal, some appear to be more equal than others.

CBT remains a largely top-down model. To listen to the more zealous CBT therapists speak, you would conclude that if the head doesn't always rule the heart, it potentially always can and probably should. CBT has encouraged a widespread and misplaced assumption that our thoughts (positive or negative) are always the root cause of our emotions and on the back of this rides the expectation that we can reliably mobilise our thoughts to subdue any emotions we don't want around.

But, as any honest CBT therapist will tell you, one of the recurrent problems that crops up in CBT sessions is the difficulty of isolating the relevant 'automatic thoughts'. Negative automatic thoughts – as the name implies – are supposedly the thoughts that inconveniently pop into one's mind as a result of

> **CBT has encouraged a widespread and misplaced assumption that our thoughts (positive or negative) are always the root cause of our emotions.**

certain biases of interpretation: 'I'm rubbish'; 'Things never go my way'; 'I can't cope with this' and so on. We are all familiar with the persecutory little voice that whispers such things to us, and your CBT therapist will be keen to pinpoint such cognitions since they are believed to be the switches that open the floodgates of unpleasant feelings.

But often these negative automatic thoughts prove surprisingly elusive. Clients will describe situations that left them flooded with feelings of panic or despair but really struggle to identify any conscious thoughts that may have been involved. Sometimes the therapist will helpfully suggest a way that the client *might* have been construing the scenario in question, or use their existing knowledge of the client to tie the reaction into other beliefs that the client has about themselves. Often they will fall back on the old cliché that these thoughts are just so habitual that while we may scarcely notice them any more, they're still there dragging us down nonetheless. But this is just cheating isn't it? What if those thoughts genuinely were never there in the first place?

It's certainly not so unreasonable to suggest they might not be. While there has been much discussion about the precise nature of the unconscious mind, most cognitive scientists agree that a great deal of our processing of the world goes on below the level of our conscious awareness. The trouble is that we can't access or exercise conscious control over cognitive processes we don't know anything about. For us this level of processing is automatic and effectively invisible, made known only by its effects. Sometimes these processes may percolate up to the surface where they appear as conscious thoughts but there is no guarantee that this is always the case, and no reason to believe that the flow of traffic is necessarily always two-way.

A fascinating and well-known finding by Benjamin Libet, replicated over many successive investigations, indicates that what goes on in our conscious minds may turn out to be far less important than we assume. There have been reliable but counterintuitive studies that indicate that our brains start to initiate movements by booting up the motor cortex 300 milliseconds *before* we are even aware of making the decision to move. This result implies that while we may believe we are making conscious choices to do things, the level of our minds that really governs some choices is operating at a pre-conscious level. According to these studies the conscious decision that we think causes the action never did: it's just an illusion our minds play on us after the event. Psychologist and broadcaster Susan Blackmore believes that these experiments indicate that 'conscious experience takes time to build up and is much too slow to be responsible for making things happen'. If our brains have a life of their own that we are not even aware of, the notion that reprogramming our conscious minds is going to alter things at these subterranean levels starts to look a little optimistic.

Then again, just which brain are we trying to reprogram? It may come as a surprise to learn that every human being has not just one brain but two. Most of us are familiar with the brain resident in our skull, but in fact your gut also has a 'mind of its own'. Its lining is embedded with some 100 million neurones, which work together to coordinate the surprisingly complex task of digesting food and expelling waste. The enteric brain has its own reflexes and senses, and although it is connected to the central nervous system through the vagus nerve, it can also operate completely independently of it. The enteric brain employs more than 30 neurotransmitters to coordinate signals and impulses across the system and 95 per cent of the body's seratonin (the hormone that the most widely-used antidepressants attempt to keep at optimal levels in your brain proper) is to be found in your bowels.

Significantly, this enteric brain plays a major role in the way we experience emotion: we all know what it is like to get 'butterflies' when we feel nervous or to feel 'sick to our stomach' when contending with distressing or shocking news. Emotion is often a visceral business, and it may be no coincidence that the ancient Taoists associated anger, anxiety, fear, worry and sadness with different regions of the soft organs that are all linked parasympathetically by the vagus nerve and sympathetically by the splanchnic nerves. The most crucial point for the current discussion is that, due to the way the vagus nerve is constructed, 90 per cent of the nerve fibres are dedicated to transmitting information *up* towards the main brain, leaving only 10 per cent committed to sending information *down* in the other direction. This may suggest that while the enteric brain may have significant input into what we experience mentally, our conscious thought life may have relatively little leverage when it comes to controlling what our guts are already screaming at us.

Then there is the thorny issue of how much purchase rationality has over our unwanted thoughts and emotions anyway. One thing that has always slightly irritated me about CBT is its tendency to define any thought that makes us feel uncomfortable as 'irrational'. This is tantamount to saying that if I don't like it then it can't be true. I'm sorry, but sometimes your most paranoid and pessimistic interpretations of the situation are entirely correct. Maybe your friend actually *was* avoiding you; it really wasn't that she failed to spot you or was rushing to the bathroom or any of the other supposedly 'rational' alternative interpretations you and your therapist come up with.

For Freud and the psychoanalysts, of course, the activity of the conscious mind was just the tip of the iceberg visible above the waterline, while the elemental forces that really drive human lives do their work unbidden and unseen within the murky depths of the unconscious. And according to Freud and Jung, the world of the unconscious mind has little truck with the niceties of logic and reason. It is an anarchic dark void of

Sometimes your most paranoid and pessimistic interpretations of the situation are entirely correct.

fleeting impressions and semi-formed ideas, a vortex of turbulent emotion populated by phantoms, fantasies and dark desires. Freud argued that the so-called 'primary process' thinking that occurs in the unconscious is marked by its complete disregard for conventional logic or the laws of causality. In the world of the id anything is possible. It doesn't have to make sense.

So if only a fraction of what originates in the unconscious bubbles up to the surface to assume the form of thoughts (negative or otherwise) there may be a great deal of highly emotive material left below that lies forever beyond the reach of reason. Jung also believed that when the contents of the unconscious mind do percolate through they can often take the form of images rather than words. This begs the question: how do you argue or reason with a picture? If the unconscious doesn't even speak the language of its more reasonable conscious counterpart, we might be on a hiding to nothing trying to reason with it.

Rationality may be of particularly limited use when facing situations that trigger our fight-or-flight reflexes, one of our most primitive protective systems. How often have you heard people who have survived disasters saying that 'there was no time to think', 'my mind froze' or that they 'have no idea how we ever got out of there'? When we feel threatened we are designed to stop thinking and let our instincts take over. The primitive reptilian brain pulls rank and does the job it has been doing successfully for over two million years: that of helping you survive. What this means though is that various unpleasant feelings, the sort we associate with danger and threat, are more likely to switch off the higher centres you need to reason with your crazed, fear-filled mind. Not only will certain negative emotions stand less chance of emerging as clear thoughts but, once in the grip of them, your rational mind may not even be fully online to address them.

Finally, I suspect that sometimes we may be trying to enlist the wrong kind of logic altogether. CBT tries to treat us all like good little miniature scientists. It assumes that we are essentially rational, reasonable creatures – a proposition that frankly even the most cursory examination of our actual lives blows clean out of the water. While scientists and philosophers may lean on the power of reason and dutifully sift and weigh evidence, in our daily lives most of us operate under the auspices of a very different kind of 'logic' and sense making. The latter has much more to do with the ethos of myth and story-telling than it does with the world of lab coats and test tubes.

CBT treats 'negative beliefs' as if they exist in discrete bubbles that can be easily detached and held up to the light of reason. But a story is more like a tapestry. Its meaning is encoded within the whole narrative and the relationship between its parts. While you can trace an individual thread, a particular theme or focus in on one area of the picture, you can't ever really examine any of these in isolation. It's as if every part of the story simultaneously touches every other part of itself so you can't pull bits out without unravelling the whole thing. One of the supposed advantages of CBT is that it allows you to ignore the past and just focus on what happens in the present. However, our personal stories, unlike abstract beliefs, extend through time. While they can be conceived as a whole, they cast shadows upon our past and illuminate a pathway towards a yet untold future.

The only consistency we require from stories is that they 'feel right' to us. This may have little to do with whether they make logical sense. Like Lewis Carroll's Queen of Hearts, when it comes to our personal narratives, we are all capable of believing 'as many as six impossible things before breakfast'. Rationality has nothing to do with it. Narrative tone and thematic coherence are what count.

> **Sense making has much more to do with the ethos of myth and story-telling than it does with the world of lab coats and test tubes.**

Logic also comes up pretty empty-handed when we are dealing with what matters most to us – our values, our ethics, our loves and hates. Shakespeare was right when he said that 'Love and reason keep little company together', and by translating the flow of consciousness into staccato abstract thoughts which are then evaluated according to how reasonable or useful they are, CBT all but ignores a crucial and all-pervasive dimension of consciousness: the fact that in everyday life the stories we weave to make sense of the world invariably carry a moral or ethical charge. Something in the makeup of the human psyche makes it almost impossible for us to experience the world and our lives except in these terms.

Pick up today's newspaper. The events that have grabbed the headlines are all issues that connect immediately with our moral awareness. As I write this, they happen to concern a sea captain who may have deserted his ship before the passengers were escorted to safety, the ethics of city bankers paying themselves inflated bonuses, and a phone-hacking scandal that has called the integrity of the press into question.

Our brains willingly and instinctively process these facts into moral fables, tales of men and women doing good and bad things. And it's not just current affairs that we tend to infuse with moral significance: we make these kinds of value judgment the whole time, applying them liberally to almost every area of life that matters to us. Yet, as the parables of Jesus and the fables of Aesop demonstrate, the moral undercurrents of life are best translated into stories rather than the kind of discrete thoughts and beliefs that end up in the bubbles in CBT formulations. When it tries to address the ethical issues that preoccupy real-life human beings, the conventions of CBT all too readily dislocate meanings from their contexts, often with really unhelpful results. It's a bit like text-speak. It leaves us trying to translate something quite subtle into a clumsy stylised language with a really limited vocabulary. It forces us to collapse, condense and delete important nuances of our experience rather than highlighting them. It's a literal case of what philosophers and mathematicians call *reductio ad absurdum*. When it comes to moral meaning often the story *is* the message. It can't be processed into some convenient abstraction, simply because that happens to be the currency CBT likes to deal in.

People often come into therapy not because they are plagued by illogical thoughts but because they instinctively feel that the stories they have sought to live by are unravelling. Something has happened that threatens to undermine the integrity of their personal narrative, or they suddenly find themselves cast by events into roles they never intended or chose for themselves. For others, the opposite is true. These clients are locked into stories and roles from which they feel powerless to escape. The stories we tell ourselves are powerful organising forces. They exercise an inexorable pull over our actions, feelings and choices, rather like a magnetic field draws scattered iron filings into alignment with its own invisible lines of influence.

When dealing with the steady undertow of someone's implicit narrative, reason and logic often prove feeble instruments. If an action, a feeling or a belief 'fits' within the dynamic of the tale being told it will be embraced, however illogical or absurd it may be. Recasting and rescripting such stories is always destined to be an art as much as a science. Therapy can be about so many things, but at its heart it is often an attempt by two people to forge a new narrative together that both therapist and client can sign up to, hopefully one that reinterprets the past or opens up new possibilities for the future. These stories certainly have to make sense, but the sense that they make is often of a very different order to the 'sense' that CBT trades in.

In 1877 the Italian astronomer Schiaparelli saw something through his telescope that looked like channels on the surface of Mars. The American astronomer Percival Lowell, greatly enthused by Schiaparelli's work, set up an observatory in Flagstaff, Arizona, and had soon not only mapped out a complete network of canals but was enthralling the public with his lectures about Martian civilisation and tales of how the inhabitants had constructed the canals in a desperate attempt to channel water from the ice caps as the planet slowly heated up and died. Unfortunately Lowell had got a bit ahead of himself. When the unmanned craft *Mariner 9* mapped the red planet in 1972 no evidence of the famous canals was found. Today it is known that they are a product of an optical illusion. Lowell was a brilliant man but he got carried away and assumed too much.

The danger with Cognitive Behavioural Therapy is that we do much the same. CBT absolutely has already made a genuinely valuable contribution to our ongoing quest to understand how our minds work and how we can best fix things when they go wrong. However, until we do have a more adequate understanding of what goes on inside our heads, let's not carry on as if we already have the whole business sussed, as fans and practitioners of CBT are rather wont to do.

You can never be
too assertive

In Hindu scriptures the Sanskrit word *ahamkara* translates roughly into 'the sound of I'. In the Western world these days, thanks to the behaviours and attitudes bundled up under the heading of 'assertiveness', we are encouraged to broadcast the personal voice with increasing clarity and persistence. Assertive behaviour is now the official gold standard of communication. It promises to teach us how to stand up for ourselves and make sure our feelings, needs and rights are acknowledged by others. It will protect us against exploitation, bullying and generally being put upon. Moreover, advocates of assertiveness (and there are many) insist that it does all this without meeting 'fire with fire'. On the contrary, we are assured that true assertiveness diffuses conflict and promotes harmony. Based on principles of mutuality and respect, assertiveness authors claim the hallmarks of true assertiveness are self-control and reasonableness. One of the key messages rammed home repeatedly in assertiveness training is that it has absolutely *nothing* to do with aggression, even though for some strange reason people continue to confuse the two.

On paper all of this looks good, so good in fact that we seldom pause to examine whether assertiveness is the virtue we usually assume it to be, either in theory or in practice. In the meantime we continue to prescribe 'assertiveness training' as an appropriate response to a variety of issues and situations. Whether you are a child being bullied at school, a grown up trying to cope with a domineering mother-in-law or an insensitive boss, or maybe just trying to stop feeling self-conscious and awkward at parties, assertiveness training is clearly the way forward.

The trouble is that the theory and the practice of assertiveness often seem at odds with each other. The ideology of assertiveness stresses the importance of maintaining a respectful attitude towards your conversational partner but, if you look at some of the most commonly practised assertiveness techniques, it is hard to imagine them coming from a very respectful place.

If you have ever been unfortunate enough to be on the receiving end of the 'broken record' technique you will know exactly what I mean. Commended by Manuel Smith in his famous book *When I Say No I Feel Guilty,* the broken record boils down to a simple reiteration of your position, usually parroting the same phrase over and over again, irrespective of the response of your opponent – sorry – partner. Smith claims that this technique is appropriate 'when your partner won't take no for an answer' but of course it is only called upon when you aren't prepared to take no for an answer either! Repeating the same position communicates a clear message: '*I* will not be moved and *nothing* you can say will change my mind. Until you concede or acknowledge *my* position I will not engage with anything you are saying and I will continue to frustrate you in your attempts to talk to me. *My* position is actually non-negotiable, and I fully intend to block and negate you by repeating it again and again until you either give up or give way.' Are we seriously supposed to believe there is nothing aggressive about this?

We seldom pause to examine whether assertiveness is the virtue we usually assume it to be, either in theory or in practice.

Get down? Get down off the table? Sounds to me like you just don't respect *men's rights.*

This gentleman clearly hasn't been taking assertiveness classes. Or has he?

To get what I want from you I might also try 'fogging'. This is where I strategically try and align myself with some part of what you are saying in order to lever my own agenda more effectively. I agree with you in part or in principle (or at least appear to) in order to take the wind out of your sails and lull you into the sense that we are actually in agreement. In the case of 'negative assertion' I appear to take on board your criticism but ensure that in the very same breath I make sure I press forward with my own demands.

I'm sorry, but this is Machiavellian to the core. It's chess, not conversation, and we should be under no illusions that the goal is not to wrestle the other person into submission.

How can we truly have a genuinely respectful interaction with someone at the very moment we are attempting to manipulate them? If we use such ploys we are fencing with the other person, not authentically engaging with them. Passive aggression is aggression nonetheless, and that's exactly what a lot of 'assertiveness' amounts to. If you don't believe me, just see what it feels like to exit a conversation with someone who has been 'appropriately assertive' with you. Do you feel empowered or validated? Probably not. But they certainly will.

Assertiveness is a game in which you subtly disenfranchise your opponent by enlisting implicit rules of engagement by which you are both bound. Put simply, like a greased-up wrestler, you prevent the other person from getting any purchase on you. By remaining calm and self-possessed you make their angry overtures appear unwarranted. By stating clearly only your *own* perspective and desires ('*I* feel unhappy when ...', '*I* would like you to ...'), you cunningly inoculate yourself against contradiction since the other person knows full well they cannot claim to have better access to your inner world than you do. I'm not saying assertiveness techniques don't work, or even that there isn't a valid place for them, but let's not pretend that establishing mutual respect is the primary agenda. Respect requires that you treat the other person at least as an equal, if not a superior. Most books on assertiveness are ultimately manuals on how to gain the upper hand.

Assertiveness is born of individualism, which of course is why it is so in vogue in the West. In Japan and other more collectivist cultures that emphasise 'we' and 'us' over 'I' and 'me', submissive, deferential attitudes are more likely to be esteemed as virtuous. In fact when it comes to the various honorific forms of Japanese, the whole structure of the language seems designed to subvert the kind of self-assertion we value in the West. Both *sonkeigo* (respectful language) and *kenjogo* (humble language) are used to signal the inferiority and deference of the speaker. One commentator – clearly not a fan of the oriental way – parodies the ethos of *sonkeigo* as follows: 'OMG, you are the greatest person ever, bestow upon me the privilege of bearing your children! Your steps cause me to bow in reverence!' while the essence of *kenjogo* is summarised as: 'OMG, I am the most incapable person ever, nothing I do matters at all. I am the most insignificant piece of garbage ever.'

While blog-writer Aaron (a non-Japanese intern working for a company that builds Japanese toilets) may have been exaggerating for effect, the point still stands. The Japanese do not generally regard it as a good thing to attempt to level the playing field as assertiveness encourages, and appear unthreatened by deferential conduct that would make many Westerners wince. Submission to the authority of others, raising others up above the self – these are strategies for ensuring group harmony which is highly prized in the East. It should be noted that ethology suggests that in many animal packs, displays of submission are just as crucial as dominance displays in ensuring the smooth functioning of the group and its ability to provide for its constituent members. Protocols of dominance and submission often forestall the need for full-on bloody fights that the pack can ill afford.

Even here in the West it turns out that you can have too much of a supposedly good thing. A study by Daniel Ames and Francis Flynn at Columbia University discovered that, when it comes to people's appraisal of leadership qualities, too much assertiveness was generally regarded by employees to be just as problematic as too little. It seemed a 'Goldilocks algorithm' was at work that left leaders at the higher end of the assertiveness spectrum just as compromised as if they were perceived as lacking in assertiveness. The authors point out that 'Although

> **When it comes to people's appraisal of leadership qualities, too much assertiveness was generally regarded by employees to be just as problematic as too little.**

a high level of assertiveness may entail instrumental benefits, it often carries social costs. Assertive people tend to be seen as less likeable and less friendly than unassertive people, even when assertive behaviour is considered effective, justified, and appropriate ... even kinder and gentler versions of assertiveness are seen as leading to worse impressions than are low levels of assertiveness.' How very surprising this is, considering that assertive communication supposedly places such emphasis on respectful interaction, mutual validation of everyone's point of view and represents a mature and moderate approach to resolving conflict ... But on the other hand, if the lines between assertiveness and aggression are more blurred than everyone wishes to believe, then perhaps we shouldn't be that surprised after all.

Intriguingly, and slightly at odds with the Ames and Flynn study, an analysis of what makes good companies become great ones identified 'level five leadership' as one of the crucial determinants. Publishing his findings in the *Harvard Business Review*, Jim Collins concluded that outstandingly successful companies often seemed to be led by individuals with two distinct qualities: personal humility and professional will power. These leaders were markedly unassuming in a way that contradicts the stereotype of what an assertive person should look like. Describing them as paradoxically 'timid and ferocious' and 'modest and wilful', Collins goes on to give examples of leaders who often proved strikingly self-effacing at interview, including one level five leader who confided (or even asserted): 'There are a lot of people in this company who could do this job better than I do.' While coming across as genuinely humble and unassuming individuals, where these men and women did not hold back was in relentlessly and single-mindedly pushing through the reforms, policies and redundancies they believed were in the interest of their companies – even when these involved controversial or unpopular choices. Here some kind of assertiveness was clearly at work, but not assertiveness geared to the service of the ego or the advancement of the individual in the way we equate with assertiveness. Instead it was applied with steely determination to the interests of the wider collective, while their own egos took a back seat.

Assertiveness in the form with which we are familiar may be warranted on occasion, but let's not kid ourselves that it's going to help us win any popularity contests or that when harnessed to advancing our personal agendas (even legitimate ones) our assertive behaviour isn't going to be interpreted by others as an act of war. I know of one highly assertive man who informed a superior that he experienced his boss's body language as anxiety-provoking. This ticked all the assertiveness boxes: the man in question was only saying what *he* felt and how he interpreted the other person's actions; he wasn't directly blaming the boss; he took responsibility for his own reactions to her. However, suffice it to say that a few days later he found that he had been marginalised within the organisation and his performance was suddenly being negatively appraised. There may be no connection at all, but you have to wonder …

It seems to me that truly effective communication is a dance in which we have to be prepared to move fluidly between different and complementary roles, even if that means sometimes holding the high status position and sometimes agreeing to be what is known in sadomasochistic circles as 'the bottom'. Ames and Flynn compare the use of assertiveness with seasoning a meal: too little and it tastes bland, but too much and the dish is ruined. Insisting that we can maintain respectful equality at all times is a pleasant fantasy, but it certainly isn't going to be realised by using techniques which often amount

Truly effective communication is a dance in which we have to be prepared to move fluidly between different and complementary roles.

to no more than a form of manipulation to get our needs met. In the Hindu faith 'the sound of I' must be silenced before you can get in touch with deeper levels of reality. Perhaps we should bear this in mind before we get too sold on techniques that ultimately are just designed to pump up the volume.

Men and women live on different planets

A basic premise of a great many relationship books is that men and women are fundamentally very different creatures. With over 70 million copies of John Gray's famous book *Men are from Mars, Women are from Venus* in circulation over the last decade, it's no wonder this particular assumption has stamped itself so indelibly upon the public consciousness in Western culture. Gray says that a lot of what goes wrong in relationships between men and women stems from our failure to appreciate just how different they are, and claims that only when men and women are able to respect and accept their differences does 'love [have] a chance to blossom'.

Now I am not attempting to deny that men and women are different in many important respects, but I would suggest that the differences have been overplayed. In my opinion this has encouraged a kind of psychological apartheid between the sexes that is just downright unhelpful. Despite what Allan and Barbara Pease may wish to tell us about (insulting both genders in a single swipe) *Why Men Don't Listen and Women Can't Read Maps* or *Why Men Don't Have a Clue and Women Always Need More Shoes*, whatever the differences, we should always remember that the basic similarities between us remain much stronger. People are people, irrespective of whether or

People are people, irrespective of whether or not they carry a Y chromosome about their genotype.

not they carry a Y chromosome about their genotype, and we are all likely to get on a whole lot better if we remember that our distinctive combinations of needs and emotions are created using pigments from a common palate.

One reason why popular-psychology books based on gender differences have proved influential is undoubtedly because their rise has coincided with a number of research studies apparently supporting the theory that men and women really are distinct, right down to the level of how their brains are built. There are a number of studies that claim to show contrasts in the processing of emotion, memories, spatial perception, faces, and the levels of aggression demonstrated by men and women. However, in her excellent and carefully researched analysis of such studies, Cordelia Fine argues that the scientific evidence is ultimately far from convincing, and that the attributed differences are more to do with social constructions of gender and the prevalence of 'neuro-sexism' amongst some of the researchers concerned.

For example, we all know that women are more emotional than men, don't we? Well not according to researchers Ann Kring and Albert Gordon who conducted a fascinating experiment in which they subjected a cohort of men and women to a series of short films selected to elicit an emotional response from the viewer and watched the results.

By and large it was possible to read the impact of the content on the women's faces. Positive and negative emotions of greater intensity and duration were writ large for all to see. The men showed much less emotional response, so no surprises there. But before you conclude that this just goes to prove what we all know, in other words that women are much more 'in touch' with their feelings than men, consider some of Kring and Gordon's other findings. When they asked their subjects to rate their emotional responses to what they had seen there was no difference between the men and the women. The men claimed they had been just as moved as their female counterparts. And even more telling (for the sceptics amongst you are thinking that the clumsy oafs were just mislabelling or misjudging their own feelings), measures of the skin's electrical conductivity showed that the men's nervous systems were, if anything, on average *more* responsive than the women's, suggesting greater activation in response to what they were seeing.

One reading of this is that while the women were comfortably emoting and discharging their feelings, the men's struggle to remain impassive in the face of equally profound emotional shifts was leaking out in other ways. Women may be better at expressing emotions (and there are many studies suggesting they are better at reading them), but men feel an equal range of emotions and studies like these suggest they feel them just as deeply.

Some additional evidence is provided by another study in which boys were much quicker than girls to turn off the sound of a baby crying. At first the researchers assumed this was because the males were just insensitive and thus indifferent to the child's distress. However, when they analysed their subjects' levels of stress hormones they found that, if anything, the boys had been *more* stressed by the crying than their female counterparts. This is why it is completely unreasonable for women to expect men to get up to their children in the night. I'm joking, I'm joking …

But what about the other way round? What evidence is there that women experience supposedly 'male' emotions like aggression to similar levels? Intriguingly, in one of the most comprehensive reviews of the gender research in 2005, Janet Hyde found that aggression, along with other so-called gendered behaviours, tended to occur differently depending upon the context. It seems both men and women step out of role when they think no one is looking! So when experimental subjects were told that all markers of their gender would be eliminated or disguised, not only did women show as much aggressive behaviour as men, they actually demonstrated more.

Incidentally, Hyde's conclusion after carefully reviewing 46 meta-analyses was that throughout the lifespan males and females were far more similar than they were different. Such differences as there were, she believes, are largely down to cultural influences. She cites examples like the fact that the first

Teen Talk Barbie included amongst its repertoire of sound bites, the immortal utterance: 'Gee, maths class is tough!' Admittedly the offending remark was later deleted following an entirely understandable public outcry.

The way in which your culture constructs gender is really powerful. Messages like 'Big boys don't cry' are unconsciously absorbed. Your culture gives you a script for what it means to be male or female, and by and large most of us find ourselves striving to obey its directives. As the anthropologist Victor Turner pointed out, culture is a big theatrical production, and any play only works if the actors stick to the script. Too much improvisation, too much deviation from the part allotted to you, creates problems for other actors since all the roles are mutually interdependent. This is why, if you happen to be conducting a study looking at what grabs an infant's attention, it's probably a good idea to conceal the gender of the subjects from your scorers – unless of course you fully intend to 'discover' that the boys spend more time looking at mechanisms like mobiles and the girls show a statistically significant preference for faces …

Yet, even if we accept that culture shapes behaviour and the interpretation of behaviour, surely the neuro-imaging studies don't lie? Well, perhaps. But then again, when MRI scans from a dead Atlantic salmon showed brain activity you have to wonder what to believe![1] Even the finding that women have a thicker corpus callosum, the neural telephone exchange between the two hemispheres of the brain, has been called into question in the last few years.

> **Your culture gives you a script for what it means to be male or female, and by and large most of us find ourselves striving to obey its directives.**

[1]For more details of the dead salmon that produced a false positive result on an MRI scan see: http://prefrontal.org/blog/2009/09/the-story-behind-the-atlantic-salmon

The scientific evidence is at best ambiguous, but of course once you accept the notion that the person in front of you thinks and feels completely differently to you, you are likely to start foundering badly when you try and relate to them. You can no longer rely upon empathy to guide you, because your opposite gendered mate is apparently nothing like you. You are now dependent upon the sketchy maps drawn by those who claim to be familiar with the territory of both your worlds: your own internal compass is pretty much useless. You are like someone with Asperger's syndrome, left having to decode the emotional aspects of your partner's behaviour purely by the book, without ever being able to fully identify with them or relate intuitively to their experience. We would do well to remember that a love letter and an instruction manual are very different kinds of undertaking.

We should also bear in mind that the typologies being offered to us ('All men prefer this … All women are like such and such …') are ultimately no more than crude, sexist stereotypes. They don't allow for how different members of the *same* gender can be from each other. We all know men who are sensitive and expressive as well as those who conform to the stereotype of the emotional dullard. In fact you can probably think of examples of masculinity all the way along the spectrum. Similarly, not every sister is eager to pour her heart out at every opportunity. Some women are 'strong, silent types', while others demonstrate other supposedly 'masculine' qualities like ambition or aggression in abundance. However, because the prospect of a more fulfilled, rewarding relationship is so alluring for us, or perhaps because the claims are apparently backed by hard science, no one ever really challenges these stereotypes. And, if we are honest, much of the popularity of such books has to do not so much with what they tell us about our Significant Other, but instead what they appear to tell us about ourselves.

These books offer readers of both genders a convenient script upon which to hang aspects of their own identity. We recognise ourselves in their pages in the same way that we like to match up aspects of our lives with the predictions of horoscopes, or the categories offered by pop-psychology quizzes in magazines. With the help of these books we can perform our masculinity and femininity in ways that other people will acknowledge and recognise – not least because they have read the same books as we have. They also let us off the hook with a convenient excuse when it comes to demands we can't be bothered to meet. It's a case of: 'Sorry, love, I just can't be expected to remember your birthday/pick towels off the floor/talk about my feelings etc. It's a man thing. Just read this book – it'll explain everything …'

Male or female, with the help of these books everyone knows what they are doing (or at least what they are supposed to be doing) and there is a great comfort in this. Having worked extensively with transgendered and gay clients, take it from me that when people are ambiguous about the script, or fall foul of society's expectations concerning gender or sexuality, a great deal of anxiety is stirred up – usually not only in them but also in the people around them.

Yet in many cultural traditions those who walk closest to the gods, such as the Greek prophet Tiresias or the shamen of the Navajo and other Native American tribes, are often characterised by their blending of both male and female characteristics and roles. In Tiresias's case, legend has it that he was compelled to spend several years as a woman after the goddess Hera objected to his rough treatment of a pair of copulating snakes. It sounds entirely reasonable to me. However, the association between heightened levels of insight and the blending of male and female identities is a strong and recurrent one across many cultures.

Of course the Swiss psychologist Carl Jung believed that legends like that of Tiresias reflect a deeper and more fundamental truth, namely that within the psyche of *every* human being there is a masculine and feminine dimension. He called these the *animus* and *anima* and claimed that they represent gendered archetypes latent in us all. The guiding principle of the *animus*, the male aspect, is logical and active, being oriented towards getting things done in the outside world. The *anima*, on the other hand, is all about establishing relationships in the inner world and is typically manifested in processes like intuition, sensitivity to feelings and capacity for meaningful connection.

Furthermore, Jung suggests that it is the very existence of this contra-sexual self (the unconscious masculine principle in every woman or the feminine buried in every man) that allows people of the opposite gender to relate to one another in a meaningful way. To some extent we intuitively 'get' how the other sex works because there is a part of us that recognises ourselves in them. As the feminist journalist and author Margaret Fuller observes in her epic treatise *Woman in the Nineteenth Century*:

> 'Male and female represent the two sides of the great radical dualism. But in fact they are perpetually passing into one another. Fluid hardens to solid, solid rushes to fluid. There is no wholly masculine man, no purely feminine woman.'

Psychological maturity, for Jung, was partly about being able to accept and harmonise these complementary aspects of one's nature. This is not about suddenly coming over all metrosexual or rushing out to get a short haircut and a pair of Doc Martens (unless you want to, of course). It is about learning to integrate the whole spectrum of who you are and connecting with the different facets of the collective unconscious in all of us. Readers of John Gray should note that Jung warned that when people of either sex repress their other-gendered self, the rejected *animus* or *anima* can take on a darker, more malevolent guise in the 'Shadow Self'. If Jung is right, then the psychological segregation of the sexes is both misguided and potentially destructive.

When the hapless Professor Higgins puts his head in his hands in the musical *My Fair Lady* and laments tunelessly, 'Why can't a woman be more like a man?' the lyricist Alan Jay Lerner

I hate thinking!

Me too!

Perhaps fans of Mars and Venus can find some common ground after all?

is providing us with a cautionary tale. Higgins' chauvinism, his underlying belief that men and women are destined to stare uncomprehendingly at each other across an impassable gulf, actually creates the very division he is complaining about. Cut off and adrift from his own feminine side, Higgins has not the least idea how to respond to the love that Eliza offers him. Ultimately he is handicapped not by his inability to understand women but by his failure to understand himself. Fans of Mars and Venus should pause and reflect before following too eagerly in his footsteps.

Your inner child needs a hug

Ihave a confession to make. When people start talking to me about their inner child I really struggle. It just makes me want to giggle (which I suspect may be largely to do with some relatively immature part of me). I don't know quite what it is about the whole inner child thing that produces this effect. After all, I regularly work with people in various states of regression in therapy, including severely traumatised individuals who genuinely dissociate into child states to which the adult personality has little direct access. This certainly isn't funny. I also believe that early childhood experiences, especially the tone of our relationships with our parents, can continue to ricochet through the years and blight our adult lives. Indeed such stuff is the mainstay of therapy.

I suppose my problem is that a lot of the literature and teaching specifically aimed at 'healing the inner child' feels so mawkish and sentimental that part of me just rebels against the whole business. Naturally, those who promote such work would probably respond that my 'issues' with the approach merely reflect deep childhood wounds of my own. Perhaps I can't bear to be in contact with my own pain? Perhaps the little guy inside just needs reminding he is the 'Divine Child' (thank you, Dr Jung) or the Wonder Child Emmet Fox assures me he really is. Maybe he needs to 'reclaim the magic that was lost in the wounding experience' as Cathryn Taylor's mystical *Seven Layers of Healing* technique recommends. Quite possibly.

Now, I think children are great. I even have two of my own at home that I'm quite fond of. I respect and value many of the qualities we quite rightly associate with early childhood: their spontaneity, curiosity and creativity, their emotional directness and capacity for playfulness. However, I do think that people who like to focus on the inner child also cling on to a beatific and saccharine view of what a child actually is.

The idealisation of childhood as a state of intellectual and spiritual enlightenment admittedly has a long heritage. Its origins can probably be traced back to Greek ideas about the perfectibility of man but certainly re-emerged with new vigour during the Romantic Movement in the nineteenth century, when poets like William Wordsworth portrayed pre-socialised children as closer to the sources of inspiration and ultimate truth than the obtuse, careworn adults they become. For the Romantics, each child arrived freshly minted from on high, 'trailing clouds of glory' before the inevitable lifelong process of forgetting sets in and 'Shades of the prison house begin to close/Upon the growing Boy …' (or presumably Girl for that matter). During the writing of this book, I attended a Neurolinguistic Programming hypnosis workshop in which Wordsworth's position was again urged upon us. The lecturer assured the delegates with quiet authority that as infants we were all confident, brilliant, perfectly adjusted little individuals. It was only once life had got its grubby hands on us that things had started to go downhill.

But the reality of children, it seems to me, is often at odds with this comforting notion. Children can be genuinely endearing, and Mother Nature ensures they draw out the protective instincts in most of us, particularly if they happen to be carrying our DNA. However, human youngsters can

> **People who like to focus on the inner child also cling on to a beatific and saccharine view of what a child actually is.**

also be hideously self-centred, tyrannical, ruthless, spiteful, aggressive, manipulative and sometimes just very hard work. They are poorly regulated, impulsive and dependent. We don't use the adjective 'immature' as a criticism of adult behaviour for no reason. Even if it were possible, would any of us really embrace our neglected younger self without at least a dash of ambivalence?

The research evidence increasingly suggests that we are not all born with well-balanced personalities that hostile life events and bad parenting subsequently chip away at. Pioneering studies of temperament conducted in the 1970s revealed that of the 65 per cent that fell neatly into Thomas and Chess's four proposed categories, only 40 per cent were 'easy' babies – in other words, generally content and sunny-natured, good sleepers and eaters – while 15 per cent were 'slow to warm up' and 10 per cent were downright 'difficult', irritable, fussy babies prone to driving their parents to distraction in a relatively short space of time. These children were like this right from the word go.

In fact, more recent research suggests that the differences Thomas and Chess observed are innately hard-wired into the brain but may have long-term developmental consequences. The child psychiatrist Jerome Kagan observed that children varied greatly in their level of arousal when presented with unfamiliar stimuli. Although the profile of many children evolved over time, those at the extreme ends of the scale remained much more likely to be diagnosed with either conduct disorder or anxiety disorders. Suffice it to say, not all infants arrive on the scene with Buddha-like serenity and the wisdom of the ages flowing through their young veins.

Of course, the main focus of inner-child enthusiasts is on the wounded child rather than the pristine one. The line is that the psychosocial injuries of childhood must be salved in order for you to fulfil your true potential as an adult. It is the neglected, rejected, criticised and ignored child who cries out for your attention and must be re-parented to properly heal your present.

Several critics have pointed out that, seen in this way, the inner child can become the focus of a victim mentality that can be highly unhelpful for the person concerned. One of the salient features of an actual child is that they often lack power to determine what happens to them, so when bad things *do* happen to them it is very clear that this is someone else's fault. Encouraging people to see themselves, or even part of themselves, in this light can subtly discourage them from taking responsibility for their own lives, or holding themselves accountable for some of the things that may have gone wrong. In my clinical experience, real therapeutic progress is usually hard if this kind of mindset is too embedded.

My very favourite response to this particular hazard of inner-child work comes from author, speaker and workshop leader Colin Tipping. Tipping has absolutely no truck with the inner child whom he describes (rather harshly) as 'the whining little brat that lives in the back room of our mind, that unhappy victim who can always be relied upon to blame everyone else for our unhappiness ...' So strong is Tipping's antipathy that he proposes a radical intervention: a guided visualisation in which the wounded child is not so much healed as euthanised! Having unearthed the inner child skulking in its bunker of resentment, Tipping proposes that you imagine throwing open the curtains and letting the sunlight blaze in. Grateful to be released from their suffering, the child will apparently wither, like Nosferatu, into a wizened, grey husk before your eyes. I will let Tipping paint the rest of the scene for you:

> 'With that, the little person dies, looking peaceful and serene. Lovingly, you wrap the little person in a white cloth and take the body upstairs and out into the light. There waits a horse

The whining little brat that lives in the back room of our mind, that unhappy victim who can always be relied upon to blame everyone else for our unhappiness...

and buggy, and angels hover nearby. A choir of angels sings softly. All the people who have ever been in your life are waiting to pay their respects. All past hurts are forgiven. Love is everywhere. The bells on the horse and buggy ring softly as the entourage slowly begins its journey to the hill where a grave has been prepared ...'

One has to ask: have the inner social services been informed?

The project of embracing your inner child can also result in surreptitiously licensing behaviour and attitudes in adults that may be acceptable in children but are pretty unbecoming in grown-ups. In our culture we are all familiar with the injunction to 'prioritise a child's needs' but if we start allowing ourselves to behave impulsively in every situation, or place too high a value on the merits of unguarded self-expression or the meeting of our own childlike needs, other people are going to pay the price. Hence one inner-child guru recommends that in order to heal the child within you must 'temporarily or permanently end all relationships in which you are being hurt'. His advice is that only after extensive therapy is it a good idea to even consider re-engaging – after all, '... you have a precious child to protect ...'. I'm all for people exiting genuinely destructive relationships, but isn't this taking things a bit too far? If we become too precious about ourselves we risk becoming self-absorbed and insensitive to the needs of those around us. Pretty soon, most likely, no one will want to know us.

We haven't yet touched upon the question of whether it is even possible to recover a previous, younger version of ourselves. There is some neurological evidence that we can. Many readers will associate the notion of the Child as a distinct persona with Transactional Analysis, the brainchild of Eric Berne who proposed that Parent, Adult and Child continue to exist within all of us and determine the dynamics of our relationships with each other. Berne based his theories partly on discoveries made by the celebrated neurologist Wilder Penfield. A maverick but brilliant Canadian neurosurgeon working in the 1950s, Penfield had pioneered a surgical technique for treating epilepsy in which he destroyed parts of the brain. In order to target the relevant brain centres only, he inserted electrical probes into various sites and discovered that when the temporal lobes were stimulated, some of his patients described vivid re-experiencing of childhood memories and other sensory experiences.

Neurologist Oliver Sacks presents a more recent case of Mrs O'C, who suffered a massive stroke that affected her temporal lobes (amongst other brain regions) and invoked 'an overwhelming sense of being-a-child-again, in her long-forgotten home, in the arms and presence of her mother'. This was all the more significant for her since before the stroke Mrs O'C had had no recollection of her early childhood prior to being orphaned before her fifth birthday. On the basis of similar evidence, Berne proposed that childhood experience and attributes most likely continued to make their presence felt in adult life.

Such observations certainly offer tantalising insights into the way the brain may process and store experience. Nevertheless, we also need to be mindful that all memory is ultimately an act of re-creation, not simply a matter of delving into accurate mental records of past events. Even very vivid and convincing memories can sometimes turn out to be unreliable. A recent study conducted at Hull University demonstrated that many of us have clear 'memories' of childhood events *that never actually happened.* In fact, the child psychologist Jean Piaget also reported having had absolutely vivid recall of being kidnapped as a two-year-old, right down to the scratches on his nurse's face as she sought to ward off the attacker. However, 13 years later the nurse confessed that she had made up the tale, even though the event continued to feel utterly real for Piaget.

Some have turned to hypnotic regression in order to try and settle whether we can revisit our younger selves, but here the waters become frustratingly muddied. The upshot seems to be that there are real limits to what aspects of the developmental clock are actually turned back. In a very comprehensive review conducted in 1987, Michael Nash at the University of Tennessee concluded that under hypnotic regression an adult's brainwaves do not resume the slow arrhythmic patterns found in infancy and childhood reflexes are not reinstated. Hypnotically regressed adults also continue to outperform actual children on IQ tests. Although in one study hypnotised subjects were able to name the day of the week when their birthday or Christmas fell aged at 4, 7 or 10 years old, later studies couldn't reproduce the result. There is some suggestion that the investigator may have unwittingly been giving participants clues in the original study by the way he asked the questions.

Cognitive abilities and reflexes are one thing, but surely the key issue is whether somewhere inside us we preserve the emotional dynamics, ego functions and personality characteristics of our early years? Some inventive studies have been conducted using projective tests (like the famous ink blot test) and, lo and behold, the hypnotically regressed subjects did produce responses that resembled those of children. The only fly in the ointment was that non-hypnotised control subjects who were asked to 'fake' childlike responses also managed to produce convincing immature reactions. However, regressed adults did interact with a variety of transitional objects in a childlike way that controls couldn't match, but the regressed subjects were actually less likely to identify the type of object they had used as a child (only 23 per cent got it right) than the non-hypnotised adults who usually had a fairly good idea. Mothers of both groups were consulted to confirm independently the accuracy of participants' perceptions (because what your mum says goes). The researchers concluded that while hypnosis seemed to activate some of the emotional responses of children, they certainly weren't reliving specific events as they had actually occurred when they *were* children.

Maybe there is indeed a child lurking in all of us: in fact I'm sure of it. I for one am capable of behaving in thoroughly childish ways at times and I know I'm not alone. However, I suspect this is often not because we necessarily carry a fully formed psychic child about with us like a live echo of our past, but rather because we have never properly grown up in the first place. This may be no bad thing: children can have a lot of fun. However, they are clearly ill equipped to cope with every aspect of life in an adult's world. Perhaps that's the real source of our fascination with our inner child. It's not just that we want to believe that all aspects of who we are continue to exist and that nothing is ever truly lost. It's that we all secretly would like to turn the clock back to a time when we had fewer responsibilities and anything still seemed possible.

If you want to give your inner child a hug, by all means go ahead. But be aware that any unmet needs you have now, whenever they originated, are now part of who you are in the present and must be dealt with as such. We can't go back, what's done is done, but our future is still unformed and unblemished. Just as it was when we were kids, it still resembles a hushed garden of freshly fallen snow, waiting to receive whatever new tracks we make across it. What children know instinctively, but adults these days seem to forget, is that it's generally a good idea to keep your gaze fixed on where you're going, especially when it's slippery underfoot. If you spend too much time looking back over your shoulder you are very likely to end up on your backside.

We all secretly would like to turn the clock back to a time when we had fewer responsibilities and anything still seemed possible.

You can learn to do anything you want

Some of you will doubtless remember the late 1960s exploits of the eponymous schoolboy-cum-super-spy, Joe McClaine, in the Gerry and Sylvia Anderson Supermarionation TV series, *Joe 90*. Each week Joe sat in a machine invented by his adopted dad and had other people's skills and experiences downloaded directly into his young brain. This enabled him to perform brain surgery, pilot various aircraft, acquire several foreign languages, and in short carry out his full range of duties as the Most Special Agent of the World Intelligence Network. It was a pretty useful trick, even if he did have to wear a pair of rather unflattering spectacles to pull it off.

Joe 90 was (and I stress) a children's science-fiction fantasy series. But even if you don't happen to have an adopted father with a Brain Impulse Galvanoscope Record and Transfer machine to hand, Neurolinguistic Programming (NLP) would assure you that it is perfectly possible for you to replicate young Joe's impressive accomplishments. As one NLP website enthuses: 'If one human can do something. then, potentially, anyone can ...' NLP has been propounding this view for some years now, but while most of us would freely acknowledge that a 'can do' attitude is likely to get you further in life than self-defeating passivity, a moment's reflection may reveal that this cherished tenet of NLP doesn't really stand up to serious examination. As blogger Diana Hartman points out: 'If that were true there would be a lot fewer janitors and a lot more astronauts.'

NLP claims that by replicating the mental habits and representations of successful people you can duplicate their success-inducing behaviours. This was the rationale behind Bandler and Grinder's original analysis of the communication style of three eminent therapists – Fritz Perls, Virginia Satir and later Milton Erickson. Bandler and Grinder believed in doing so that they had uncovered the 'deep structure' of effective communication, a psychological grammar that could be learned and copied by just about anyone. Now it is one thing to identify and imitate behavioural techniques employed by the great and the good. It's quite another to suggest that by doing so you will replicate their results. Knowing the rules of chess may enable me to move the pieces around the board in a legal fashion, but it won't necessarily turn me into a Grand Master overnight.

Perls, Satir and Erickson were all masters of their craft. Quite apart from having put in the requisite hours, one strongly suspects they were used to making subtle and complex judgments at the instinctive, unconscious level deployed by the true expert. Ironically, as educational researchers and brothers Stuart and Hubert Dreyfus explain, as people develop real expertise they move beyond any structure of knowledge that can be readily formalised or communicated to someone else. As they put it:

> 'If one asks an expert for the rules he or she is using, one will, in effect, force the expert to regress to the level of a beginner and state the rules learned in school. Thus, instead of using rules he or she no longer remembers, as the knowledge engineers suppose, the expert is forced to remember rules he or she no longer uses ... No amount of

It is one thing to identify and imitate behavioural techniques employed by the Good and the Great. It's quite another to suggest that by doing so you will replicate their results.

rules and facts can capture the knowledge an expert has when he or she has stored experience of the actual outcomes of tens of thousands of situations.'

The more expert we become, the more the relevant processes fade from the view of consciousness. Expertise therefore cannot be taught or even adequately described by anyone, not even the expert themselves. It has to be developed through experience and immersion, and is encoded within the evolving structure and function of our brains. To borrow one of Bandler and Grinder's computational metaphors, the software and the hardware become merged into one. Since I can't have your brain, I can never really have your expertise either. The best I can hope for is my own approximation of it.

Way before we run into the difficulties of replicating expertise, we face the more fundamental problem of how even basic skills are to be installed in our heads. Bandler and Grinder are a bit vague on this point, but since we lack a convenient disk drive to allow the instantaneous upload of new 'programs', we are instead forced to rely on the more laborious, hit-and-miss process called education. Skilled teachers know that when it comes to learning anything, one size does not fit all. They have to adapt their approach to the strengths and thinking styles of the particular pupils they are dealing with. Perhaps the student is a visual learner, or an auditory learner, a converger or a diverger. Good teachers have to use different strategies to communicate knowledge effectively to different students. This would suggest that learning takes place within the parameters set by individual brains, and that knowledge is not necessarily constructed in an identical way by each of us. If the way I process information is different to you, why should I be able to do everything you can do?

Then there is the thorny issue of innate talent or aptitude. Are all brains really created equal? It is undeniable that some people arrive on the planet predisposed to pick up certain skills with particular ease, while for others they will always remain a significant challenge. The electrochemical messages that travel between neurones go faster in the brains of clever people. Mice who have their RGS14 gene disabled remember objects better and navigate mazes better than regular mice, perhaps giving us a glimpse of the role that genetics might play in constricting or enabling individual learning abilities.

A team from the Cognitive Neuroscience Research Group in Barcelona has some convincing experimental evidence that people naturally better at differentiating between subtle auditory distinctions in vowel sounds are naturally much better equipped to acquire other languages. Furthermore it will come as little surprise to anyone who has spent time in a classroom that scientists are also discovering innate differences in very young children that suggest some of us are just born better at maths than others. Have you ever been at a fête where you have tried to guess the number of marbles in a jar or ping-pong balls in a car? Dr Melissa Libertus found that pre-schoolers whose superior 'number sense' allowed them to judge more accurately whether they could see more blue or yellow dots on a flashing computer image later also performed better on more formal measures of mathematical ability.

Although there has been a lot of emphasis recently on the role that sheer practice plays in developing superior performance capabilities, other factors are clearly involved. As Paul McCartney pointed out when asked about Malcolm Gladwell's book *Outliers*, the Beatles were by no means the only band to have put in over 10,000 hours on the road. However, they certainly made more of an impact on popular culture than their peers.

It is undeniable that some people arrive on the planet predisposed to pick up certain skills with particular ease, while for others they will always remain a significant challenge.

Did you know...

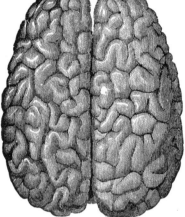

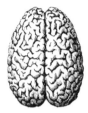

The brain on the right is the same size as the brain on the left. Is is simply farther away.

No two brains are exactly alike.

The 1,400 or so grammes of spongy grey matter in people's skulls may look very similar but brains are different, and thank goodness they are or the world would be a very dull place indeed. It is highly unlikely my brain physically resembles Einstein's in terms of shape or detailed structure. It probably doesn't lack a parietal operculum, or have an enlarged Sylvian fissure like his did. It's unlikely to have his above-average concentration of glial cells. We know all this, incidentally, because the physicist thoughtfully left his brain to science. The pathologist Thomas Stoltz Harvey helpfully removed it, dissected it, photographed it from every conceivable angle, and preserved it in formalin. Somewhat less helpfully he then diced it up into 240 pieces. Gruesomely, he also gave the dead man's eyes to Henry Abrams, his optometrist. Einstein's eyeballs are currently rumoured to be sitting in a safe-deposit box somewhere in New York.

It may be that certain features of his neurobiology gave Einstein a head start, although it should be noted that he was considered very average at school. But even if these gross structural differences count for very little, the brain he started with was undoubtedly physically and functionally altered as a result of his experiences and the many hours he spent in that Swiss patent office pondering the mysteries and mathematics of space-time. We now know that neural pathways that are strengthened through repeated activation tend to become permanent, while redundant circuits atrophy and die away. Literally. In fact, during adolescence our brains undergo a massive paring down of their less frequently used connections. Nature and usage sculpts your brain into a one-off masterpiece.

However, brains are wonderful things and, within limits, continue to adapt structurally to the purposes to which they are put. Thus Dr Sara Lazar and colleagues found that the brains of regular meditators demonstrated thickening in the cortex in those areas associated with attention and emotional integration, while only half an hour of mindfulness meditation over eight weeks produced greater density of grey matter in brain centres associated with self-awareness, compassion and introspection.

Similarly, the brains of London taxi drivers generally have larger than average hippocampi, the centre that helps mammals navigate. The hippocampus also plays a significant role in memory and the coordination of neural relays between the two hemispheres. When you think about what they do, and the fact that they spend on average three years learning the maze of roads within a six-mile radius of Charing Cross, it is perhaps unsurprising that their brains respond by generating a greater density of connections in the relevant areas. Or maybe in some kind of urban version of natural selection only the taxi drivers with a larger hippocampus were able to assimilate The Knowledge in the first place? But before we get too carried away we should remember that three-quarters of all those who embark upon acquiring The Knowledge never complete their training. Again, this would suggest that rehearsal and practice can only take you so far. Nature imposes limits that have to be respected.

But, you might object, the high failure rates don't mean that these drivers *couldn't* acquire the relevant skills, merely that they *didn't* acquire them. Perhaps they weren't that keen in the first place? Maybe they got bored or distracted, or needed a change? You could well be right. However, the point is that exactly these kinds of factors also impose real restrictions when it comes to picking up new skills. We now know that learning isn't just a matter of raw intelligence. It is strongly influenced by factors like attentional resources, motivation levels, memory, mental flexibility, and even personality factors – all of which can vary significantly between individuals and many of which may have strong biological roots. Physiology alone would stop me from ever running a mile as fast as Usain Bolt, but I suspect I might not even have the will-power to stick to his training regime. The truth is that aspects of my personality and temperament may also present equally significant obstacles to any prospect of my developing his unique skill set.

It may also be that I can't learn to do what you can do because my brain has already become specialised to do the things that *I* can do. In an episode of *The Simpsons*, Homer Simpson reminisces: '... every time I learn something new, it pushes some old stuff out of my brain. Remember when I took that home winemaking course, and I forgot how to drive?' While this is a parody and your brain actually retains sufficient capacity to learn new skills late into life, there may be a grain of truth in Homer's lament. Cognitive scientists are becoming increasingly interested in the interference effects that take place when new knowledge and old knowledge compete for processing and storage space.

Proactive interference takes place when previous knowledge disrupts the ability to assimilate new knowledge. Have you ever changed your bank account and tried to learn the new account number? It proves to be much harder because the old account number has become so firmly ingrained. Or have you ever found yourself standing in a garage able to call to mind the number plate of your old car but completely at a loss to recall the new one? These are relatively trivial examples, but can you imagine the issues that arise once brain circuits have been dedicated to certain tasks and you suddenly expect them to accommodate totally new skills? The human brain is plastic, but not infinitely so. While most of us can have a stab at most things, it is unrealistic to assume we are necessarily going to be able to achieve the same level of performance as someone whose neural wiring reflects their devotion to rehearsing and honing particular talents and habits.

Are we really so vain or insecure that we need to believe that we can do and be anything? Has political correctness reached a point whereby we can no longer admit to ourselves that some people are just better at certain things than others? Why do we allow ourselves to be cast into the wretched state described so well by Shakespeare in his 29th sonnet:

'Desiring this man's art and that man's scope,
With what I most enjoy contented least ...'

Why can't we focus instead on being good at the things we are built to be good at, and celebrate the talents and skills of others without feeling the need to grab them for ourselves? I remember meeting a twin once who told me that when his brother learned how to do something he would step back, not because he didn't want to compete, but merely because as a pair they now had that particular skill in their repertoire. Perhaps we could start thinking more along these lines? I am happy to let Usain Bolt run 100m on my behalf and cheer when he blasts across the line. I am content to be transported by Murray Perahia's virtuosity on the keyboard without feeling I have to

Are we really so vain or insecure that we need to believe that we can do and be anything?

try and duplicate it. I strongly suspect that my own time would be better spent discovering what I most enjoy doing, even if I never become that competent at it. I'm not denying it would be great fun to be Joe 90, but it's not realistic. NLP's promise is an empty one. In any case, perhaps the real question is not 'If someone out there is doing something really well, can I do it too?' but rather, 'Why would I need to?'

I feel you, man. Some days I'm just like, sure, I could change to the same color as this tree, but where does it really get me in the end?

You'd better get yourself sorted

'It is best to do things systematically, since we are only human, and disorder is our worst enemy.'

HESIOD, CIRCA 800BC

Two thousand years after the Greek poet first penned these lines, I wonder what Hesiod would make of the throng of trainers and self-help authors so willing to help us put his advice into practice today? Whether it be Steven Covey commending to us *The Seven Habits of Highly Effective People* or David Allen advising us on the art of *Getting Things Done*, helping people to get their lives organised and become more productive is still big business. As loyal citizens of the People's Republic of Psychobabble, we have been reared to believe that productivity and efficiency are virtues upon which our success and happiness depend. While I do admire Stephen Covey for his holistic emphasis on ethical living, it's telling that his famous book seamlessly blends moral responsibility with techniques for administering all aspects of life more efficiently. The result is that the dividing line between them becomes increasingly blurred. Psychobabble's version of the good life is one that increasingly resembles the perfect time and motion and study. The message is clear: there can be no inner harmony without external order. The optimal life is one of smooth, seamless efficiency, and one in which we must exercise continuous control over all aspects of ourselves and the immediate environment. But is disorder *really* our worst enemy?

One important criticism that has been levelled against the strident chorus of lifestyle 'clutter-busters' is that too much emphasis on order can end up stifling our creativity. A. A. Milne, creator of the children's classic, *Winnie the Pooh*, remarked astutely that 'One of the advantages of being disorderly is that one is constantly making exciting discoveries'. Psychologists investigating the phenomenon of creativity have found that more creative people tend to be divergent thinkers, relying on a relatively fluid and spontaneous process of free association that is certainly hard to reconcile with the convergent, logical, flow-chart approach recommended by most productivity manuals.

Picasso insisted that 'Every act of creation is first an act of destruction.' Existing structures of thought and perception have to be deliberately dismantled, or even smashed beyond recognition, so that novel possibilities can breathe and new combinations arise from the resultant disarray. Albert Rothenberg studied the creative processes of 22 Nobel prize-winning scientists and reviewed the biographies of giants like Niels Bohr, Max Planck, Albert Einstein and Charles Darwin. He agreed that radical innovation did indeed require people to deconstruct existing categories and juxtapose seemingly contradictory ideas no one else would have thought of putting together. He christened this feat the 'Janusian process', after the two-faced Roman god who was able to face in two directions at the same time.

Since the turn of the decade, psychiatrist Nancy Andreason has been using the latest neuro-imaging techniques to study creative processes at a physical level. She has discovered that the brain is at its most creative in its 'resting' state, since this is when multiple regions of the association cortex spring to life. Andreason describes this as a fluid process. She speculates: 'It is as if the association cortices are working actively, throwing our feelers for possible connections between unrelated capacities – verbal and visual spatial associations, abstract and concrete associations, colours, images, concepts… a veritable primordial soup of thought'. Her description concurs with the French mathematician and physicist Henri Poincaré's account of how he made a breakthrough discovery:

'One evening, contrary to my custom, I drank black coffee and could not sleep. Ideas rose in crowds; I felt them collide until pairs interlocked, so to speak, making a stable combination. By the next morning I had established the existence of a class of Fuchsian functions ...'

Thus it would appear that creativity involves a kind of letting go, abandoning oneself to a free-floating unconscious process that has little to do with formal logic, schedule or systematic analysis. It's a world away from the kind of structured, deliberate strategies that Covey and others endorse ('Draw a time management matrix and try and estimate the percentage of your time you spend in each quadrant ...' etc.).

So is it just coincidence that in their studios and workrooms, creative people often tend to surround themselves with chaos? Do their environments mirror the internal processes that contribute to their originality? Or do they just spend more time than most in a state of reverie that doesn't particularly lend itself to a preoccupation with tidiness, structure and colour-coded index cards?

Even for we less creative types, retired psychology professor Jay Brand believes that keeping our desks tidy is unlikely to boost our productivity and may even impede it. His argument is that the capacity restrictions of your working memory mean you can only hold a limited number of chunks of information on your mental desktop at any one time (seven items plus or minus two in fact). Therefore, he suggests, spreading information pell-mell across your physical desktop creates an extension of your thinking space and means that 'you are using the environment to think as well'.

An alternative recent take on the potential virtues of a messy desk comes from a German research team headed by Jia Liu, who found fascinating experimental evidence that our innate instinct to screen out extraneous information from environmental static can actually mean that working in a messier environment focuses our attention more closely on the task in hand. Whatever the reason, the philosophy of 'Mess for Success' may have something going for it. Two surveys found that in practice more disorganised workspaces tended to belong to the people taking home the higher salaries.

One journalist remarked with glee that such recent studies revealing the positive face of disorder also '… confirm what you have known, deep down, all along: really neat people are not avatars of the good life; they are humourless and inflexible prigs and have way too much time on their hands'. However, this is a bit strong. I suspect it may have been penned from a very untidy desk by someone who has a few organisation issues of their own … What we *do* know about these people is that the desire to keep things tidy and organised is strongly associated both with one of the 'Big Five' personality traits called 'conscientiousness' (usually a good thing) and, in psychoanalyst Karen Horney's book, with 'neuroticism' (almost invariably a bad thing). Conscientious people 'tend to be more organized and less cluttered in their homes and offices …' while the presence of planners and to-do lists are apparently also tell-tale signs.'[1] Now there's much more to conscientiousness than this: there's certainly nothing wrong with being reliable, industrious and disciplined. In fact conscientiousness is actually one of the strongest predictors of performance in the workplace.[2] However, there is also a shadow side to this virtuous trait for those who have it in excess: they can easily become obsessive perfectionists or 'workaholics', who never enjoy a moment's peace.

---

[1] As indeed (bizarrely) is better lighting in their homes! I have no idea what that's all about …

[2] Higher levels of conscientiousness are also positively associated with better health. Jennifer Lodi-Smith (see Lodi-Smith et al. 2010) believes the latter is due to the fact that 'the conscientious individual is actually going to go out and do the things their doctor says they should be doing to stay healthy'.

If we take the message of the productivity authors onboard, our grim determination to stay in command can very easily turn against us. Obsessive Compulsive Disorder (OCD) is one of the most destructive manifestations of the need for order and control and it is on the increase. Sufferers develop an unrealistic sense of personal responsibility that can lead them to become hyper-vigilant, either continually checking or creating magical control rituals to help them manage the unmanageable. These can be paralysing, as anyone who suffers from OCD knows only too well.

Conventional thinking about OCD is that there is a significant genetic component underlying it. Your genes create vulnerability to certain thought processes that you then develop compulsions (like hand-washing rituals) to try and manage. However, recently researchers at Cambridge University have produced evidence that makes it look as if it may be possible for compulsive behaviours to cause obsessional thoughts, rather than the other way round. Claire Gillan and colleagues found that, even in the absence of worrying thoughts, people vulnerable to OCD were more prone to keep on reacting habit-ually to selected stimuli, even once the rewards for doing so were withdrawn. These OCD sufferers were on an automatic pilot, and the researchers are speculating that the obsessional thoughts may be generated, as it were, *after* the event to help 'join up the dots' and make sense of the compulsive behaviour.

Now while people who suffer from OCD may well have predisposing vulnerabilities to the condition, is it completely far-fetched to imagine that persuading someone to act 'as if' they had OCD might not galvanise any latent tendencies in that direction? This might be analogous to the way that when you starve someone, they often start producing the thought distor-tions and attitudes characteristic of an anorexic. You have to wonder, when you consider the salutary tale of self-confessed former 'clutter criminal' and blogger, Art Gould, who finally caved in and dedicated a week of his life to getting himself organised. After clearing the backlog of work that had built up while he was sorting things out (!), Art sensed a new problem:

'My new desk was beginning to take on the characteristics
of a shrine. I dared not do anything that might alter the
pristine image that had made such a profound impression on
me once I had finally cleaned it. My obsession with keeping
it immaculate soon became an additional task added to my
already long list of tasks.'

As Art shows us, once we dedicate ourselves to the cause of
Order, it has the potential to enslave us, turning us into obsessive
neat freaks. Just as people with social phobia resort to 'safety
behaviours' like wearing dark glasses that only compound
their problems, it would appear that waging war on chaos
and the causes of chaos can make any anxieties surrounding it
even greater. Thrill to the rising panic in no less a person than
Stephen Covey himself when Mother Nature cruelly intervened
to disturb his writer's idyll on the north shore of Oahu, Hawaii:

'Suddenly the breeze started picking up and blowing
my papers about. I remember the frantic sense of loss
I felt because things were no longer in order, including
unnumbered pages, and I began rushing around the room
trying desperately to put them back …'

I'm sure it's probably just mean-spirited jealousy that makes
this such a pleasing scenario for me, but the point still holds:
however hard we try and indulge our fantasies of control, there
are forces out there in the world that are all too able to rip those
illusions away.

This may give us important clues as to why organisation
appeals so much to a certain type of person. When confronted
with an efficient, well-run life it can be hard to work out what's
really going on. For some people, especially those with an
inbuilt instinct for it, maintaining order is simply a pragmatic

*Once we dedicate ourselves to the cause of
Order, it has the potential to enslave us.*

issue: it keeps stress levels down by helping them keep life on track and juggle demands on their time with some semblance of composure. For others, one suspects, a preoccupation with neatness and order may be a defence against more deeply-seated anxieties about death, decay and impotence. If neuropsychologist Jerrold Pollak is right that 'Total organisation' is indeed '… a futile attempt to deny and control the unpredictability of life', then we might do better to abandon this particular form of socially-validated denial and reconcile ourselves to our ultimate helplessness.

For others, preoccupation with orderliness appears to serve a very different function. While organisation helps some people get more done, for others it becomes a stealthy way of doing less, or at least doing it later. How many of us, presented with a daunting project or unpleasant task, mysteriously find ourselves several hours later with a stack of freshly ironed clothes, an immaculately tidy house and a newly-ordered sock draw but have made little progress with the task that's supposed to be commanding our attention? Not that I am talking from personal experience, you understand, but I gather such people often convince themselves that they will be able to focus much better once these extraneous acts of order have taken place. The truth is it's just displacement activity. This latter kind of obsession with order doesn't promote efficiency at all: it just sucks up energy that would be far better invested in the job in hand.

And make no mistake: keeping things in order does cost us. As David Freedman and Eric Abrahamson, authors of *A Perfect Mess: The Hidden Benefits of Disorder*, explain, 'It takes extra effort to neaten up a system … Things don't generally neaten themselves.' The second law of thermodynamics would firmly agree with them. It states that, left to their own devices, *all* systems have a natural tendency to become more disorganised rather than less. Even if we want to chase after structure and order, Newton is clear that ultimately we are on a hiding to nothing. Perhaps we should consider whether we would do better channelling our finite energies into the things that really matter to us? In fact, to be accurate, Newton's second law claims that 'in general the total entropy of any system will not decrease other than by increasing the entropy of some other system'. My reading of this is that if you tidy your desk, somewhere in the world some poor person's desk is getting messier as a result. You're virtually littering! Stop it! My desk is messy enough as it is ...

More seriously, we also have to ask ourselves whether we want to be the kind of people who always have a system and a place for everything? These principles may seem harmless enough, even necessary at times, but as society embraces orderliness as the norm they can have an insidious effect on our collective identity. Productivity guides and time-management bibles, however insightful or helpful they may appear, clearly belong to the tradition of rationalisation. This was set in motion during the industrial revolution of the nineteenth century, enshrined in the principles of scientific management popularised by Frederick Taylor, and culminated in Henry Ford's famous Model T production line. Reflecting on the experience of workers on Ford's production line, organisational analyst Larry Hirschhorn wrote:

'Nothing seems more brutalizing, not because of felt pain or discomfort – for many studies show that workers do adjust to the rhythms of movement imposed by the line and may derive pleasure from the experience of continuity – but rather because experiences and potentials are lost forever and intelligent people are robbed of their ability to think, puzzle out, and discover.'

As the sociologist Max Weber warned us, in a world where the principles of instrumental rationality prevail, life is soon reduced to an endless cascade of means and ends. Calculation and efficiency prevail as our most cherished virtues, and even time itself, becomes a commodity to be apportioned out according to the law of maximum returns. Before we rush to the shelves to pick up our copy of the latest productivity blockbuster (the one that's *really* going to help us get our act together) let's just consider whether we might not be adding our own momentum to what Marx and Engels chillingly described as 'icy waves of egotistical calculation'. Failing that, let's at least try and live by the compromise suggested by David Freedman to Penelope

Ugh. Don't waste your time, Carol. Every single god-damn page that comes out of this thing is the same.

Excessive rationalisation can make life rather dull and predictable...

Green, a journalist from the *New York Times*: 'Almost anything looks pretty neat,' he told her, 'if it's shuffled into a pile.'

As a fan of the sci-fi classic *Star Trek*, I was always secretly impressed by how Captain James T. Kirk and his various successors ran not only a tight starship, but a very tidy one as well – despite the fact that you never saw anyone putting anything away, going to the toilet or doing any kind of sorting, let alone dusting. It may be true that in space '... no one can hear you scream ...' but it would appear no one can hear you clean either. However, the ergonomically streamlined, clutter-free lives of the crew of the *Enterprise* are just not a realistic template for most of us.

Sure, you can try and get yourself organised, put all those clever systems, fancy file boxes and smart disciplines in place. We all need to sort ourselves out a bit every now and again. But equally, we may sometimes need a bit of creative chaos around us, and to be comfortable with turning a blind eye to the trivial stuff so that we can devote our resources to what really matters in life. By constantly dangling in front of us the prospect of a life that runs with the articulated, jewelled precision of a Swiss watch, the productivity gurus really aren't helping, quite apart from setting standards to which few mere mortals can realistically aspire. I don't necessarily always agree with the philosopher Friedrich Nietzsche that 'the will to system betrays a lack of integrity' but we do need to ensure our various systems are serving us, and not the other way round.

You are stronger than you know

'Our deepest fear is not that we are inadequate …,' intones the motivational speaker Marianne Williamson, 'Our deepest fear is that we are powerful beyond measure …' These celebrated lines[1] from *Return to Love* have been embraced so enthusiastically by so many that it feels churlish (and possibly even heretical) to be casting doubt upon the basic assumption on which they rest. And yet, while many have drawn consolation and inspiration from Williamson's words, I have to suggest that the expectations they create may be doing us all as much harm as good.

The idea that we all have limitless, untapped resources within us is one of popular psychology's most enduring leitmotifs. Anthony Robbins, for example, urges us to *Awaken the Giant Within* and to unleash our *Unlimited Power*. He assures us that: 'Most people have no idea of the giant capacity we can immediately command when we focus all of our resources on mastering a single area of our lives.' Robbins is only one voice among a swelling chorus of self-help authors who want us to embrace inventor Henry Ford's conviction: 'There is no man living that cannot do more than he thinks he can.'

---

[1] They have even been attributed to Nelson Mandela, although the common belief that he quoted them in his inauguration speech turns out to be an urban myth. Williamson herself graciously concedes: 'As honored as I would be had President Mandela quoted my words, indeed he did not. I have no idea where that story came from, but I am gratified that the paragraph has come to mean so much to so many people.'

We are naturally flattered by this idea. It feels comforting to think that we are all sitting on this great wellspring of human potential, and that beneath our faded street clothes there is a Superman or Superwoman poised to soar into the stratosphere. Unfortunately, accident and emergency departments the world over already have to deal with a steady stream of injured children in capes who also managed to convince themselves of powers they didn't actually possess.

Rather than affirming that we are all stronger than we know, a more honest bumper sticker for the human race would probably read: 'Most of us are weaker than we could possibly imagine.' How many of us have told our children that they can accomplish anything they set their minds to? Is that how it's panned out for us? Maybe it has. Or, do we find ourselves somewhat less successful, less fulfilled, and less accomplished than this brazen piece of wishful thinking encouraged us to believe? Worse still, in view of the generally reliable but unglamorous observation of psychologists that past behaviour is the best predictor of future behaviour, the adults amongst us should probably resign themselves to the fact that things are unlikely to change much any time soon.

Of course *some* people can and do accomplish amazing things – and formidable will-power or single-minded determination often features as a crucial part of the equation, although a generous sprinkling of exceptional natural talent and good old-fashioned luck also usually play a part too. In his book *Outliers,* Malcolm Gladwell is only the most recent modern prophet to rediscover the age-old truth of Edison's well-worn maxim that genius is 'one per cent inspiration and ninety per cent perspiration'. But while this may be true, it doesn't mean

The idea that we all have limitless, untapped resources within us is one of popular psychology's most enduring leitmotifs.

Children! Stop crying or you'll have to start from the beginning! Your fingers are supposed to bleed. That's how you know you're getting good.

Only another 8,770 hours to go...

we all have it in us to be like little David Beckham, 'scarcely seen without a football' throughout a childhood obsessively dedicated to logging up endless hours of practice.

Will-power, determination and focus are not distributed equally among Mother Nature's offspring, any more than her other desirable gifts including brains and beauty. Gladwell's 'outliers' are exceptional not just because they put in the hours, but because there was something unusual about their psychological make-up (or sometimes that of their parents!) that *enabled* them to put in those hours. Psychologically, most of us are just the unfit kid puffing away at the back of pack in the school cross-country race, desperate just to sit down and make the pain stop.

Anyone who has tried and failed to give up smoking, broken a New Year's resolution or rewarded themselves for two noble hours in the gym with a generous slab of chocolate cake already knows this to be true. And talking of chocolate cake, if you ever needed convincing that your will-power is not an unstoppable force in the world, perhaps you should drop in to Professor Baba Shiv's laboratory at Stanford University.

In one of Shiv's more unnerving experiments, people simply asked to memorise a seven-digit number proved *twice* as likely to opt for cake over fruit salad a few minutes later, compared with a sample asked to commit only two digits to memory. What this reveals is how quickly our will-power is eroded when we tax our prefrontal cortex with additional tasks – even relatively trivial ones. Then again, Roy Baumeister has also demonstrated that our level of will-power is surprisingly dependent upon our blood-sugar levels. So perhaps those greedy cake-eaters in Shiv's study just needed those extra calories to replenish their energy reserves after the mammoth mental exertion involved in memorising a sequence no longer than the average telephone number? Either way, these studies underline that if will-power is like a muscle, as Baumeister maintains, the majority of us are six-stone weaklings rather than iron men.

Rather unfairly, it is often at those very moments when we are trying our hardest to resist temptation that the cognitive processes involved in doing so leave us most vulnerable to relapse. Something in us snaps, or we find ourselves being 'pinged back' in the opposite direction. As aspirational dieter Edward Ugel comments:

> 'Control is a funny thing. It comes and goes. Some days I had it, some days I didn't. It felt like every time I did something healthy, I had this insatiable need to counterbalance it by doing something unhealthy.'

Ugel is not alone. Wolfgang Stroebe found skipping meals often predicts weight gain rather than loss while, according to Daniel Wegner, efforts to banish all thoughts of certain foods ends up in more rather than less of them.

Nevertheless, because we are having it drummed into us the whole time that we have it in us to move mountains and that even our wildest dreams lie within our reach if we would just put our backs into it, we place ourselves under enormous pressure to keep going, even when things are not working out. Labouring under the burden of Anthony Robbins' grim injunction that '... life's greatest rewards are reserved for those who demonstrate a never-ending commitment to act until they achieve' we no longer feel we are allowed to give up. We lose sight of the option of calling a halt to something simply because we no longer want to continue doing it.

Psychobabble assures us that anyone can make it, providing they are prepared to make the necessary sacrifices and commit to the hard, painful slog. Want to become an expert in your field? Then roll up your sleeves and start logging those 10,000 hours of deliberate practice Malcolm Gladwell says it's going to take. Yes, of course you may feel bored, disillusioned and desperate at times – but no one said it would be easy, did they? And think of how great you'll feel when you succeed ... Unfortunately, even if we *do* succeed, sometimes the biggest pay-off is the cessation of the pain we could have saved ourselves by never setting out in the first place. This was certainly my personal experience of running the Brighton marathon two years ago.

Our belief in our invincibility has encouraged the modern world to develop a perverse relationship with pain. You will undoubtedly have seen T-shirts and towels emblazoned with the legend from the Second World War propaganda poster, 'Keep

We place ourselves under enormous pressure to keep going, even when things are not working out.

calm and carry on'. The first part sounds like generally good advice to me, but I have serious reservations about the 'carrying on' bit. If a situation is that anxiety-provoking or painful, then sometimes the best thing to do is *not* to carry on, precisely because those feelings may be Nature's way of telling you to reconsider and do something else.

All around us we are presented with examples of people 'carrying on' and successfully defying their natural impulses in order to push themselves to the limit (and sometimes beyond). Turn on your television and you will see celebrities submitting themselves to 'trials' of various kinds, whether it be comedian Eddie Izzard running an improbable 43 marathons in 51 days, *Little Britain*'s David Walliams swimming the channel, or some hapless reality TV star battling his gag reflex while consuming kangaroo genitals in the Australian outback.

Now these feats are all genuinely impressive in their own way (although the kangaroo might beg to differ, of course) and it would be a lie to claim that suffering doesn't sometimes bring its own rewards. However, these stunts also play into our culture's conviction that its normal and even desirable that life should feel like some kind of an endurance sport. Ever since Jane Fonda first encouraged us to 'feel the burn' back in the 1970s, we have come to view chronic discomfort not as a warning sign but as reassuring evidence that we are getting somewhere. This is not always the case.

The pain barrier isn't always there just to be crashed through. Like all barriers its message to us is, 'Stop! Don't go any further' or, at the very least, 'Proceed with caution'. When you feel physical pain in your body and carry on regardless, sooner or later something is going to break. The same is true of your mind and heart. Yet because endurance has become such an aspirational activity, we don't always pay enough attention to the warning signs.

No one wants the stigma of being branded a 'quitter' or a 'loser' but the constant pressure to fulfil this immeasurable potential of ours can prove extremely costly for us. As the phrase implies, people who pursue any objective with 'single-minded' determination inevitably risk becoming rather one-dimensional creatures. Dedication to our overriding mission sometimes leaves little room in our lives for anything else. Before we know it, other activities have been squeezed out and we find ourselves neglecting friends and family. We become depressed and miserable. Instead of blossoming, our lives contract.

But under such circumstances, paradoxically, our reliance on the project to which we have unwittingly enslaved ourselves becomes all the greater. We set in motion a vicious circle that makes it even harder to abandon ship when we should. We convince ourselves we can no longer afford to quit because the endeavour has already proved so emotionally costly that we need to feel our sacrifice has not been in vain. Although depleted, we therefore redouble our efforts to succeed. Running on empty, we are now at increasing risk of experiencing the rising levels of inefficiency, exhaustion and cynicism measured by the Maslach Burnout Inventory.[2] Soon we find ourselves functioning even less effectively than before and drifting ever further from achieving the goal we have set ourselves. It's not a pretty tale.

I suspect there may even be a more sinister legacy of this belief that we are always capable of more. There is a real possibility that we sometimes keep going when things get tough not because we are still determined to succeed, but because unconsciously we need to keep punishing ourselves for failing. Inflamed by the unrealistic expectations you find in popular psychology, our impossible standards sometimes drive us to persecute the vulnerability and weakness we have uncovered in ourselves. What better way of achieving this than to keep our nose forced to the grindstone? In the true spirit of making the punishment fit the crime, we sentence ourselves to enduring

---

[2]This is a structured psychological questionnaire for measuring the symptoms of stress associated with the state of long-term exhaustion and diminished interest, colloquially know as 'burnout'.

the very hardship that exposed our flaws. We adopt the role of Sisyphus in Greek mythology, who was condemned by Queen Persephone to the back-breaking and fruitless task of pushing an enormous boulder up a hill, only to have it repeatedly roll back down again as he approached the summit. The rage we feel as a result of our humiliation is turned back in on ourselves. By submitting ourselves to a slow process of self-destruction we also take surreptitious revenge on all who have dared to demand more of us than deep down we felt able to give.

So if our will-power is more dilute than we were led to believe, and if the reality is that we are not 'powerful beyond measure' as Williamson and others have promised, where does this leave us?

Well, first we need to recognise that we might be wise to conserve our scant resources. This means not overextending ourselves. If we cannot content ourselves with realistic people-sized goals, then at least increase the odds by not trying to excel in more than one or two areas. Also, however busy we are, we must ensure we take time to do the things and nurture the relationships that will replenish our resources. If Baumeister is to be believed, from time to time this may even include eating the odd Mars bar, but boring stuff like adequate sleep, regular meals and a bit of physical exercise will also help.

Secondly, we should probably reconcile ourselves to our human frailty rather than denying it or (even worse) berating ourselves for it all the time. While it is perfectly healthy to aspire to greatness and goodness, we need to accept that our collective mental and moral frailty means we will inevitably and frequently fall short. We can't all be the fastest runner or the most successful entrepreneur or the cleverest in the class. Nether are we all cut out for sainthood. So when we turn out not to be, rather than endlessly berating ourselves for having 'let ourselves down', perhaps we should cut ourselves a bit of slack. We are seldom very good at forgiving ourselves for our own shortcomings, even when the standards we have set ourselves are too ambitious. Fortunately, compassion and forgiveness, however difficult they may be to achieve, don't appear to place excessive demands on our mental powers. They are freely available but underutilised talents that we would all be wise to cultivate: after all, most of us are going to have plenty of opportunity to use them.[3]

Finally, we need to get our heads round the fact that if we are doing the right thing it just shouldn't feel that hard or difficult. Of course there is effort involved in achieving anything worthwhile and there are storms that absolutely should be weathered. However, life shouldn't feel crushing. As psychologist Mihaly Csikszentmihalyi has explained, when we find what works for us, we are naturally drawn into a state of 'flow' in which we become effortlessly attuned, absorbed and fascinated by the task in hand. Rather than feeling like we are setting our faces against a gale, under these conditions we find the wind forever at our back, propelling us forward or even plucking us into the sky like mad, dancing kites.

If the state of flow is an energised joyride on a sunlit country road, but mentally we find ourselves continually stuck in a traffic jam on the M25, it makes sense to start looking for the next available exit rather than just keep trudging along. Of course we sometimes need to keep working at things, but we mustn't fool ourselves that chronic distress, even at a low level, is a necessary down payment on a better life ahead. It's a warning sign we should heed, even if the prospect of change makes us nervous. Sadly, many of us choose to keep plugging away at our impossible dreams, thankless careers or doomed relationships rather than admit to ourselves that we no longer have it in us to keep trying. In its efforts to force us

Life shouldn't feel crushing.

[3] If you want more genuinely helpful advice on how to go about this, have a look at Paul Gilbert's work on compassion-focused therapy, distilled into a readable form in *The Compassionate Mind*.

to acknowledge our potential, Psychobabble has made giving up very hard to do. After all, quitting or throwing in the towel are not the behaviours of invincible people. Ultimately though, I guess it all depends on how we choose to understand what strength is. This is surely what agony aunt Ann Landers was driving at when she wrote:

> 'Some people believe holding on and hanging in there are signs of great strength. However, there are times when it takes much more strength to know when to let go and then do it.'

Neither accepting our limits nor calling a halt are easy options in today's world. But sometimes our psychological health may depend upon our ability to do precisely that.

In its efforts to force us to acknowledge our potential, Psychobabble has made giving up very hard to do.

MYTH 15

You are a master of the universe!

The alleged power of mind over matter is a common enough theme in the self-help genre. In its 'weak' form it appears as techniques like positive thinking, Cognitive Behavioural Therapy, and the use of confidence-building affirmations. All of the above are premised on the understanding that mental shifts translate into effects in the real world, but they are always mediated through changes in your behaviour: in other words shifts in attitude alter what you do and how you respond and it is your actions that ultimately change your life for the better. Nothing too fancy or esoteric going on here, folks: just plain old common-sense pathways of cause and effect that sit reasonably comfortably within our traditional view of the world.

But there is a second, far more challenging 'strong position' of mind over matter that recurs in a surprising number of self-help books, courses and presentations. According to this genre, the mind has innate metaphysical powers to manipulate reality in ways that lie far beyond any current, orthodox understanding of the way the physical world works. Buckle up, gentle reader: we are now entering the twilight zone of the paranormal.

The concept of controlling aspects of the world remotely and manifesting our desires by literally willing them into being is, as the author of the bestseller *The Secret* keeps reminding us, a very old idea. Some psychologists would argue that its ancient pedigree is due to the fact that it is likely to originate in early infancy as a universal, primitive fantasy. The helpless human baby counteracts its intuitive sense of dependency by conceiving itself, in the words of an exuberant Leonardo DiCaprio on the prow of the *Titanic,* as 'King of the World'. The narcissism of infancy is usually well supported by direct experience. Hungry? Send up the distress flare and any half-attentive carer will be on hand to feed you. Nappy feeling a bit soggy and clammy? No worries: just make your displeasure known and Dad will be along in a jiffy for a quick change. In our culture, when you are tiny you call the shots. Everyone rushes around trying to meet your needs and if you are being well looked after there is scant evidence to suggest that the world does not revolve around you, especially when your brain and understanding are too underdeveloped to grasp the whys and wherefores of how this all happens. Is it any wonder that the notion that the cosmos might be equally accommodating once we grow older remains such an alluring prospect?

I'm going to be picking on *The Secret* for a while because although it is by no means the only self-help book built on the foundation of these kinds of ideas, its huge commercial success lies in part in that it presents them in a remarkably pure (some might say blatant) form. It therefore offers a particularly transparent and instructive insight into the way the strong version of the mind-over-matter position operates.

The principles of *The Secret* – which according to author Rhonda Byrne have been known and practised by creative pioneers and leaders throughout history – amount to picturing the universe as a kind of cosmic Argos. And please don't think this is some disparaging metaphor I've dreamt up for humorous effect. It's pretty much precisely the one used in the book by Dr Joe Vitale, who cheerfully explains:

> 'It's like having the universe as your catalogue. You flip through it and say, "I'd like to have this experience and I'd like to have that product and I'd like to have a person like that." It is You placing your order with the Universe. It is really that easy.'

Who knew? Apart, of course, from Plato, Bacon, Beethoven, Shakespeare, Newton and Einstein obviously – the latter two of whom would doubtless be turning in their graves to be associated with the rather dubious metaphysics of all this. Someone really ought to tell the starving children of Africa and the oppressed peoples of the world that they need to buck up their ideas and start ordering the right things.

The 'Law of Attraction' upon which *The Secret* is based apparently states that we inevitably draw to ourselves the things with which we fill our minds because, as Byrne assures us, 'unfathomable magnetic power is emitted through your thoughts'. The implication one might read into this is that each and every one of us is entirely responsible for our own fate. In my personal opinion, the idea that some of us might be willing suffering and disaster upon ourselves is a pretty repugnant doctrine. As a psychologist, I fully accept that we all have self-destructive urges and I frequently encounter people who seem unconsciously bent on sabotaging their lives. However, surely conjuring up a tsunami, famine or plague lies beyond even the most pathological of us?

Books like *The Secret* are full of authoritative proclamations about the nature of man and reality that are just not in any way backed up, as far as I can see, by satisfactory evidence. And the brilliant catch of it is that the very nature of the claims makes them irrefutable. This belief system (and that is what it is) can account for every outcome with impunity. If you don't get what you ordered then that's because at some level you haven't really focused your thinking or committed your mind to the desired outcome to the exclusion of all other possibilities. You may think you psychically ordered that Series 5 BMW in racing green, but the fact it hasn't materialised means either (a) the timing isn't right yet or (b) *unconsciously* you actually didn't want it so your order was cancelled – sorry about that, or (c) your lack of belief left you focused on your state of *not* having the car in your life yet, and unfortunately the universe obligingly manifested precisely that: you not having the car!

Basically you got distracted, you didn't really know your own mind or you didn't have enough faith. Whichever way you look at it, you are at fault, not the system. Suddenly the feel-good factor in all of this is draining away pretty fast. But of course, remember if you are thinking 'guilt trip' or 'disillusionment' right now, Rhonda and her friends can't be held accountable if that's exactly what you get.

It is undeniable that discoveries in the realm of quantum mechanics have completely transformed our understanding of the nature of reality over the last few decades. Scientists like Heisenberg, Schrödinger, Born, Dirac and Witten have established beyond all reasonable doubt that the universe is far stranger than we could ever possibly have imagined. The philosophical implications of theories like quantum entanglement, string theory or even the notion that things can exist simultaneously in more than one state are mind-boggling and leave us constantly falling down intellectual rabbit holes into a wonderland of truly bizarre and surreal possibilities. The ordered clockwork of Newton's elegant universe has been smashed to bits so irretrievably we could be forgiven for concluding that in the strange and counterintuitive landscape of particle physics all bets are off and anything is now possible.

But this is precisely the point. Just because something seems theoretically possible, as the lyricist Ira Gershwin reminds us, 'it ain't necessarily so'. However, the metaphysics of self-help often doesn't trouble itself with that finicky distinction. If the dots don't quite join up yet, well, never mind: the fact that such possibilities even exist show we're clearly in the right ballpark. Didn't Arthur C. Clark famously once say that magic is just technology we don't quite understand yet? Maybe if we just throw around a bit of choice scientific terminology and broadly sketch out the territory then that'll be quite sufficient to convince a gullible reader. We can't all be particle physicists after all. Too many speakers and writers towards the more esoteric end of the self-help spectrum rely rather too heavily on the truth of the refreshingly honest and reliably brilliant

Mr. Darwin, you may indeed believe that we came from monkeys... but dare you disbelieve in... MAGIC?!

The self-help gurus throw down the gauntlet ...

Richard Feynman who commented: 'I think I can safely say *nobody* understands quantum mechanics.'

But while it's playing fast and loose to try and recruit quantum physics to bolster the strong form of the mind-over-matter argument, it may come as something of a shock to discover that there is a whole body of carefully collected, rigorously analysed data that actually does – albeit by a very slim margin. Over the last 30 years, experiments have been repeated time and time again under the most stringent controlled conditions that are consistently supportive of the hypothesis that people can indeed remotely change the outcome of physical events using the power of their minds.

The story begins in 1979 with Robert Jahn, who was the Dean of Princeton University's prestigious School of Engineering and Applied Science. He set up a programme to investigate the possibility that human consciousness might be interacting with machines, causing them to function in ways that appeared to defy the balance of probability. At the heart of the research run at the PEAR (Princeton Engineering Anomalies Research) lab was endless trials using random number generators. When left to their own devices, these machines electronically produce either a one or a zero in a completely random sequence, a bit like flipping a coin. And, as with flipping a coin, you would expect ones and zeros to come up in approximately equal numbers once you repeat your exercise enough times.

However, what Professor Jahn and his colleagues found was that when people concentrated on willing the generator to produce more 'heads' or fewer 'tails' they were able to skew the results (albeit ever so slightly) away from the pattern predicted by pure chance. The shifts were minuscule – equivalent to demonstrating that on average people were able to influence the outcome of two events out of every 10,000 above chance. Not great odds admittedly, and the paltry scale of the effect alone has naturally invited scepticism from baying critics who feel that there must be some other explanation for the results. However, the results were statistically significant and the more trials they did throughout the years (and they did millions), the more these tiny fluctuations persisted, eventually leading colleagues of Jahn to conclude that the odds were less than a trillion to one that the overall pattern of results from two decades of work was itself due to a freak occurrence.

Now, for the strong version of the mind-over-matter position the PEAR results are both good and bad news. Good news insofar as *any* consistently demonstrable effect, however small, genuinely supports the idea that it may be possible for people to affect the physical world with their minds. The bad news, however, is that the effects are so infinitesimally small that, even if genuine, one cannot begin to imagine how they might have the least meaningful impact on our lives. We're a long way from telekinetically flinging knives around the kitchen like Sissy Spacek in *Carrie* or even bending the odd spoon. In the individual studies we are looking at a hit rate of barely two-hundredths of a single percentage above chance (50.02 per cent). I'm not being mean but it's practically a slither of nothing and would mean absolutely nothing had it not then occurred thousands of time more. To argue that this research proves that books like *The Secret* are on to something amounts to saying that your lucky find of a 20-pence piece on the street this morning means you will now be able to pick all the winning lottery numbers in the EuroMillions draw.

Interestingly, although PEAR closed its doors in 2007, it paved the way for the Global Consciousness Project that is currently using random event generators to novel and even more controversial effect. Dr Roger Nelson and colleagues collate the data from approximately 70 of these boxes placed in locations all over the world. What he has apparently found is extraordinary. He is not instructing anyone to try and influence anything, but by combining and cross-referencing the continual flow of results from the boxes he has discovered that the law of averages seems to get significantly ruffled during periods that coincide with major world events. Around the time a plane flies into the Twin Towers you get a blip in the random distribution of the ones and the noughts. Princess Diana dies and you get a significant peak. What Nelson's team believes is that in some way the boxes are responding to emotive experiences shared by millions of people that amount to ripples in a shared global consciousness.

This is all very bizarre stuff, but while the scientific community has understandably raised a collective eyebrow at the claims of the Global Consciousness team, thus far it has struggled to provide a satisfactory alternative account for its data. One fairly compelling criticism is that the group has broken the golden rule of statistics which says that if you sift through data looking for correlations long enough you will inevitably find them (so perhaps Rhonda Byrne is right after all: you do get what you expect!). Cynics argue that the fact these probabilistic anomalies coincide with the timing of certain world events is just coincidental; after all, the world is a busy place and there is a lot going on at any particular moment. The chances of finding a momentous event that coincides with your statistical glitch, they argue, is therefore reasonably high. However, it is much more of a challenge to explain why these admittedly delicate fibrillations in the flow of chance appear to be happening simultaneously in several independent boxes at the same time.

And if all this doesn't read like an *X Files* script already, a further jaw-dropping twist is that Nelson's team claims sometimes these statistical anomalies occur just *before* the events to which they are assumed to refer. That's right: a few hours in advance. If the team's hypothesis that this process is driven by something human beings are doing is correct, and assuming that the fluctuations do indeed correspond to the events in question, this would mean that people are unconsciously anticipating those events before they happen. In effect these boxes are predicting the future. Allegedly, data from the random event generators scattered throughout the world anticipated the Twin Towers attack by four hours and also the Asian tsunami. How strange would this be if true? We would have to rip up everything we know about time, consciousness and material physics. But then again, how many of us had the more mundane experience of thinking about someone just before they ring or we bump into them in the street?

Spookily, in 2010 a research team at Cornell University also generated disconcerting evidence that we may be able to see into the future. Psychologist Daryl Bem used the technique of reverse priming to demonstrate what look like precognitive abilities. In normal priming, if you show someone a negative word followed by a positive image it will take people slightly longer to identify the image as a positive one because there is a mild interference effect. Their 'negative association' schemas are up and running already so it's not so easy for the brain to access positive material. This is a well-established effect. However, what Bem found was that if you reversed the whole process and showed people a positive image first and only *afterwards* showed them a negative stimulus, they still took longer to identify the positive image than a control group, even though the interference effect technically hadn't yet occurred! In trials subjects have also performed better than average at detecting the presence of an image behind closed curtains, but only when what was concealed was particularly salacious or stimulating.

Of course, going back to the Global Consciousness team results, it must be stressed that once again we are considering tiny fluctuations in the balance of probability that would be virtually undetectable if not cross-referenced with data streams from the other boxes. And why chance should be so sensitive to outpourings of human emotion is another question altogether. However, for self-help adherents of the 'strong' mind-over-matter school, the Global Consciousness data does introduce the theoretical possibility that under certain conditions our minds could have some psychic impact upon the physical world.

I have neither the statistical skill, the anorak nor the time to evaluate Nelson's data with any authority, but if you are intrigued by all of this, as I was, I suggest you have a look at the Global Consciousness project website for yourself. Time and scientific hard graft will tell how seriously we should be taking all this.

Interestingly, Nelson and colleagues claim that the largest blips in probability coincide with events that evoke empathy

The Global Consciousness data does introduce the theoretical possibility that under certain conditions our minds could have some psychic impact upon the physical world.

or compassion. Fear-based events apparently do not register as strongly, and the Global Consciousness team has wondered whether this is because emotions like pain, fear and terror tend to turn us inwards, making us self-focused and thereby isolating us from other people, whereas emotions like compassion incline us to 'connect' with others, thereby presumably amplifying the potential impact on the probability fields of the cosmos.

This might fit quite well with data reported from Lynne McTaggart's Intention Experiments, which she bills as one of the largest scale mind-over-matter investigations ever conducted. Apparently thousands of volunteers have signed up to her web-based experiments and again the results reported so far are certainly thought-provoking. Whether they provoke you to wonder or ridicule is another matter.

Author and speaker Lynne McTaggart is, of course, a true believer in the power of mind over matter and positions herself as someone attempting to bridge the existing gaps between science and spirituality. To her credit, although not formally trained as a scientist, she is well informed and does not shy away from data that does not fit with her preferred view of the world. One of the refreshing things about her is that, while she accepts psychic influence as given, she is pretty dismissive of attempts to use it to order up new cars or widescreen TVs. Her spirituality focuses her on more altruistic goals like psychokinetically purifying water supplies and promoting peace between warring countries. Let's turn now to some of the more striking findings of the Intention Experiment.

Gardeners who put their prize-winning marrows down to chatting away to them while they grow might be fascinated to discover that McTaggart's most impressive results concern the use of intention to promote the germination and growth of plants. Working in conjunction with Dr Gary Schwartz from the University of Arizona, she came up with an elegant and carefully controlled experimental design. In the experimental conditions McTaggart's volunteers allegedly beamed the intention for one of four selected sets of seeds to grow by 'at least 3cm by the fourth day of growing'. McTaggart reports that, on average, seeds receiving these waves of intention ended up 8mm higher than the controls. The statistical analysis of the results gave only a 0.7 per cent probability that this result occurred by chance which is pretty good going (or growing?). However, as far as I am aware, these results have not yet been replicated or the findings submitted to any academic peer-reviewed journal.

Also of interest is an experiment in which McTaggart's army of volunteers tried to influence events in the northern stronghold of the Tamil Tigers in Wanni, Sri Lanka after 25 years of bloody civil war. The claim is that, after an initial striking *increase* in the levels of violence following the week of focused intention in September 2010, the death rate of casualties fell by 74 per cent and injuries by 48 per cent in the following week, completely bucking the general trends of weekly violence data provided by Dr Kumar Rupesinghe of the Sri Lankan Foundation for Co-existence. McTaggart goes on to speculate about the possible connection between key events that occurred around that time (such as the recapturing of the Elephant Pass) and the final expulsion of the separatist guerrillas and liberation of the Wanni territories some three months later.

Now McTaggart is the first to acknowledge the possibility that these results may be entirely down to coincidence, and the impossibility of applying the kind of controlled conditions you can aspire to in a laboratory setting mean we will probably never really know what was going on. However, at the very time the Peace Intention experiment was conducted, Roger Nelson's random number generators were once again flicking gently away from their baseline counts. Now that's spooky.

So where does this leave us? Well, it certainly doesn't preclude the very real possibility that the strong form of mind over matter might still be complete nonsense. The results of all this painstaking research could still be due to the effects of chance, experimental static, conspiracy, or could even be a testimony to the subtle power of experimenter bias.

However, even if we suspend our natural disbelief and accept these phenomena at face value, I would point out that none of this amounts to a convincing case for the grandiose claims of many self-help books, seminars and tapes. It would appear that even if we *do* have latent psychic powers they are very far from formidable. What influence we supposedly have seems only to very faintly bias processes that are going on all around us anyway – plants growing, diodes switching on and off in random number generators, rival political factions grappling for supremacy. And that's with lots of us all simultaneously bending our attention towards the same object.

The scale of the reported effects is mostly pretty feeble, insofar as no supernatural intervention is required to explain the processes involved. Apparently, even when lots of us unite together, our combined mental efforts produce no more than statistical blips on devices with hair-trigger sensitivity to psychokinetic disturbance. People like Uri Geller, who claim to be able to suspend laws of nature, are thankfully comparatively rare – a fact that should perhaps also give us pause for thought.

To judge from the data collected so far, trying to reorganise the universe using the psychokinetic resources of a single mind, however focused, is akin to trying to redirect the course of a speeding car by blowing gently on the bonnet. If you really want that BMW or glossy new kitchen you would probably do better to make a plan, work hard at your job or take out a loan. My strong suspicion is that if you order one up using mind power alone you may be waiting for a long, long time.

Even if we suspend our natural disbelief and accept these phenomena at face value, none of this amounts to a convincing case for the grandiose claims of many self-help books, seminars and tapes.

There is no failure, only feedback

I am very fond of Thomas Edison's response to cross-examination regarding his quest to find the right filament for his prototype light-bulb. It had been proving a laborious, expensive and unrewarding business, so you have to admire the inventor's pluck when he responded: 'I haven't failed. I've found 10,000 ways that don't work.' The inventors of Neurolinguistic Programming (NLP) would have approved strongly of Edison's attitude, not least because his eventual success appears to validate NLP's cherished maxim that 'there is no failure, only feedback'. But can we really apply this principle unilaterally without turning ourselves into something scarcely recognisable as human?

By all means let's learn from our mistakes, but I am uncomfortable with the underlying desire to deny that failure even exists. This smacks of the kind of unflinching positivism that can easily make us look even more ridiculous than the failure itself. Why aren't we allowed to fail sometimes? Aren't both failure and success part of the natural punctuation of a life, responsible for the beats and pauses that lend it its distinctive rhythm and cadence?

> **Aren't both failure and success part of the natural punctuation of a life, responsible for the beats and pauses that lend it its distinctive rhythm and cadence?**

Sometimes you need a failure to act as a full stop, a no-entry sign that decisively terminates one phase of your activity and nudges you in new, as yet unexplored, directions. Walt Disney is a classic example. Had he not failed as a newspaper editor (ironically because he 'lacked imagination and had no good ideas') and gone on to found several spectacularly unsuccessful businesses, the world might never have been introduced to Mickey Mouse. If Isaac Newton hadn't made such a pig's ear of running the family farm, his uncle would never have sent him off to Cambridge where he became the world-renowned scholar we've all heard of.

If you want to insist that the 'feedback' from these pioneers' early experiences was, 'You're a bit rubbish at this so chuck it in and do something completely different', I can agree with you, but the point was that Disney and Newton benefited from this invaluable input only because they genuinely did fail in the first place. And I mean *really* failed: the crash-and-burn type of failure, not the sanitised NLP Failure Lite, i.e. the failure-that-isn't-really-failure sort of failure.

Failure shunted these men unceremoniously towards their destinies. It also proved a gift of sorts for the world's most successful author, J. K. Rowling, as she freely acknowledged during a commencement address she gave to Harvard students in 2008. She focused on her writing because she had lost everything else. Her marriage had failed, her parents disapproved of her, she scarcely had enough money to keep herself above the poverty line. As a result, with everything else gone, she clung to the one thing she had left. She discovered not only a purity of focus but also a heightened sense of herself. As she put it: 'Failure meant a stripping away of the inessential. I stopped pretending to myself that I was anything other than I was and began diverting all my energy into finishing the only work that mattered to me.'

But failure is helpful and necessary in its own right, not just as a stepping-stone to ultimate success, as NLP teaches. It shows us who we are and, perhaps more importantly, who we

Even scientists sometimes make mistakes ...

are not. Our failures define us just as surely as our successes do. Failure can be good for the soul – often far better for us than success, which tends merely to inflate our egos and leaves us back on the treadmill scrabbling after new prizes. We need real failure to knock the pretensions out of us and show us our limits. Without failure, what will puncture our bubble of self-delusion, downscale our expectations and put our plans for world domination on hold?

Sometimes when this happens, having to rein in our ambitions and work on a more modest scale is not the tragedy we anticipated. It can have unforeseen benefits: what is lost in grandiose breadth is made up for in new depth. By not pushing ourselves to our limits and finding ourselves unexpectedly liberated from our ambitions, we can take time to appreciate, to focus on what we're doing, to enjoy simpler pleasures. It is very

> **Our failures define us just as surely as our successes do. Failure can be good for the soul – often far better for us than success.**

difficult to have true peace of mind when you are constantly striving towards some luminous goal over the horizon, however worthy it may be.

Our inbred fear of failure is often arrogance in disguise. We dread failure because Psychobabble has conditioned us to believe that we can, indeed deserve to be, anything we want. If we let it, failure can teach us a becoming humility, but somehow I don't think this is the kind of feedback that the NLP crowd is referring to.

The collusion that exists between narcissism and popular notions of success was deftly exposed by a recent comment from Jason Fried, the co-founder of 37 Signals, a Chicago-based web application company. He remarked that obscurity can be a good thing because failing in private removes a large part of the associated fear. This implies that our fear of failure is actually a fear of public humiliation, fear that people will think less of us and that consequently we will think less of ourselves. Maybe we need to get over that?

Although the NLP maxim looks like it offers us a life raft, the refutation of failure is ultimately a denial of ourselves. When we experience failure we recognise that we have been unable to meet goals and standards that we ourselves have set, that we invested in, that we believed were worth something. Since we set the parameters of success in the first place, to refuse to acknowledge failure is tantamount to denying our own reality. When we brush aside the web of values and hopes we have carefully spun as matters of no importance we kill off a bit of ourselves too. Sometimes we need to accept and mourn the death of our dreams, not just casually dismiss them as inconsequential. NLP's reframe casts us into the role of a widower avoiding the pain of grief by leap-frogging into a rebound relationship with a younger woman, never pausing to say a proper goodbye to his dead wife.

When we demote the consequences of all our actions, including our worst mistakes and transgressions, to mere 'feedback' we also risk disengaging ourselves from any meaningful moral responsibility. We place ourselves firmly at the centre. Incoming data from the world becomes relevant only insofar as it is useful in helping us progress towards our goals. In NLP's self-referential vision of life as a cybernetic loop, other people don't ultimately matter very much. They are just part of the data stream.

But the distress that our transgressions and mistakes cause other people is not just feedback to help us make more appropriate, adaptive choices in future. In the moral arena, as we are all painfully aware, you absolutely *can* fail. Is the angry husband who stabs his wife just collecting feedback? Is the rogue trader who defrauds his bank merely gathering information? From mundane, petty acts of spitefulness to acts of mass genocide, our conscience is there to confirm for us that these acts are indeed failures of a fundamental kind, sometimes on a grand scale. To treat the pain of others merely as fascinating information is a symptom of psychopathy.

Rather than distancing yourself from moral failure or treating it as an exercise in data collection or an opportunity to figure out what does or doesn't work too well in life, it is crucial for our well-being as individuals and as a species that we own these sorts of failures. Rather than rationalising them, we need to let ourselves inhabit them, feel their sting, and allow them to connect us to the pain we have caused. Only when we acknowledge and submit to them can these failures change us and allow us to grow.

NLP wants a world without shame. This may sound appealing, but unpleasant though shame can be, we probably all need a good dose from time to time. It's definitely okay to make mistakes and mess up and there is always a possibility of

NLP wants a world without shame. This may sound appealing, but unpleasant though shame can be, we probably all need a good dose from time to time.

redemption. The wise Canadian actress Mary Pickford knew this, and I warm to her definition of true failure as 'not the falling down but the staying down'. Just as the human tongue has receptors to detect both sweet and sour tastes, we need to learn how to savour both success and failure in their turn. Failure is not just something to be managed away and transmuted into the down payment of ultimate success. Failure is not just feedback, because we are not mere machines. Failure is part of a process that makes us human. As James Barrie, the children's author, said: 'We are all failures ... at least the best of us are.'

Given that failure is generally a more plentiful commodity than success, we need to embrace it rather than keep manically trying to beat it off with a stick or hiding our faces from it in terror and shame. When the time comes, as it surely must, let's make no bones about it. Let's look each other squarely in the eye and announce to ourselves and anyone who cares to listen: 'Want to know what I've done today? I've failed! And what's more tomorrow there's a very good chance I may do it all again ...' Try it for yourself. You might be surprised how liberating it feels.

It's all your parents' fault

It takes a stoic and selfless parent these days to receive the news that their offspring is about to enter therapy without some trepidation. However pleased and relieved they might feel that their child is demonstrating commitment to overcoming their difficulties, part of every parent dreads the inevitable dissection of their children's upbringing. Parents know full well that they are more than likely to end up in the frame as the chief culprit and author of their child's problems and failings, however old they may be. If there is one great myth to rule them all in popular psychology it is this: that the kind of adult you become is almost exclusively determined by what happened to you when you were younger, particularly at the hands of your hapless parents. It's for this reason that the Canadian writer Dr Laurence J. Peter joked that, 'Psychiatry enables us to correct our faults by confessing our parents' shortcomings.' In fact, I know of more than one case where the parents of perfectly affluent adult children have fallen on their swords and offered to pay upfront for their offspring's therapy precisely, one suspects, because they felt obliged to take personal responsibility for whatever may have gone wrong in their children's lives. Usually, alas, their sons and daughters were only too quick to agree with them.

If there is one great myth to rule them all in popular psychology it is this: that the kind of adult you become is almost exclusively determined by what happened to you when you were younger.

147

However, such pre-emptive parental attempts to 'settle out of court' may be misguided. Whatever mistakes they may have made bringing you up, your parents can't really be held accountable for your genetic make-up over which, after all, they had very little control once they had chosen their respective mates. Independent scholar Judith Rich Harris, for one, has little time for those who succumb to what she calls *The Nurture Assumption*:

> 'The classic case is the poet Philip Larkin, who famously griped, "They fuck you up, your mum and dad." Though he admitted that he shared most of his faults with his parents, he never entertained the thought that he might have inherited them.'

Harris is a formidable woman. Possessed with a fierce intelligence, a refreshingly open mind and buckets of dogged determination to spare, she has stormed the citadel of accepted wisdom and ruffled more than a few feathers in the academic community. Holed up in her home in Middletown, New Jersey, where she is largely confined by health problems, with no stipend or formal academic qualifications, she has pored through the minutiae of the existing developmental research and come up with some pretty incendiary conclusions.

Much of her scholarship draws from the research of evolutionary psychologists and the genetic studies that use twins, siblings and adopted children to work out how much variation between people can be attributed to the influence of the environment, and how much to inherited characteristics. Her brutal conclusion is that once the impact of genes have been accounted for, 'the home environment and the parent's style of child-rearing are found to be ineffective in shaping children's personalities.' Although her figures are slightly different, the direction of her findings very much agrees with those of other authors like David Cohen, who also compares the cases of identical twins (same genes, obviously) reared together and identical twins reared apart. Whereas various characteristics of

Twin studies are helping us understand the respective contributions of nature and nurture.

the twins raised apart correlate approximately 75 per cent of the time, those reared in the same home correlate just 85 per cent, leaving only 10 per cent of variation that can be attributed to their so-called shared environment. Intriguingly, of course, this also leaves a substantial percentage of variability that cannot be explained by either, an enigma explored by Harris in her latest book, *No Two Alike*.

But what about all those studies demonstrating the impact of adverse life events on children? Surely it has been established beyond all reasonable doubt that if your father is a violent drunk, or your mother depressed and unresponsive, there are going to be negative knock-on effects for you further down the road? This may be so, and there is certainly a very large pile of thorough research suggesting this is the case. However, we have to be careful. Most of these studies assume that just because two or more factors occur together there is probably some kind of causal relationship between them.

For example, if we know, as psychologist Diana Baumrind reminds us, that children of dominating, authoritarian parents are prone to lower self-esteem, reactions of fear and aggression and tend to emulate their parents' coercive behaviours, it is natural enough to assume that the children have turned out like this *because* of the way they were treated. But what if they turned out this way because they had simply inherited these tendencies from their parents? Might this not explain why aggressive, controlling parents often produce aggressive, controlling offspring just as plausibly as the notion that they became this way as a consequence of their upbringing? In fact, aggressive tendencies turn out to be quite highly heritable. You can see the problem.

If you still need convincing, consider the salutary case of one study of adopted children whose original biological mothers had criminal records. If their mother had a conviction, compared with a sample of adoptees whose biological mother had no record, these adopted children were more likely to have been arrested (15 per cent compared with 2 per cent), convicted themselves (13 per cent versus 1 per cent) and put in prison (10 per cent versus 0 per cent). The unpalatable reality is that in studies that control properly for genetic factors, Harris's conclusions are consistently upheld: it would appear that, generally speaking, parenting has much less impact on how we turn out than we might all wish to believe.

If you are a parent, like myself, you may find the implications of all this a bit mind-blowing. If, like me, your work

> **It would appear that, generally speaking, parenting has much less impact on how we turn out than we might all wish to believe.**

also involves child protection cases in which huge emphasis is quite rightly placed on trying to safeguard children from the adverse effects of early environments, then Harris's work raises profound concerns. Nevertheless, she makes a compelling case that I would strongly urge you to read for yourself, however tempted you are to dismiss it out of hand (as many of her critics have).

The first-hand evidence of my own clinical experience means I am certainly not quite ready to dismiss the influence of environment just yet. Some fascinating findings are coming through suggesting that exposure to parental stress can actually modify your genes, turning off the stress hormone receptor sites. This would seem to be a pretty strong piece of evidence for the line that environment is far from toothless although, to give Harris her due, she has never claimed otherwise – merely that things don't necessarily work in quite the way we assume they do. If you are committed to the value of nurture, you might also want to look at some of the persuasive neuropsychological evidence from brain scans of emotionally deprived children presented in Sue Gerhardt's very well written book *Why Love Matters* before you chuck the baby out with the bathwater (presumably an environmental event that even Judith Rich Harris might expect to have some impact ...). I am also somewhat reassured by developmental psychologist Sandra Scarr's recent suggestion that it is perhaps only *extreme* environmental conditions that may tend to affect us, depending on our predisposing vulnerabilities. This would certainly start to cover the cases of some of the damaged children I work with. But what Harris and others are telling us implies that if we are muddling along in a fairly average home, even if things feel far from ideal and we have a list of grievances as long as our arm, we can't really lay the blame at our mum and dad's door for the grown-ups we become. The bar for what constitutes 'good enough parenting' may just have got a whole lot lower.

Bracketing for a moment the cases where parents do truly terrible things to their children, let's look in a bit more detail at the grounds for our prevailing sense that our mum and dad have messed us up. What do we mean when we say they are to blame, and what exactly are they to blame for?

One of the charges frequently made against parents is that the way they have treated us as children has left us feeling bad about ourselves. However, research into self-esteem suggests that while a critical, unsupportive environment can damage our self-image, self-esteem is far from fixed in childhood. Reviewing the findings of over 130 studies, psychologist Chiungjung Huang discovered that across the board self-esteem ratings continue to fluctuate up until the age of 30, after which group effects tend to plateau out. The first decade of young adulthood turned out to be a time of particular turbulence. Huang didn't look at individual cases, so it is likely that there were hidden and local fluctuations the study didn't pick up. However, let's not forget that the way we feel about ourselves often owes a great deal to factors that have little to do with home. We know, for example, from Susan Harter's work how powerfully peer relationships orchestrate the rise and fall of adolescent self-esteem. Satisfaction with physical appearance is another strong predictor of self-esteem levels within this age group. However, peer factors and media-propagated ideals of beauty turn out to be more significant in determining how satisfied young girls are with their bodies than any input from their parents.

There is another idea, essentially psychoanalytic in origin, that continues to exercise the popular imagination: namely that our various 'hang-ups' are due to the way our parents dealt with issues like sex, rules, and self-indulgence. Freud believed that repeated parental injunctions about such matters give rise to the 'superego', our childhood programming about how things *should* be done and the conditions under which we can experience pleasure or pain. The superego is the repository of all the times our actions met with our parents' delight, disapproval or anger. It's the basis of our conscience, and it's not to be trifled with. To resist its demands is to risk flooding oneself with guilt. According to Freud, the battle between our pleasure-seeking drives and the disapproving superego can set up eddies of unconscious conflict that result in all manner of neurotic symptoms, leaving us feeling nervy and rotten. We all know people who are prissy, controlling and 'anally retentive' and the fact that they are like this is supposedly a lot to do with how they have been brought up. According to Oliver James, just the right blend of strictness and empathy from your folks produces a benign conscience that won't trouble you overmuch but keeps you on the straight and narrow, while parenting styles that stray too far towards the punitive and authoritarian on the one hand, or that are too relaxed and liberal on the other, can create serious problems for us. However, once again Judith Rich Harris springs up to insist that parenting style makes little odds, pointing out that, 'Of the large number of correlations the researchers calculated between maternal practices and child outcomes, only 6 per cent – about the percentage you would expect to occur by chance – were statistically significant.'

Freud and Klein both believed that issues of sexuality can be especially troubling for developing children, especially since sexual desire for the opposite-sex parent has to be repressed. This supposedly leads to the development of the Oedipus complex in boys and the matching Electra complex in girls. We might be tempted to dismiss this as a lot of psychoanalytic claptrap but, as the following anecdote amusingly illustrates, the unconscious mind can still make fools of us all:

> Freda Cohen is having a very torrid time with her
> teenage son. They are always screaming at each other
> and sometimes even fighting. So Freda takes him to see
> a psychoanalyst. After several sessions, the doctor calls
> Freda into his office and tells her, 'Your son has an Oedipus
> complex.' 'Oedipus Shmedipus,' answers Freda, 'As long as he
> loves his mother …'

The truth is that these days few people take Freud's theory of psychosexual development very seriously. Evolutionary psychologists Martin Daly and Margo Wilson found little evidence of the Oedipus complex when they went hunting for it in the data, and concluded that the lack of evidence made it virtually impossible to test predictions about it. Meanwhile, Walter Mischel argued that the flexibility of our moral standards within different contexts (for example children cheerfully cheating and lying at school who would never dream of doing so at home) weighs against the likelihood that 'a unitary moral agency like the superego' even exists. With no superego to tie us up in knots, this really lets our parents off the hook.

But what about our relationships? Your parents' messy divorce is bound to have blighted your prospects of future happiness, surely? Maybe not. Alison Kirk found that while being a child of divorcees made people more anxious/realistic about the likelihood of relationship breakdown, this didn't affect young adults' self-esteem, anxieties about intimacy or their reported levels of satisfaction in their relationships.

However, perhaps your childhood experiences are influencing your personal life in more indirect and subtle ways? Many of us have now heard of 'attachment theory' and how the quality of your early relationship with your carer could potentially be affecting your relationships later in life. If not, let me offer the briefest of introductions. Attachments come in two main flavours – 'secure' and 'insecure'. There are several subcategories of the latter. A 'securely' attached infant is confident that their parent will respond to their needs. They seek comfort when required, enjoy being close, but can also tolerate brief separations without undue distress. In fact, securely attached children use their parents as a dependable base from which to explore the world, apparently confident in the knowledge that their mothers will welcome them back when they return.

However, some children (in fact about a third to half of them) don't behave like this. Some are hopelessly clingy. Others come across as withdrawn, passive and indifferent, as if they gave up on any hope of getting what they need from adults long ago. Yet other children respond to separations by blowing hot and cold and, when their mothers do return, alternately demand cuddles and then angrily reject them when they're offered. Then there is a fourth group of infants whose behaviour seems completely random and incoherent. These poor children are all over the show, often making little distinction between people they know really well and total strangers.

On the basis of these kinds of responses, infants are classified under one of four main attachment styles. The received wisdom is that their behaviour reflects what they have unconsciously learnt about the world from the parenting they've received. If their mother is reliable, affectionate and responsive, then this is likely to promote a 'secure' attachment. If not, they will fall into one of the other four 'insecure' categories. With about 40 per cent of the population classified as 'insecure', a naive reading of this would be that that there must be a lot of ropy parenting going on out there. Worse still, statistical studies show that those of us who don't enjoy the privileged gold-standard 'secure' status are more vulnerable to all manner of psychological problems and social disadvantages. So maybe your parents really *are* to blame for all your hang-ups and neuroses? To add insult to injury, Cindy Hazan and Philip Shaver found evidence of equivalent attachment styles at work in adults' romantic relationships. Once again, if your adult attachment style is 'secure', then you're laughing. But if you happen to fall into one of the other categories (as about half of us still do) – well, there may be fireworks, heartbreak or substantial solicitors' fees ahead …

Of course, I'm parodying the whole business: researchers know that it's by no means as cut and dried as that. But what if one's style of relating really was set in stone in infancy? Then surely your parents *must* shoulder responsibility for your volatile or disappointing love life? This is certainly the impression given by certain popular-psychology authors who haven't done their homework properly. The idea that attachment is the 'missing link' that neatly ties up an individual's past and present is so elegant and convenient that some very important loose ends are often ignored.

For a start, the similar distribution of the various attachment styles amongst children and adults doesn't mean that individuals necessarily keep the same attachment style over the course of their lives. The best estimate is that about two-thirds of us stick with the same attachment style, but that still leaves a third of us who are chopping and changing. One study that followed the attachment behaviours of children from infancy through to maturity found only 17 per cent still demonstrated the same attachment style in their adult romantic relationships as they had when they were little. Another found correlations of security ratings between parents and current romantic partners of under a third. Other researchers have found (not surprisingly) that the attachment style of adults often wobbles quite dramatically in the wake of stressful life events. It also appears that people don't necessarily demonstrate the same attachment style across the board in their various relationships, which poses a bit of a challenge for those who subscribe to the most basic version of the 'internal working model' – the theory that the mental template we inherited from our mum and dad is applied indiscriminately to everyone.[1] As Paula Pietromonaco and Lisa Barrett concede, 'From this perspective, people do not hold a single set of working models of the self and others ...', while Mark Baldwin acknowledges that 'Within romantic relationships, expectations might then vary significantly depending on the specific partner, or the specific situation, or the specific needs being expressed'.

This makes a lot more sense and sits more comfortably with our everyday experience. Sure, we may know individuals who just seem to repeat the same disastrous pattern with each successive partner, but haven't you also encountered people who miraculously blossomed into someone very different when they stopped dating disaster stories and found someone who

---

[1] You can check out for yourself how differently you relate to the significant people in your own life by logging onto Chris Fraley's quiz at www.your personality.net/relstructures

was a Mr or Miss Right for them? Or, conversely, friends who slowly drifted away from the open, relaxed warmth of a secure attachment style once they fell under the sway of a controlling, jealous partner? Having seen how different people can become under the influence of new relationships, I really struggle with the concept that we have one predetermined style of relating, as some of the more simplistic attachment literature suggests. There is certainly little evidence to support popular-psychology authors Amir Levine and Rachel Heller's bold assertion that 'Understanding attachment styles is an easy and reliable way to understand and predict people's behaviour in any romantic situation'. If only it were that simple!

It would hardly be very adaptive if we all responded to everyone in the same way. The fact is, even babies don't. Babies whose mothers are depressed may very well exhibit a concerning pattern of behaviour in their mothers' company, and then behave entirely normally in the company of other non-depressed caregivers. As Judith Rich Harris points out, 'A baby whose mother is depressed doesn't expect everyone to be depressed.'

The security of attachment in infancy is also a poor predictor of how well we get on with others later on in life. For example, infant attachment doesn't necessarily anticipate how we will relate to our friends, and Dinero and colleagues discovered that even having a secure attachment style in your mid-twenties was no guarantee of the quality of your interactions with your romantic partner.

In any case, for most of us the attachment system may be less relevant than we assume. As Professor Pat Crittenden explains, attachment behaviours are primarily activated only under conditions of threat, since that's what evolution designed them for. It's quite possible that even if these powerful internal programs do exist, providing things are ticking along okay and we are on a relatively even keel, they may well leave us alone. Crittenden's Dynamic-Maturational Model is thankfully sufficiently flexible to accommodate the possibility of different ways of relating in different contexts.

The truth is, we currently understand less about attachment than you might assume from the blasé way the term is thrown around these days. We are certainly not clear about the pathways by which our parents might bequeath us a specific style of relating. What we probably shouldn't overlook is that our attachment status is closely linked to our belief system – specifically beliefs we hold about ourselves and other people. Bartholomew and Horowitz have managed to reformulate the whole taxonomy of adult attachment in precisely these terms (as you can see from the diagram opposite). For example, if you have a positive attitude towards yourself and other people you are likely to be 'secure', whereas if you have low self-esteem but think well of others you will end up in the 'preoccupied–insecure' quadrant.

The point is that as adults we should be taking personal responsibility for *all* our beliefs – even those that might underlie our so-called attachment style. Babies may not be able to artic-ulate their beliefs clearly but adults can. If they are of a mind to, they can even work on changing them. Since it is clearly far more adaptive to hold the attitudes associated with 'secure' attachment styles, we might want to think about challenging and re-scripting any unhelpful attributions linked with an 'insecure' attachment status. Perhaps we could educate ourselves to see the outside world as less threatening, and ourselves as being a little more worthy? We probably owe it to ourselves to do so. To resign yourself to being stuck with beliefs you arrived at when you were knee-high and – even worse – to blame someone else for them, is both defeatist and unnecessary. There's a whole load of other stuff you used to believe that you have revised perfectly successfully: I presume you no longer subscribe to Father Christmas, the Easter Bunny or the Tooth Fairy? If your beliefs about yourself and other people aren't helping you, then maybe you should put a bit of effort into changing them? There are many good resources out there to show you how.

Moreover, before you call your parents to account for what they did to you, take a moment to consider what you may have

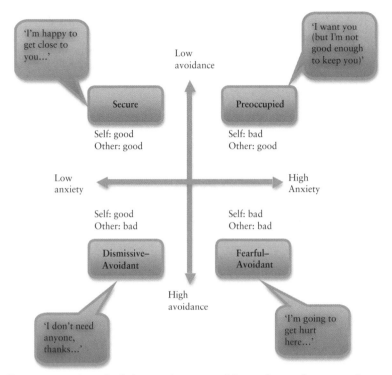

Four categories of adult attachment and how they reflect our views of self and others.

done to them. The type of child you were (by nature) may well have helped condition the sorts of responses you were met with. Temperamentally tricky infants do put pressures on parents who sometimes find themselves hard-pushed to cope and it doesn't necessarily get easier with older children either. In 2006 David Huh and colleagues tracked the behaviour of 500 teenage girls. They found that the parents of girls who had initially scored highest on measures of antisocial behaviour such as fighting and

> **If your beliefs about yourself and other people aren't helping you, then maybe you should put a bit of effort into changing them?**

cruelty at the start of the study were demonstrating less and less momentum in trying to keep their daughters' behaviour in check by the end of the study. The 'mean girls' won out. The parents of the most difficult girls appeared to be being progressively worn down and had abandoned their efforts to control them.

Perhaps you feel aggrieved because you weren't Mummy or Daddy's favourite, or that you got a raw deal because of where you ended up in the birth order? And it is true that parents do treat their children differently. Attractive children get doted on. Clever ones get kudos for it. However, Oliver James's claim that 'Each parent treats each child so differently that they might as well have been raised in completely different families' is pushing it a bit, I feel. Often, such claims are made by supporters of environmental causes who are only too well aware of data suggesting differences between siblings comparable with those that actually might have been found if they *had* come from different families. The effect is there but it is much smaller than you might imagine. Harris claims that differential treatment by their parents accounts for only two per cent of the variance shown between siblings. Furthermore, what differential treatment existed was linked exclusively to the genetic differences between them rather than the non-genetic differences. What this indicates is that 'the parents were *reacting* to the genetic differences between their children, rather than *causing* their children to be different'.

The bottom line logically is that if you have been instrumental in shaping your own environment, then maybe you have to carry some of the responsibility for its effects on you? Generally, recognising that any relationship is a dynamic system in which both parties exert a mutual influence over each other can sometimes be an important step towards laying down arms and calling a truce.

In trying to make sense of all of this data, and regardless of whether you wish to hold nature or nurture accountable for where you find yourself in life, it is probably crucial to hold on to the fact that you are not a helpless child any more. Biology alone might not constitute destiny as Freud once claimed, but neither does upbringing. After all, as you grow older you have more and more freedom to choose your own environment, even if your genes may still influence the environments you select. As Edward Miller, a professor of economics, comments in relation to psychologist David Cohen's work:

> 'All over the world, teenagers are choosing friends, and
> even mates, that their parents disapprove of. A person who
> is smart and who enjoys intellectual activities will engage
> in intellectual activities, read books etc. By adulthood
> individuals are picking their own environments and the
> influence of family is minor.'

There comes a cut-off point when it no longer makes much sense to keep blaming someone else. We have to face the fact that our current circumstances are likely to be largely of our own making. It is definitely true that we are the only ones who have any realistic chance of shaping our future.

The nature–nurture debate is certainly not resolved yet to anyone's satisfaction, but what is now clear is that the whole picture is far more complex than it appears. It doesn't allow for any knee-jerk apportioning of blame. Whatever sins of commission or omission committed against us, let's try and keep in mind that the majority of our parents were doing their best. Sometimes it is not we who need to forgive our parents, but our parents who need to forgive themselves; it is heartening to think that perhaps they have not done as much long-term harm as they may have feared.

People are people – baffling, perverse, and laws unto themselves in many cases, which is why psychological researchers have such a hard time getting adequate purchase on them. Sometimes the things that should affect us don't, and the things that shouldn't matter send shockwaves rippling through the rest of our lives. The truth is we can't always tell which is which. Judith Rich Harris makes a good point that the revolution in childcare practices and attitudes towards children that has taken place in the last 50 years doesn't appear to have translated into measurable global differences between the personalities of those born in the first and second halves of the twentieth century. Even in cases where parents have palpably let their children down very badly, I have encountered several truly remarkable people in my work who have still defied the odds. Despite having had the cards of the environmental lottery completely stacked against them, and having done battle with horrors most of us, fortunately, can scarcely conceive of, they have still found within themselves the resources to go on to become loving, brilliant, and impressive human beings. This gives me hope. And generally speaking, hope and blame don't make very companionable bedfellows. We should choose carefully which we are going to kick out.

You can heal your body

It makes intuitive sense to most of us that what goes on in our minds is going to affect what occurs in our bodies. After all, we use mind power to change our bodies all the time, albeit via the millions of pulsing signals we send out through the central nervous system in order to activate muscles and stimulate organs. It's definitely a miracle of sorts when you think about it, but admittedly not one likely to make the front page of *Time* magazine. Also, illness inevitably makes us feel rubbish, and because we associate physical decline and discomfort with low mood and anxiety, we are easily conned into miscalling the direction of cause and effect.

However, these days we are also actively encouraged to believe that the mind–body connection controls our somatic destiny. There are some experimental studies supporting the idea that mind power can indeed produce physical changes. Guang Yue, an exercise psychologist from Ohio, reports that a group of volunteers who regularly pictured themselves flexing their biceps while *never* actually visiting the gym, increased their muscle strength by nearly 14 per cent after a few weeks. This is pretty impressive, especially considering that a control group who actually *did* exercise their arms apparently only achieved a 30 per cent increase in the same time period. However, it looks as if you may have to 'feel the burn' and tolerate further lycra-clad exposure if you really want that body beautiful: brain scans conducted during the visualisation sessions suggested that these improvements might have been due to the brain's increased efficiency in sending nerve signals to the relevant muscles rather than any change in the muscles themselves.

There are some intriguing studies suggesting that hypnosis and visualisation can increase your bust size, possibly by stimulating blood flow, and it appears that hypnosis can help with weight loss, albeit by helping people ward off thoughts and behaviours that would otherwise sabotage their more conventional diet and exercise regimes.

All this is harmless enough, but slightly more worrying is the widespread conviction that what we do with our minds can help us successfully combat even the most serious disease. The fight against illnesses like cancer or heart disease, for example, is often portrayed as being as much a mental battle as a physical one. But is this helpful for us?

The belief that we can retain ultimate control in situations seemingly designed to impress upon us our frailty and helplessness is of course comforting, but it can also work against us. As the author Barbara Ehrenreich points out, it is all too easy for already sick people to be left feeling like utter failures when they ultimately prove unable to rid themselves of their symptoms, which is clearly the last thing anyone needs under such circumstances.

Particularly challenging in this regard is the position adopted by writers like Louise Hay, who staunchly regard physical illness as a direct manifestation of destructive thought patterns and negative emotions. Hay makes no bones about holding individuals ultimately responsible for their physical condition. She states in the introduction to her bestseller, *Heal Your Body*:

> 'When cancer or any other illness returns, I don't believe it's because the doctor didn't "get it all out", but rather, that the patient has made no mental changes and so just recreates the same illness.'

The belief that we can retain ultimate control is of course comforting, but it can also work against us.

The doctrine of 'metaphysical causations' that Hay encountered at the Church of Religious Science taught her that 'for every effect in our lives, there's a thought pattern that precedes or creates it'. She goes on to make some fairly specific claims about the emotions and attitudes that she believes underlie illnesses of various kinds. Thus criticism fosters arthritis, resentment literally 'eats away' at us in the form of cancer and so on. Incidentally, by Ms Hay's reckoning, I am personally due for a particularly nasty case of haemorrhoids since she links these specifically to the stress of missed deadlines! Hay claims that she cured herself from cervical cancer by releasing the bitterness, anger and resentment she unwittingly held towards the parents she holds responsible for her childhood abuse, and that consequently she *knows* that if people are 'willing to do the mental work of releasing and forgiving, almost anything can be healed'.

Many find such claims far-fetched, and rebel against the notion that we bring diseases upon ourselves by harbouring hostile thoughts and indulging our darker emotions. However, books by Louise Hay and other authors writing in a similar vein continue to prove hugely popular. The idea that you can magically reverse even the most severe physical illness through a diet of corrective self-affirmations sadly lacks any convincing empirical backing. However, there is persuasive evidence that psychological factors can affect your physical health and predispose you towards particular forms of illness.

We do know beyond all reasonable doubt, for example, that stress really is a killer. Study after study indicates that it compromises the immune system, slows healing rates and can contribute to heart disease and a host of other illnesses. Therefore it seems reasonable to suppose that attitudes and habits of mind that leave us chronically stressed are strongly implicated in all sorts of physical problems. According to psychologist Johan Denollet, so-called Type D personalities (characterised by negativity, depression, anxiety, anger and social isolation) are at three times more risk of heart problems than people from other groups and make up half of all cardiovascular patients in the

United States. It also turned out that among over 5,000 villagers sampled from sleepy villages on the picturesque slopes of the Lanusei valley in Italy, those who scored as the most angry and antagonistic in their dealings with others often demonstrated pronounced and ominous thickening of their neck arteries.

So doesn't this support the case for 'you can think yourself well'? Possibly not. As our understanding of human physiology expands, we are starting to make sense of the biological processes linking stress to disease, without requiring any help from principles as esoteric as Hay's laws of 'metaphysical causation'. For example, we now understand the damage that long-term exposure to stress hormones like cortisol (ideally released in short, sharp bursts when we need to fight or run for our lives) does to our tissues. In 2008 some fascinating research conducted by Jenny Choi, Steven Fauce and Rita Effros demonstrated how cortisol inhibits immune cells' ability to use telomerase, an enzyme that helps keep the cells young and dividing normally. In people with HIV, osteoporosis, and heart disease the telomeres within their cells become prematurely shortened and this restricts the number of times these crucial cells can divide. It is as if the biological clock inside the cells is advanced so the cells age more rapidly. Interestingly, it has just been discovered that in flatworms the length of telomeres remains the same however many times they divide, so perhaps immortality is just round the corner for us all, God help us!

But while avoiding certain types of stress-inducing negative thoughts may be extremely important in preserving your health, unequivocal evidence that you get much independent added value from positive thinking and an upbeat approach to life is lacking. In one controlled study that looked at people's immune response to a flu vaccine, researchers found that while getting people to write about distressing experiences did produce a notable reduction in the production of antibodies, writing about life-enhancing, happy experiences seemed to make no difference to antibody levels whatsoever. This may suggest that the chief value of thinking happy thoughts is in keeping health-depleting unhappy thoughts at bay, not necessarily because they produce additional physical health benefits in their own right.

This is only one isolated and very limited study so we mustn't leap to conclusions. The implication that negative thoughts and emotions may have more power to damage our health than positive ones do to enhance it is admittedly a bit of a downer. However, it may have a bearing on how we approach and manage diseases we have already contracted. Filling your mind with sunny thoughts, watching endless comedy films or picturing your white blood cells gobbling up cancer cells may make you feel better psychologically, but as yet there would appear to be few empirical grounds to believe they will necessarily have that much impact on what's wrong with your body.

Dr David Hamilton would strongly disagree, however. Hamilton is interesting because, although a massive advocate of visualisation and other aspects of New Age spirituality, he has a PhD in organic chemistry and spent four years working in the pharmaceutical industry developing drug treatments for cardiovascular disease and cancer. He makes the compelling point that while treatments have to outperform placebos in drug trials in order to establish efficacy, the bar is set pretty high because placebos themselves tend to produce improvements in approximately 35 per cent of cases. This makes them pretty powerful agents of change. Moreover, the effect is fairly consistent, regardless of the condition being treated. This could indeed suggest that the patient's expectations alone are catalysing and coordinating a broad range of physical changes in the body.

Hamilton proffers various speculative mechanisms by which the mind might contribute to the healing of the body. He implies that thoughts may cause the brain to release specific combinations of neuropeptides that in turn influence cellular DNA throughout the body, even prompting the production of the relevant stem cells within the bone marrow to promote healing.

Neuropeptides, as the name implies, are protein-like substances that chiefly influence other neurones in the brain by binding to their receptor sites. Neuropeptides do seem to play a crucial role in influencing our emotions and anything that affects the brain could quite plausibly affect the body's systems. However, although I am no expert in molecular biology, my layman's understanding is that their effect is an *indirect* one. It relies on the brain sending out prompts via the central nervous system or galvanising the release of hormones with their powerful but limited effects on other organs and tissues. While it is the case that neuropeptides may indeed stimulate DNA synthesis in certain cell types, it seems to me potentially misleading to picture them as genetic antibodies, rushing round the bloodstream reprogramming DNA in damaged cells throughout the body. Ironically, certain cells outside the brain also manufacture neuropeptides which *do* influence the brain when they reach it, so with regard to this particular mechanism, it looks like the argument for the body influencing the mind is rather stronger than the one for the other way round.

In my view, Hamilton is also relying heavily on the established destructive physiological impact of stress to validate claims about the mind–body connection. Stress may well dysregulate DNA in normal cells but that doesn't necessarily mean that neuropeptides can therefore programme them to combat disease. And while the world on a quantum scale is a truly mysterious place where the distinction between energy and information dissolves, it is surely pushing well beyond the current bounds of scientific understanding to claim that our thoughts operate directly on the quantum field itself, as Hamilton encourages people to picture during his Quantum Effect Healing sessions.

Having conducted a careful and comprehensive analysis of the relevant existing studies, James Coyne and Howard Tennen certainly concluded that the benefits the mind can offer to cancer patients has been overplayed. Patients who displayed fighting spirit did not, sadly, fare statistically better against the disease, and psychological interventions of various kinds seem to make little difference to survival rates. Coyne and

Tennen believe that the widespread acceptance of views to the contrary are the product of 'bad science, exaggerated claims and unproven medicine'.

I am really open to the mind's role in healing the body, but if the claims of the likes of Hay and Hamilton were true, surely we would we expect to see more compelling results when systematic investigations into faith-healing, prayer, and alternative therapies are conducted? Yet, in study after study, the effects are either non-significant or, if they are present, tend to be explicable in terms of reduced stress levels or the patient's perceptions rather than measurable physiological improvements.

Perhaps such studies disappoint because, as Louise Hay implies, people are not working hard enough to change destructive patterns or applying their mental energies with sufficient conviction. Who knows? There are certainly many anecdotal accounts out there of people making dramatic recoveries using visualisation techniques and affirmations, but I have yet to find a decent controlled study looking specifically at the use of these approaches. I guess therefore the most reasonable stance is to remain agnostic.

Science certainly doesn't know everything, and I would be the very worst kind of psychologist if I undermined the hope of anyone facing a life-threatening condition. If I were given bad news by my doctor I would probably be the first to try anything and everything in the hope that it might work. After all, what have we got to lose? But maybe we should hold back, because there is some merit to cultivating only realistic expectations.

> *In study after study, the effects are either non-significant or, if they are present, tend to be explicable in terms of reduced stress levels or the patient's perceptions rather than measurable physiological improvements.*

Otherwise we risk putting ourselves under enormous and unnecessary pressure and may have to contend with crushing disappointment. As we have seen, such emotions may well counteract any attempts our body *is* making to heal itself.

You are in control of your life

Most psychologists would agree that we all share a need for some level of control in our lives. In fact, as I know only too well from treating people suffering from post-traumatic stress disorder following a car crash or an assault, one of the things that shakes people up the most is the unwelcome revelation that we actually have far less control over what happens to us than we generally imagine. Without control we are not only left vulnerable, but we also have our noses pressed up against the prospects of chaos, dissolution and death – possibilities that really frighten us.

In the face of these huge primal fears, we tenaciously cling on to our attempts to reassert some kind of order, even if that means having to impose sense on random events. Some ingenious experiments conducted in 2008 by Jennifer Whitson and Adam Galinsky discovered that people deprived of control are far more likely to see images in patterns of random dots, and resort to superstitious beliefs and conspiracy theories. Curiously, once their sense of control had been restored, these effects went away.

The harsh reality is there are many things in life we cannot control and from which we cannot adequately protect either ourselves or those we love. However, our brains are remarkably reluctant to accept this. In recent experiments in which participants were asked to estimate the chances of various significant misfortunes befalling them such as getting cancer or breaking a bone, even once they had been given accurate statistical information they stubbornly continued to underestimate the risk. However, when the likelihood of positive events turned out to be higher than they had assumed, subjects mysteriously proved more than capable of assimilating the new information and updating their estimate accordingly. We are biased towards disbelieving our own vulnerability, even in the face of the evidence.

We like to maintain the fantasy that we can even influence events that are completely down to chance. Ellen Langer conducted a celebrated experiment in 1975 in which she sold lottery tickets to two groups of people. Members of the first group were just assigned tickets as they came, while the second group was allowed to choose the numbers on their tickets. Bizarrely, when asked to sell them back the following day, those who had chosen their tickets charged *up to four times* the amount of those who had been assigned them! One explanation is that this group believed that their number selection had somehow added value, suggesting they also secretly believed that these tickets now stood a better chance of winning.

Incidentally, it may well be that the very survival of financial institutions like Wall Street relies on our need to believe that even complex systems can be mastered and managed and their outcomes predicted. The economist Burton Malkiel explains that if you had indiscriminately purchased all of the 500 stocks in the Standard and Poor's Index and just held onto them throughout the 1970s you would have made more money than 80 per cent of the account managers on Wall Street and more than half of them in the early 1990s. In other words, random chance performs as well, on average, as the very highly paid experts who continue to ascribe any intermittent runs of success to their own skill and judgment. Yet still we pay their huge salaries rather than rely on the toss of a coin. It seems we would

We are biased towards disbelieving our own vulnerability, even in the face of the evidence.

prefer to hold onto the illusion rather than tolerate the implications of the alternative.

However, being too controlling is bad for our physical and mental health. You may have heard of the Type A personality. This was based on a cluster of common characteristics that Meyer Friedman and Mike Jordan identified in a longitudinal study of coronary disease patients. Type A personalities emerged as driven, ambitious individuals with all manner of control issues. Now while it turned out that being a Type A per se doesn't inevitably put you at greater risk of heart disease (following the 'all spaniels are dogs but not all dogs are spaniels' line of argument), many Type As nonetheless did turn out to be smouldering volcanoes of stress and anger. Both characteristics have been strongly linked to serious health problems of various kinds, including heart disease, and both have their roots in issues directly related to control. Anger and stress are instinctive responses to perceived threat, and the threat rockets when you feel you don't have the resources to deal adequately with the situation. In fact Richard Lazarus specifically defines stress as what occurs when 'individuals perceive that they cannot adequately cope with the demands being made on them or with threats to their well-being'. Seen this way, it's clear that any attempts to control and micromanage everything are inevitably going to flood us with stress simply because, as novelist J. K. Rowling appreciates, 'Life is difficult and complicated and beyond anyone's total control'.

In the 1970s Jonathan Rotter discovered that all of us tend to fall into one of two camps: either we believe we are puppets on the world's stage and that the things that happen to us are down to outside forces that we can do little about (external locus of control) or conversely that we are masters of our own fate and can shape our own destinies (internal locus of control). The Protestant work ethic powering our culture of Psychobabble generally encourages us to regard an internal locus of control as the much healthier of the two options. Generally it is indeed emotionally healthier for people to regard themselves as having some influence over their lives, because they often tend to become passive and defeatist otherwise. However, as Uncle Ben famously says to Peter Parker (a.k.a. *Spiderman*), 'With great power comes great responsibility' – even if that power is more perceived than actual. People with a really strong internal locus are consequently vulnerable to guilt, perfectionism, anxiety and self-recrimination. Believing that it is solely their own actions that determine the outcome of every situation, they feel obliged to work incessantly to make sure things turn out the right way, and feel ultimately accountable when they don't. And the trouble is, Psychobabble, with all its blithe assurance about how strong and capable we are, inevitably encourages us to think like this.

People who believe they are in control, who believe that life is determined solely by their choices, automatically feel under pressure to get it right all the time. Under such circumstances they can easily become frozen and stilted in their decision-making processes, when they might be far more productive if they eased off the brakes and went with the flow a bit more. We are often poor judges of which of our choices are going to be significant and, as Daniel Gilbert has shown us, spectacularly bad at predicting which options will secure our happiness. We might do better to adopt a more laid-back scattergun approach, not waste too much time thinking through the minutiae, seize opportunities when they present themselves, take chances and see what sticks. It's a bit like arriving at the answer to an equation via a successive series of approximate guesses and a process of elimination that gradually narrow the field of possibility and steer you closer to the correct answer. However, over-controlled people are so terrified of making a mistake that they find it almost impossible to act in the moment.

People who believe they are in control automatically feel under pressure to get it right all the time.

In fact, controlling people always tend to have one eye on the future. They have to anticipate the possible contingencies that could affect them or those close to them and, let's face it, there's a lot that could potentially go wrong out there ... This is the perfect recipe for severe anxiety. Ironically, more and more research is emphasising that our mental health is far better protected if we can learn to locate ourselves as much as possible in the present. This is the essence of Mindfulness training, which is proving to be a very effective antidote for depression and many other psychological problems. There is a Zen koan which states simply: 'Chop wood, carry water.' This encapsulates the wisdom of an Eastern tradition that encourages us to simply be in the 'here and now' as much as we can, allowing ourselves to experience life without necessarily trying to control our responses to it. As the actress Nicole Kidman has discovered: 'When you relinquish the desire to control your future, you can have more happiness.' Far better to be like this than the unfortunate, but very funny, Tina Fey who pokes fun at the notion that we solve anything by worrying too much about it. As she confesses in her autobiography, *Bossypants*: 'It's a burden being able to control situations with my hyper-vigilance, but it's my lot in life.'

In some contexts there is evidence emerging that it may even be a good thing to have less control. Researchers Evan Apfelbaum and Samuel Sommers found that when they deliberately depleted subjects' reserves of self-control using a demanding mental task, they subsequently coped much better in a potentially stressful interracial group discussion. Not only were Caucasian participants under these conditions less inhibited and stilted in their interactions, but they were also rated as being less racist by independent black observers. As

More and more research is emphasising that our mental health is far better protected if we can learn to locate ourselves as much as possible in the present.

Sandra Sanger stresses, flexibility at a behavioural and mental level is a hallmark of good mental health. 'When you need control,' she observes, 'you forgo flexibility and place a lower than necessary ceiling on your capacity for engaging in and enjoying life.'

Letting go also teaches us to trust ourselves and the universe a bit more. In his discussion of the 'wisdom of spontaneity', Dr Leon Seltzer argues that speakers who feel able to rely upon their judgment and experience can afford to cut loose and go off-piste, ad-libbing and making off-the-cuff remarks at will because they trust themselves to do so effectively. And of course the feedback loop between our thoughts and behaviour means the opposite is equally true: like the tribe who thinks the annual rain dance it performs is responsible for the rain when it comes, controlling people never have the opportunity to discover that things might still be okay if they let go of the reins from time to time.

We need to be in control because we are frightened – frightened of the consequences if we are not; of what we might lose; of what could happen to us. Because modern society offers us a greater prospect of control through increased choice and technological advances, we are conned into believing that we should be able to control *everything* that happens whereas, of course, this is impossible. As Ed Smith argues, chance plays a much bigger role in our lives than we care to admit. We seem to believe that if we can only stay in control then we can engineer our own happiness but, as the wise philosopher Epictetus pointed out many centuries ago: 'There is only one way to happiness, and that is to cease worrying about things that are beyond the power of our will.'

I also suspect we could make things a little easier for ourselves if we didn't take ourselves quite so seriously. In our modern age we have become terribly sold on the idea that our lives matter rather more than perhaps they do, and I don't think we appreciate the degree to which this ties us up in knots. We can stress over every little detail, overanalyse every minor event

This existence, this cursed planet, all of its billions of people clawing and screaming for a single moment of true happiness, is temporary. All is temporary, all must end eventually. Pass it on.

Let's try and keep things in proportion, shall we?

and strive to make the 'right' choices as if something momentous depended upon it. Or, alternatively, we can accept the fact that in the great scheme of things *nothing* we do probably matters that much. We are tiny, insignificant creatures on a pinprick of

In our modern age we have become terribly sold on the idea that our lives matter rather more than perhaps they do, and I don't think we appreciate the degree to which this ties us up in knots.

a planet, only one speck of cosmic sand on an endless beach. The paltry 28,000 days of the average human life scarcely register in the cosmic drama of an infinitely vast, majestic and expanding universe that is itself already nearly 14 billion years old. Okay, admittedly this knowledge should probably humble us and it might even scare us a little. However, really get to grips with it and it can be a remarkably liberating perspective. It can release us from the burden of our own self-importance, and certainly makes the risk of giving up the control we never really had anyway seem much less extreme. We need to trust life and ourselves a bit more and see how things unfold rather than trying to grab the wheel the whole time. Our lives aren't just jewels to be fastidiously cut and polished through our pains-taking efforts. They are not something to be *made* so much as something to be *experienced*. As the web-comic author Randy K. Milholland advises us:

> 'Think of life as a giant, fat cat you're in charge of. Sometimes you can control it but other times it's going to do what it wants and you have to roll with it. And sometimes you can do everything – everything you're s'posed to do – and it'll still shred all the things you hold dear …'

There's no denying that life can hit us with the occasional tsunami from time to time, but perhaps we also need to recognise that it's probably a good job we don't have as much power as we think we do. You don't want the inmates running the asylum, after all … Sometimes, if we can only relax and just allow ourselves to drift downstream, life obliges by taking us on interesting and diverting journeys to exotic lands. The great mythologist Joseph Campbell once shrewdly observed that 'We must be willing to let go of the life we have planned, so as to accept the life that is waiting for us.' But how many of us are brave enough to relinquish control to that degree? Go on. I dare you.

Married bliss: a matter of give and take

'Given all that we know about relationships', enthuses one of the many websites offering advice in this area, 'there really is no excuse for tolerating one that is less than fantastic.' Well, I'm glad we've got that straight. I'm truly relieved to learn that our scientific understanding of the human heart is now so comprehensive that we can finally lay to rest the misgivings expressed in the pessimistic musings of novelist Erica Jong: 'Men and women, women and men. It will never work …'

So what's the secret? Well, apparently one of the key points is that we must insist on getting our needs met. While 'your partner doesn't need to meet 100% of your needs' say the team from *The Relationship Gym*, '… they will almost certainly need to support all of the *important* ones for you to be truly happy in your relationship.'

This view, that a relationship is some kind of romantic cooperative forged primarily to meet the emotional needs of the two people in it, underlies many of the varied takes on love and dating within the self-help genre. Many of the books and DVDs offering advice on the subject boil down to variations of the old adage, 'You scratch my back and I'll scratch yours'. In fact, some of the more hardcore dating books, including the charmingly titled, *Why Men Love Bitches*, actually recommend withholding further 'scratching' as a bargaining counter in order to get your own needs met. This is the essence of Sherry Argov's 'Jujube installment plan'. No, I'm not going to spell it out. Just use your imagination.

A more benign example of this position is Dr Emerson Eggerichs' *Love and Respect*, a book whose cover bears the epic tag-line: 'the love she most desires … the respect he desperately needs.' Dr Eggerichs is a Christian minister claiming to offer a definitive biblical blueprint concerning the respective psychological needs of men and women. The basic premise of Eggerichs' book is that if you are a married woman, then you need to practise unconditional respect of your husband in order to win his love. As Dr Eggerichs explains: '… without love from him she reacts without respect; without respect from her he reacts without love.' Through each party seeking to meet the relevant need of their partner, Eggerichs maintains that couples can break free of their 'Crazy Cycle' and enjoy the transformative effects of the 'Rewarded Cycle' in which everyone is kept happy.

It's certainly true in my experience that most people who don't feel respected by their partners will probably struggle to feel particularly loving towards them. As to whether or not you agree that women have *less* need for respect than they do for love, or that men would always prioritise respect over love is another matter altogether – perhaps one, you might wish to take up with Aretha Franklin and several generations of feminists. However, while you might balk at the specifics, the fundamental vision of a relationship as a vehicle of exchange for meeting needs remains widely accepted. We are not a million miles away from the utilitarian ethos of 'social exchange theory', a model in which 'the guiding force of interpersonal relationships is always the advancement of both parties' self-interest'.

It certainly doesn't sound terribly romantic, but that may well be the least of the drawbacks to this needs-based model of human attraction. For a start, there appears to be an assumption in place that the 'needs' in question are fixed and finite. However, people have a tricky capacity to change over time, as do the dynamics within their relationships. Consequently, what people think they need can change too. The nervous and uncertain young woman who enters a relationship

Newspaper, sir?

Louise, we've worked the same street for over twenty years. You don't want a broom and I don't want a newspaper, remember?

Understanding the needs of others can be a real challenge ...

in her twenties may grow in confidence over time and no longer require or desire the protective patronage of her older lover in her thirties. The script has to be amended. The partner who formerly fulfilled this role and enjoyed the image of himself as a strong provider and protector, may have to accept that he is out of a job, and that he will have to find other ways to meet his own need to define himself as her knight in shining armour.

You may also have noticed that it may not take a decade for new needs to surface. People sometimes change moment by moment. We are not nearly as consistent as we would like to believe. And as different sub-selves push to the surface they often bring with them a host of conflicting priorities. Childlike aspects of ourselves may insist upon more fun or spontaneity in the bedroom, while an internal Parent might get irritated with a partner who won't buckle down, take their responsibilities seriously and check methodically through the bank statements. As we move through these constantly changing states it can be hard for our partners to keep up with us, or indeed for us to know precisely what they want from us at any given moment.

People are highly complex, inconsistent creatures who reveal very different aspects of themselves in different contexts. We can only explore our full range within a variety of relationships. Friends, relatives, colleagues all have a role to play. The notion that one person (however marvellous) can respond to every dimension of your multifaceted nature is frankly unrealistic. It can put enormous pressure on a relationship. The phrase 'They mean the world to me' is not supposed to imply that any one person can be an adequate substitute for the collective. If we cling to the idea that our partner can be everything we may seek from life, we are setting ourselves up for a fall.

Also, when the needs of a couple are in the foreground, the result is often not very pretty. Not all needs are healthy, and relationships constellated around implacable emotional drives are often played out within horribly destructive scripts. For example, individuals classified as having dependent personality disorders suffer from an exaggerated fear of isolation. Terrified that they will be unable to cope on their own, they are usually pathologically clingy. They are often highly amenable, submissive, and self-sacrificing. They often put up with a great deal, and never seem to fight their corner. To put it bluntly, they behave like doormats a lot of the time. But while Dependents may *appear* dedicated to setting their own needs aside, scratch

The notion that one person (however marvellous) can respond to every dimension of your multifaceted nature is frankly unrealistic.

the surface and you will see that this kind of behaviour is far from altruistic. It's just that getting their personal needs met comes with a large price tag attached. In fact Dependents are prepared to purchase the security they crave at almost any cost, even if that involves submitting themselves to a life of emotional servitude.

Ironically, such people often end up with partners who are either narcissistic or sadistic personalities. The former need to see themselves as deserving the special treatment they are given by their willing dependent partners. The latter feed their need for power by dominating them and treating them in degrading, aggressive or cruel ways. It's easy to see how there is a ghastly 'goodness of fit' in such relationships. The personality disorders on both sides are complementary. Both sides are bent on getting their needs met, it's just that most of us would consider those needs pathological. But what such cases demonstrate all too clearly is the truth of relationship counsellor Rinatta Paries' astute observation: 'Unfortunately, approaching a relationship to get your needs met tends to attract partners who require you to give up or alter some part of you.'

Even those of us who are lucky enough not to meet the criteria of personality disorders can easily get sucked into patterns of relating to each other that, while they may work for us at a superficial level, are still pretty negative. In his famous book, *Games People Play*, the transactional analyst Eric Berne gives a number of illustrations showing how when we try to get certain needs met, we can easily get caught up in degrading and juvenile trade-offs. Berne describes the dynamics of various psychological games with worrying titles like 'Ain't it awful?' and 'Kick me'. All these games originate in misguided efforts to get unacknowledged needs met by other people. But, because the roles are formalised and the games mostly destructive, they forestall any possibility of real intimacy.

When we give someone else the responsibility for meeting our needs, we inevitably start to regress. In the parent–child dyad it's entirely legitimate for the infant to look to the adult to meet their needs because the dependency is all too real. Since human infants are born immature and unfinished (unlike the young of some animals), they have to rely on the care and nurture of others. As John Bowlby explained in 1969, the psychological attachment mechanisms that binds infants and their carers together is designed to make sure those needs are met consistently. But while it is one of the luxuries of being in an intimate relationship with an adult partner that we can occasionally indulge our child side, and it's unavoidable that we all recreate the dynamics of our early years with our partner from time to time, there is nothing like deliberately focusing on our needs to bring out our most annoyingly immature and demanding aspects.

Another fundamental problem with the whole needs-based approach is that the term 'need' is so emotive. Transferred over from the biological sciences, a need is usually something which an organism cannot survive without. Unlike a wish or desire, a need is effectively non-negotiable. It's a priority, and consequently when 'needs' are at stake, there is far less room for manoeuvre or compromise. One relationship counsellor, Larry James, lays it on the line: 'You have a responsibility to yourself to get your needs met in your love relationship,' he explains. However, when I look at the example he provides I have to wonder whether all this talk of 'needs' doesn't sometimes make people rather hardline. Would you necessarily kick into touch a lover who smoked? Apparently so, if you follow Larry's advice. You may well ask how, if you love someone unconditionally, you can walk away from the relationship because they smoke? '... Because smoking is unacceptable behaviour, period!' retorts Larry, before going on to add (rather confusingly) that 'Making a choice about getting your needs met has nothing to do with love.'

Funnily enough, a measured voice from the ancient past echoes Larry James' sentiments, although I am not sure Aristotle was approaching the topic from quite the same angle. He is, however, very clear that true love and getting your needs met have very little to do with each other. In fact, he claims these impulses pull in opposite directions. In his great treatise on *Nicomachean Ethics*, Aristotle wrote:

> 'Those who love because of utility love because of what is good for themselves, and those who love because of pleasure do so because of what is pleasant to themselves, and not in so far as the person is the man he is, but in so far as he is useful or pleasant. And thus these friendships are only incidental; for it is not as being the person he is that the loved person is loved, but as providing some good or pleasure.'

Aristotle makes an important point, and one that has been reinforced in our own century by the humanistic psychologist, Abraham Maslow. Many readers may be familiar with Maslow's famous 'hierarchy of needs' so it might come as a surprise to learn that Maslow is rather wary of what happens to us when we view the world, or other people, through the lens of our own needs.

Maslow draws out some of the key features of needs-based perception (or Deficiency Cognition as he termed it) by contrasting it with its opposite, Being Cognition. For Maslow, Being Cognition is a state of heightened awareness only made possible once all needs are out of the equation. Only then, he argues, can the perceiver fully attend to the essential qualities of the object or person in front of them. With no agenda, Being Cognition allows the perceiver to see what is *really* there and thereby appreciate the true nature of the object. This kind of perception, he suggests, is 'gentle, delicate, unintruding, undemanding, able to put itself passively into the nature of things as water gently soaks into crevices …' On the other hand, Needs-motivated perception, Maslow warns us, 'shapes things in a blustering, over-riding, exploiting, purposeful fashion in the manner of a butcher chopping apart a carcass'. I'm pretty clear which approach I would rather be met with when I come through the front door tonight …

In other words, a need-oriented approach is the enemy of

true intimacy. The point is that two people attempting to relate on the basis of their needs can never be fully known to each other. The closeness they can achieve through their interlocking needs is partial, even if superficially the pieces appear to fit. True togetherness requires a good dose of Being Cognition, because, according to Abraham Maslow, it is only under these conditions that empathic fusion becomes possible: 'the mother feels one with her child, the appreciator *becomes* the music (and it becomes *him*) or the painting, or the dance' or indeed 'the lovers come closer to forming a unit rather than two people'.

We may all have needs, but that doesn't automatically make it the responsibility of anyone else, even our partner, to meet them. We also have to be careful about labelling our urges, desires, wishes and preferences as 'needs', simply because the second we do so it's very easy to become enraged with a partner who proves resistant or inattentive to them. Sometimes just changing the language you use in your own head can be an important step forward. Replacing 'I *need* to feel more appreciated' to 'I really *want* to feel more appreciated' or 'I *expect* to feel appreciated' is a subtle but significant shift. It places as much onus on you as it does on your partner; it might even prompt a helpful examination of how legitimate that desire or expectation might be, a bit of soul searching as to its origins, and even whether it's necessarily your partner who needs to do the changing.

I'm not saying that you shouldn't feel able to ask for what you want in your relationship – of course you should – and indeed you might want to think twice about staying in a relationship in which such requests are consistently dismissed, disregarded or denied. However, it's also a mistake to assume that your partner has to make your life okay for you. Ultimately, the only person who can do that, the only person who carries the responsibility for doing that, is you and you alone.

All too often people look to their relationships as a makeshift coping mechanism, a sticking plaster for psychological wounds they should be addressing in therapy. Ironically, people who do manage to take more responsibility for themselves tend to only strengthen their romantic appeal: their independence sets them free to be more caring, spontaneous and responsive partners. When two such people find each other, the whole business of relating becomes less intense, more rewarding and more fun.

Inevitably we all do make psychological contracts with each other, but often these are implicit. The danger is that while we may assume an unspoken understanding that our partner is committed to render certain services, they may be completely oblivious to the fact! This is why your mutual hopes and expectations of each other should be negotiated openly. Moreover, since hopes and expectations are liable to change, we need to make sure that the process of negotiation is an ongoing one. There's nothing wrong with having a wish list, but ultimately we would be well advised to operate within the parameters of John Le Carré's premise that: 'The only reward of love is the experience of loving.' Is there such a thing as truly unconditional love? I don't know. But my clinical experience leaves me fairly confident that a relationship based on what you can get out of the other person is never going to end well.

I remember very clearly the case of one client who came in to see me week after week trying to make up her mind about whether or not to commit to a relationship. She kept reassuring me (and presumably herself) that Pete was the perfect guy for her. He ticked 95 per cent of all her boxes and she frequently reiterated the catalogue of qualities that made him *exactly* the person she needed in her life. Yet despite this she still prevaricated. Finally she came in one day and announced she was leaving Pete for a man she had met the night before. This man, it turned out, met virtually none of her former requirements but she felt they had just 'clicked'.

> *Ironically, people who do manage to take more responsibility for themselves tend to only strengthen their romantic appeal.*

Was she just phobic about commitment and using Mr Five Per Cent to escape a lifetime of wedded bliss with Pete? I can't answer that because I never saw her again. However, I like to think that something momentous had happened that night that had finally shaken her free of her shopping list approach to love. My hope is that, despite herself, she had opened her heart to something altogether more compelling that had convinced her to cast herself adrift and embark courageously on a potentially life-changing adventure.

Discover the real you!

'Know Thyself.' This was the stark admonition greeting every worshipper crossing the threshold of the temple of Apollo at Delphi in the sixth century BC. Many centuries have passed since then but, thanks to Psychobabble, our modern age holds tightly to the myth that such an undertaking is indeed possible and, more specifically, that we all have a core self sitting there waiting to be known. However, this is certainly not the view of a new breed of 'postmodern psychologists' who insist it is about time we dispensed with the idea of the self as we currently know it.

Discovering the 'real you' is a recurrent motif in popular psychological lore. Thanks to the legacy of humanistic psychologists like Carl Rogers, it is widely accepted that most of our emotional tribulations stem from a failure to inhabit our true selves. Psychobabble has convinced us that our authentic selves lie hidden beneath the surface, obscured by the grime and dust of the endless adaptations and compromises that life has forced upon us. By various ways and means, self-help books urge us to excavate them. They promise us that once we have shed those unhelpful defences and pathological habits, escaped the legacy of our troubled past or learned the recommended life skills, then our true nature will shine through.

If we can't quite bring our true selves into sharp focus yet, that's apparently because cleaning ourselves up can take time, possibly even a lifetime. The premise of traditional analytic psychotherapy is that finding the real you can be a long, gruelling process of self-discovery during which we must confront our demons, resolve our unconscious conflicts, and gradually learn to embrace who we really are. In popular parlance, people who opt for the psychoanalytic route don't 'go' to therapy, they are 'in' therapy. The phrase suggests that, rather like finding yourself stuck 'in' mud or 'in' quicksand, it may take a while (and possibly a second mortgage) before you're going to be able to extricate yourself. Although therapy promises change, in this model growth ultimately is a matter of restoration rather than innovation; the therapist's job is to bring us back into alignment with the people we were always meant to be, but haven't fully managed to realise yet.

The humanist psychologist Carl Rogers, on the other hand, believed that given generous lashings of empathy and unconditional regard, our positive 'true' selves will emerge spontaneously like Athena from the head of Zeus. I really like Rogers but it has always struck me as a rather optimistic assumption that if people are true to their real nature then only sweetness and light will issue forth. The greed and bloodshed of over 6,000 years of human history might suggest otherwise, although maybe the conditions haven't been altogether favourable. Perhaps none of us has been feeling quite ourselves for the past six millennia?

However, when self-help authors talk about becoming 'the real you', they are not so much talking about shared characteristics as what makes each of us unique. As individual as your fingerprints, this authentic self is presumed to be a recurring and distinctive pattern of characteristics, drives, and preferences. It is thought to be this true self that lends continuity to our sense of personal identity and that makes each of us uniquely and consistently who we *really* are. Whilst the enduring tyranny of the 'false self' may mean that the real you is not fully visible just yet, it is assumed to be already there in waiting, as fixed and consistent a property of your nature as the words running through a stick of rock or the genetic blueprint in each of your cells.

We remain very strongly wedded to the idea that some core essence of our nature remains constant over time. Older people are often heard to claim that while their bodies may have changed over the years, inside they feel just the same as they did when they were 18. But is this just an illusion, a relativity effect forced upon us by the fact that we can only view the past from the perspective of the present? Do we end up extrapolating ourselves then from the people we know ourselves to be now? If memory is reconstruction rather than accurate recall, how can we ever know how we really felt in the past? You only have to look at old photos or film of yourself from previous decades to be left with a disconcerting sense of how alien it all looks and how far removed you are now from the version of yourself staring out at you from the screen or photo album. Perhaps we are all strangers to younger and older selves without ever being aware of it. Our personal narratives may create a sense of continuity for us – that's their job, after all – but in order to achieve it we edit them heavily all the time. How much of our experience are we are forced to bracket or put to one side because it doesn't fit with the official version of our lives or because 'uncharacteristic' acts or experiences disrupt the sense of our lives as one smooth, continuous flow?

Sociologists have been pointing out for a many years now that the conditions of modern life increasingly require us to shift through any number of settings, in each of which we may have to assume new roles, new identities. Am I really the same person when I am at work, with my children, with my friends? Some have seen this kind of switching as a negative thing, causing a fragmentation of identity, but some radical sociologists like Kenneth Gergen argue that as new selves are continually birthed through this expanding repertoire of relationships, life only becomes richer and more expansive. He suggests we should embrace what he calls the 'pastiche personality':

The conditions of modern life increasingly require us to shift through any number of settings, in each of which we may have to assume new roles, new identities.

'The pastiche personality is a social chameleon, constantly borrowing bits and pieces of identity from whatever resources are available and constructing them as useful and desirable in a given situation. If one's identity is properly managed the rewards can be substantial – the devotion of one's intimates, happy children, professional success, the achievement of community goals, personal popularity, and so on. All are possible if one avoids looking back to locate a true and enduring self, and simply acts to fulfil the potential of the moment at hand ... Life becomes a candy store for one's developing appetites.'

Where then is this real self of ours to be found? In what we believe? What we value? Our beliefs change and evolve over time and even values that we may consider non-negotiable prove in reality to be remarkably vulnerable to shifts in our circumstances. Spare a thought for those brave pioneers of science recruited by Dan Ariely and George Loewenstein for their experiments into the impact of sexual arousal and decision-making in 2001, a study that makes precisely this point. For this project, Berkeley students were paid $10 a session to expose themselves to a stream of pornography on specially plastic-shrouded laptops (a nice touch ...) in order to compare their anticipated attitudes to various sexual practices pre- and post-arousal. What the researchers discovered was eye-opening. The students' reported preparedness to participate in more 'exotic' sexual practices – sexual contact with animals for example – was 72 per cent higher when aroused than they had predicted in a non-aroused state. More worryingly perhaps, they also found themselves 25 per cent of a mind not to use condoms. Perhaps we don't know ourselves quite as well as we think, or maybe who we are is just less stable than we think. As Euripides tried to warn us over 2,500 years ago, we are all creatures of circumstances. Like it or not, as they change, so do we.

Just as some of our moral values and convictions turn out to be more transient than we can probably afford to believe, it now appears that even our personalities may be in a state of flux. It has long been one of the axioms of personality research that people's core personality traits remain fairly constant over time. However, a new study of over 7,000 Australians discovered that by the end of four years key dimensions of participants' personalities had altered as much as other more visible aspects of their lives such as their jobs and marriages. This latest study by psychologist Chris Boyce and colleagues is just one of a number indicating that people give different responses to personality questionnaires over time. This may be because the questionnaires aren't very well designed, or because people are careless when they fill them in, but against this is the fact that people's self-rated evaluations tend to match the independent ratings they are given by others. Bizarrely, if you ask a bilingual person to fill in the same personality question-naire but present it in each of their different languages they often generate strikingly different profiles. Asking the 'real' self to step forward seems an increasingly futile gesture.

All this may suggest that rather than thinking of ourselves as just one person with a latent 'true self' waiting to be discovered and expressed, it may make more sense to embrace Walt Whitman's position when he proclaimed jubilantly: 'I am large. I contain multitudes.' If they believe in it at all, clinicians tend to think of cases of Multiple Personality Disorder (or Dissociated Identity Disorder, as it is now formally known) as a rare and extreme reaction to inconceivable levels of pressure and trauma. Such cases are conceived as desperate fragmenting of the whole personality in a last-ditch attempt to salvage and preserve some kind of functioning. But maybe shifting between different selves or 'alters' is more common and normal than we imagine: perhaps it's just that in everyday life we don't tend to notice the joins because they are less abrupt and dramatic than they often are in clinical presentations.

Drs Hal and Sidra Stone would certainly agree with such a view. They have spent the last 40 years developing a therapeutic technique called 'Voice Dialogue' aimed at developing patients' awareness of the different sub-personalities that they believe coexist within them. The Stones believe that: 'We are made up of many selves, identifying with some and rejecting others' and add that '... over-identification with some selves and the loss of wholeness that comes from the rejection of others, can create imbalances and blind spots.' As yet there has been little proper empirical exploration of this phenomenon, but when Rowan (1990) and Lester (1992) asked people to list their different sub-selves, both researchers found that their subjects were able to identify at least two or three with relatively little effort. You might want to try it for yourself. It could be a revelation. I am not saying that you should take any of this as gospel, but it is an intriguing proposition worth exploring.

If we are prepared to relinquish the idea that we have to have a 'real me' then some interesting possibilities open up. Perhaps we should be abandoning the quest for an integrated sense of self as one of the desirable outcomes of therapy? As Professor Edward Sampson of California State University points out: 'There are people who can live very comfortably and successfully with a multiple vision of who they are, and they don't go to traditional therapists unless they want to get that knocked out of them.'

Yes... yes! I did it! Nobody can tell me I'm not a horse now!

Perhaps there is more than just one side to your personality?

Coming from a slightly different angle, in a recent TED talk the philosopher and journalist Julian Baggini drew on the idea of the brain as a self-evolving neural network to refute the notion that we have any kind of a fixed or core self running the show. He does, however, point out that even if this is the case we are still in a privileged position to direct our own growth. He maintains that, 'If you think of yourself not as a thing, as such, but as a process, that's actually quite liberating.'

Letting go of the 'real you' might also change the way we see mental illness. If we have not one but several selves, who is to say that some are not healthier than others, or that getting better is actually a matter of choosing carefully which of our selves we spend time being?

One of the things that has surprised me most working with patients over the years is how quickly and profoundly some people can appear to change. After a few sessions the issues that brought the client to the therapist's door no longer seem so pressing. The depression lifts or the difficulties in the relationship magically disappear. Although this may sound like good news, such overnight success stories are rarely welcomed by therapists who are more likely to interpret them as examples of a so-called 'flight to health' rather than evidence of genuine recovery.

But does a rapid recovery always mean that something untoward is going on? What if healthy mindedness and psychopathology are not two ends of a spectrum but simply alternative arrangements of the same set of mental factors? What if we move fluently between different configurations all the time, in much the same way as a twist of a kaleidoscope can produce different patterns? This was a view propounded by Gestalt therapist Andras Angyal, who came to a similar conclusion back in the 1960s. In his theory of the Ambiguous Gestalt,

If you think of yourself not as a thing as such but as a process that's actually quite liberating.

Angyal argued for the existence of both a healthy and a neurotic self, claiming that both of these twin patterns involved the full spectrum of the components of personality, just organised in very different ways. As he explained, 'Each and every characteristic within the personality has a position, status and value in both organizations.' So in the negative 'neurotic' configuration, the characteristic introspection might appear as social withdrawal and timidity, whereas in the 'healthy' self, the very same trait might manifest itself as an impressive capacity for thoughtfulness and reflection.

I can't offer you any kind of clinching scientific backing for this, but this model certainly makes sense of the sorts of shifts one often witnesses in the context of clinical sessions. For several years Diana, a very anxious woman in her fifties, would regularly enter the sessions very down at heel, telling me that her symptoms were as bad as they had ever been and how she despaired of ever getting any relief from them. She looked genuinely fed up, exhibited a full range of depressive symptoms, and I got no sense that she didn't believe 100 per cent that she was truthfully representing her experience and mood. She was struggling and it showed on her face and in her whole demeanour.

Nevertheless, after a few weeks in the course of sessions she would sometimes switch out of what I uncharitably christened her 'doom and gloom' persona. Her face would brighten and she would become animated and enthusiastic, making observations about herself and her family with a dry, laconic wit that often had us both in stitches. Rather than the deflated, world-weary version of herself she had brought through the door, in this mode Diana was very much a force to be reckoned with, someone with a great appetite for life who proved a vital, effervescent companion. It was literally like sitting with two different people.

Sometimes Diana could maintain her 'healthy' self for a significant part of the session, sometimes she would phase in and out, periodically collapsing soufflé-like back into her despair. But as therapy went on it became clear that she was getting better and better at inhabiting the life-affirming self for longer outside sessions, and was spending less and less time feeling despondent, frightened and overwhelmed as a result. And as Diana became aware of her capacity to flip between the two states, that knowledge seemed to weaken the hold of Mrs Doom and Gloom, because Diana knew that a healthier version of herself, whole and intact, was not only possible but close at hand.

Clients like Diana have convinced me that in many people states of genuine health and genuine pathology coexist, and that rather than being opposite ends of a continuous spectrum, sometimes they simply represent alternative states of mind and being. In fact, I strongly suspect that we don't have just two ego states, a healthy and unhealthy version, but many different ways of organising ourselves and our personalities. But for now let's stick with the uplifting possibility that even when you are at your lowest ebb and making a mess of pretty much every-thing in your life, the possibility of a more capable, stronger, more admirable version of yourself may be closer at hand than you think.

I am not claiming that therapy is always a quick fix. In fact, even when a healthy ego state is evidently there to be courted (and it isn't always even formed), it can take a long time to stabilise and identify the cues and triggers that so easily can bring it crashing down again. However, it's equally not inevi-table that the transition from pathology to health is always going to be a grinding, inexorable journey. Sometimes it's not so much a question of taking the first step on that journey of a thousand miles but a matter of nipping into an adjacent room in your mind, a different version of you. The trick, of course, is then to stay there.

Having said that, we should also acknowledge the possi-bility that many of our problems might actually stem from our instinct to hole up in particular rooms rather than move freely through the whole house. Maureen O'Hara, president of the Association for Humanistic Psychology, gave an example of one patient whose symptoms were only relieved once she stopped striving for consistency and accepted the contradictions between her different selves.

The fact that the question 'Who am I?' may not have a single answer but many parallel possibilities is as exciting as it is nerve-wracking. If we want to live full, rich lives perhaps we need to embrace the multitude within, even if that means tolerating contradictions and paradoxes that can make some parts of ourselves downright uncomfortable. We need to accept that our different selves may not always see eye to eye and may have different values, different priorities, different styles of relating. However, rather than trying to force the illusion of an integrated self by banishing the dissenting voices, we need to make room for all of us at the table. As the Israeli politician Moshe Dyan once said: 'If you want to make peace you don't talk to your friends. You talk to your enemies.' In all likelihood the 'real you' is just a mirage. By trying to hold on to it for dear life we may actually be stifling rather than cultivating our true potential as human beings.

Make every second count

Attitudes towards time can tell you a lot about a society. We are so used to our own linear conception of time as a river flowing in one direction, or a neatly segmented path along which we move at a fixed rate, that it scarcely occurs to us that not everyone in the world experiences time in the same terms. In some cultures such as those in Latin America and South-east Asia, polychronic time is not a straight line at all, but more like a circle, a spiral or a series of elegant intersecting curves. In such cultures the past and present coexist alongside each other rather than displacing each other. For the Piraha Tribe, deep in the Amazonian rainforest, the past doesn't exist at all. The tribe has no past tense in its language and, unusually, no creation myth. Again, in many cultures, time doesn't follow the constant beat of a metronome but can be stretched and flexed as required. The Indonesians even have a term for this – 'jam karet' – which literally means 'rubber time'. Yet for we Westerners, time has now become a tightly regulated commodity, a currency that must be precisely measured, apportioned and invested. Once industrialisation took hold, the gentle rhythms of nature that used to provide the pulse of an agrarian society were deemed no longer fit for purpose. We all had to synchronise our watches, metaphorically and literally.

With industrialisation, time became a precious resource that now had to be maximised. Prior to the nineteenth century, the concept of 'wasting time' didn't even exist. Nowadays we are obsessed with the notion. Popular psychology has duly taken up the baton and the shelves are consequently full of books telling us how to use time more efficiently, work smarter, conquer our procrastinating tendencies and squeeze the very most out of every waking minute.

Psychobabble is encouraging us all to become 'Type As' in our attitudes towards time. As one online article explains, these driven individuals

> 'have limitless problems with time …. They need to avoid running out of time, they need to have a watch or clock handy so they can measure time, they invest time, measure the value of time spent and time left available. These folks have an issue with deadlines, as they are restricting, yet they feel they must have them and they must be met. Time is a tool for measuring and a means of limiting, confining and defining …'

Under Psychobabble's direction, we are turning our lives into personal time-management projects, the aim being to pack as much as we possibly can into both work and leisure so that we can become fulfilled, happy people. Ironically, I strongly suspect that the very opposite is true. We are running around like lunatics. What rest we allow ourselves often comes in the form of a depleted exhaustion.

We may think of ourselves as a nation of couch potatoes, but the truth of the matter is that often we flop in front of the TV because our working lives are so demanding that it leaves us little inclination or energy to do much else. People in Britain now work longer hours than employees in Japan, and only slightly fewer than their counterparts in America. Between 1998 and 2005 the number of people working over 48 hours a week doubled to include over a quarter of the workforce.

Why are we doing this to ourselves? The stupid thing is that the research suggests this kind of overcommitment is

People in Britain now work longer hours than employees in Japan, and only slightly less than their counterparts in America.

not only unnecessary, but even counterproductive. Professor Carey Cooper points out that numerous studies demonstrate lower working hours are invariably related to higher levels of productivity, while working over 45 hours a week has been consistently linked to all manner of physical and psychological ill effects, including hypertension, depression, infections and musculoskeletal problems.

Even when we do have 'free' time available to us, our instinct is to fill it with purposeful and self-improving activities: we go the gym, attend language classes, music lessons and book groups. Social engagements are scheduled way into the future because the pace of our lives leaves precious little opportunity for impromptu hanging out with friends and loved ones. Our lives are so busy and full that some married couples have to book date nights to keep their romance alive. It's not that any of

Welcome to the modern world …

these things are wrong, or that these activities aren't genuinely enriching at one level. It's just that our lives have become so frenetic that we are now virtual strangers to the art of idleness. We no longer know how to savour unstructured time, recharge our batteries, or allow ourselves to daydream and play in a spontaneous, non-goal-directed fashion. It's a great shame, and over the next few pages I want to try and show you why.

I think the wrongness of it all is most graphically illustrated by the way we now treat those who have traditionally had the most unstructured time at their disposal. They also happen to be those who, from a developmental point of view, have had most need of it: our children. Childhood has changed beyond all recognition over recent decades. According to a survey conducted by the University of Michigan, children have just half as much free time as they did 30 years ago. Increasingly, kids from middle-income homes spend more and more time in adult-led activities and researcher Sandra Hofferth sees them affected by the same 'time crunch' as their parents. 'As a society', claims Kathy Hirsh-Pasek, 'we have talked ourselves into believing that we have to make every moment count. And that we have to fill our children as we would empty vessels.'

On the back of this belief, many of us have committed our offspring to gruelling regimes of educational and extra-curricular activities. Inevitably, this massively accelerates the pace and stress of parents' lives too, as they dutifully ferry their children from football matches to piano lessons, Taekwondo gradings to Scouts. And are our children grateful? Apparently not. Alvin Rosenfeld reports that: '... many overscheduled kids are anxious, angry and burned out'. A study which examined the performance of pre-schoolers who received extra reading tuition before starting school, found that by the end of the first year their performance was no better than non-hot-housed children who had been allowed to play freely. Significantly, the early readers were also more depressed. Psychologist Brian Sutton-Smith concluded grimly: 'The opposite of play is not work. It's depression.'

Play isn't just beneficial for young minds. Older ones need it too. Play is a natural appetite in all of us, just like eating and sleeping. If we don't make regular opportunities to indulge our appetite for relaxation and playfulness, we can end up in a boom-and-bust cycle, alternating periods of intense activity with total collapse. We have a breakdown, we burn out, or sink into a numb, dissociated state in which nothing seems enjoyable to us. Alternatively, our need for play sneaks in through the back door where it manifests itself as procrastination. We deconstruct our working lives, sabotaging our productivity with tiny rituals of immediate gratification: another round of *Angry Birds* while the boss isn't looking; a quick nap in the car if it looks like you might get back to the factory early; an extra cigarette break round the back of the warehouse. To have a genuine need that isn't met feels psychologically threatening, and play-deprived people easily become resentful and rebellious. This may underlie Gary Chick's observation that: 'Playfulness has been replaced by aggressiveness and the feeling that more needs to be crammed into less time.'

Ironically, playfulness and even idleness are not necessarily incompatible with success or productivity. In fact in some circumstances they may even help advance it. Self-confessed slacker Marc Allen claims that, despite conducting himself in a way that many would regard as 'lazy', he has still managed to achieve considerable success in his professional life. He believes that, 'in the long run, it's far better to be relaxed than stressed and you do much better work.' He points out that the opposite of activity and drive is not stagnation or death but stillness – 'wonderful, relaxing, rejuvenating stillness' as he describes it.

Psychologist Kathy Hirsh-Pasek concurs that doing nothing is far from being a 'waste' of time. She also regards idleness as a helpful precondition for renewal and creativity. Several major corporations appear to agree with her. In the working day the search-engine giant Google offers its employees 20 per cent unstructured time for what the poet John Keats termed 'diligent indolence', while all-weather clothing manufacturer

Goretex quaintly offers its workers 15 per cent 'dabble time'. When interviewed about their work lives, many of the world's richest people reported treating their professional activity very much as a game to be relished for its own sake, rather than as any kind of means to an end, including making money. Richard Branson is a good example. He once said: 'A business has to be involving, it has to be fun, and it has to exercise your creative instincts.' This enjoyment of activity for its own sake is very much a distinctive feature of play. Even work can feel like play if you do it right.

Play has been linked to cognitive flexibility, better emotional processing, superior memory and the enhancement of problem-solving capacities. It also alleviates stress. Play 'refreshes and recharges us. It restores our optimism. It renews our ability to accomplish the work of the world' claims Hara Marano. Play must be doing something helpful, because among Lewis Terman's cohort of gifted children born in the 1920s, those who played the most are more likely to be alive today.

Yet despite its self-evident benefits, we remain strangely reluctant to dedicate much of our time to it. Why is this? Cindy Aron detects a 'deep ambivalence' towards play and idleness in the modern world, which she puts down to puritan assumptions about the assumed value of labour within the context of the Protestant work ethic. However, I suspect there may be another explanation.

Perhaps we attack our lives at such a frenetic pace because we don't want to confront what rises up in us when we hit pause. We are genuinely frightened of what we might discover once all our business is laid aside. Perhaps we are ashamed, instinctively recognising that all our furious activity to build lives we can be proud of is inevitably alienating us from ourselves. Paradoxically, this sense of discomfort often pushes us to chase even harder after the accolades, job promotions, accomplishments and possessions on which we are relying to salve our wounded psyches. To look into the mirror of silence is to encounter ourselves. And, frankly, it scares us. We worry that, like Victor Frankenstein's monster staring into the pool, we will find ourselves facing a disfigured patchwork, the image of a life cobbled together, one that doesn't somehow quite cohere. It's a painful possibility. But if we can just use the gift of unstructured time to sit with ourselves in repose, or let our spontaneity guide us to self-discovery through play, then maybe, just maybe, we can even start to recover some of what has been lost.

There is a real danger for our generation that we live lives of perpetually deferred gratification, promising ourselves that we will start enjoying life once we have accomplished our goals or completed certain tasks. Meanwhile the days, months and years flow by. The great thing about the mindset of play is that it delivers instantaneously, because the activity itself is rewarding and delightful. It is 'a free connection to pure possibility' as Hara Marano puts it, and any goals are always subordinate to the means for achieving them. Life is short. This is precisely what Nadine Stair tried to stress in a poem written at the very end of her life, in her 85th year:

'Oh, I've had my moments,
And if I had it to do over again,
I'd have more of them.
In fact, I'd try to have nothing else.
Just moments, one after another,
instead of living so many years ahead of each day …

If I had to do it again,
I would travel lighter than I have.
If I had my life to live over,
I would start barefoot earlier in the spring
and stay that way later in the fall.
I would go to more dances.
I would ride more merry-go-rounds,
I would pick more daisies.'

There is a real danger for our generation that we live lives of perpetually deferred gratification.

We pay lip service to the cliché that the best things in life are free, but how many of us let this affect the way we actually live? Has it occurred to us that it might actually be *true*? Idleness, spontaneity, playfulness – the riches of these resources are available to us right here and now and, as Stair implies, they don't need to cost us a penny. Equivalent moments are freely available to all.

As I write this there is a song playing on the radio by Bruno Mars entitled 'The Lazy Song'. It's a graphic celebration of unstructured time. The protagonist announces that today, he doesn't feel like doing anything. He's going to turn off his phone, not bother getting dressed and hole up in his flat, doing whatever takes his fancy. The song has proved popular. However, I suspect for many of us it feels like an impossible dream, a nirvana to be glimpsed wistfully over the fence, whereas the reality is that the sense of freedom captured by the song is completely achievable and realistic. We just have to give ourselves the opportunity and permission to stand down.

The Greek historian Herodotus believed that if we are always serious, never giving in to our basic need for fun and relaxation, we 'would go mad or become unstable without knowing it'. In view of our packed, purposeful lives, can we be sure we haven't already lost the plot? From where I'm sitting, the world sometimes looks a mighty odd place. You may not feel you even have the time to relax but, as the journalist Sydney Harris reminds us, that is *precisely* when we need to prioritise relaxation the most. Let's not get to 85 to find ourselves run ragged and raw, just because amidst all our hectic activity we never made time for quite enough 'moments'.

We must all strive to be happy

Ask any parent what they want most for their child and the answer you will hear in the overwhelming majority of cases is a simple one: 'I just want them to be happy.' There is a general consensus out there that happiness is the supreme good, and that the pursuit of happiness is a legitimate objective, if not *the* most important objective, of every human being during their lifetime. Not every culture has shared this conviction, but it's certainly not a view you are likely to find being challenged by the self-help industry, which has played a significant role in perpetuating it. Greater happiness is the golden carrot perennially dangled in front of us by popular psychology, and so seductive is it that we keep going back for more, even when our self-help books and CDs repeatedly fail to deliver.

It's ironic that, despite its apparent significance for all of us, not that much effort has been dedicated to defining precisely what happiness is. It is assumed that we all instinctively know and, for most self-help authors, happiness is simply what you are left with once the problem has been dealt with. Whatever form it takes – the damaging legacy of your poor social skills, the difficulties experienced in your relationship, the strain caused by your disorganised lifestyle, or the blocks you encounter as you attempt to fulfil your ambitions at work – the 'problem' is always assumed to be the obstacle on the road leading to this common destination. The position is reminiscent of the logic of the ancient Greek philosopher Epicurus, who taught that pleasure is to be achieved by the removal of suffering.

The 'problem state' and the 'happiness state' are presented as mirror opposites of each other, rather like matter and antimatter. And since we know only too well that problems make us feel bad (which is usually what alerts us to the fact that they are problems in the first place) it stands to reason that the absence of problems will surely make us feel good. Happiness has become so strongly associated in the modern mind with *feeling* good that the two concepts are becoming increasingly hard to tease apart. Ask most Westerners if they are happy and they will consult their feelings. Urged on by popular psychology, we are becoming unapologetic subscribers to the eighteenth-century philosopher Jeremy Bentham's 'greatest happiness principle' whereby we consider it a moral duty to maximise our pleasure and minimise our suffering at every turn.

Nothing wrong with that, you may think. However, new research is showing that even positive emotions can have a downside. Experimental evidence from studies observing how people play games suggests that happy people tend to be more selfish than their less happy but more even-handed peers. Joseph Forgas also provides evidence that happy people can be more gullible. Also, experiencing high levels of euphoric feelings is significantly associated with disinhibited and risky behaviour such as alcoholism and drug use. Happier people also appear less likely to do as well in their careers as their less upbeat compatriots, possibly because their high levels of satisfaction leave them unmotivated to push themselves particularly hard.

Maybe this is no bad thing, and I suspect most of us would sacrifice a promotion and a few grand a year in order to have a more enjoyable life. But of more concern is the way positive

Happiness has become so strongly associated in the modern mind with feeling good that the two concepts are becoming increasingly hard to tease apart.

mood seems to have a variety of undesirable side effects on the way we process information. Not only are happy people more slapdash about detail, but the journalist Marta Zaraska cites several studies that indicate more upbeat, happy moods can make us more prejudiced in our judgments and reactions. Being too happy, it turns out, may well make you more racist and sexist!

After the induction of a happy mood, a student jury in a mock trial held in Northwestern University became considerably keener to convict a suspect named 'Juan Garcia' than in the control condition in which the ethnicity of the suspect had no effect on their willingness to find him guilty. Down south in Australia some seven years later, researcher Joseph Forgas found that 'happy' participants were more likely to judge an essay written by a man to be of higher quality than if they believed it was written by a woman.

Even if you regard becoming a self-centred bigot as a small price to pay for increasing your flow of positive emotions, be aware that however much you desire them, there may be a number of factors that could impose a glass ceiling on the level of happiness you can actually achieve. There is growing evidence to suggest that the more we pursue it, the more happiness tends to elude us.

Psychology professor Jonathan Schooler found that of the 83 per cent of his sample who had expressed disappointment with their New Year's Eve celebrations in 2000, the most disappointed were those who had invested the most emotionally and practically in their preparations. Similarly, Professor Iris Mauss, reporting on the 'paradoxical effects of valuing happiness', discovered that people who rated happiness as particularly important to them were likely to feel especially lonely after experiencing stressful life events. Sometimes we may be better off not trying to feel great all the time. Some of these findings endorse the view of the American writer Laura Moncur who declared that 'the key to happiness is low expectations', thereby echoing the sentiments of Edith Wharton who exhorted: 'If you make up your mind not to be happy there's no reason why you shouldn't have a fairly good time.'

Introspection and self-analysis are consistently associated with lower levels of self-reported happiness, according to Sonja Lyubomirsky, one of the foremost psychologists researching this area. The philosopher John Stuart Mill warned that you only have to 'Ask yourself if you are happy and you cease to be so', and psychological research would agree. A number of studies that used mobile alarms to prompt people to report on their mood at points throughout the day discovered that people reported higher levels of contentment when they were absorbed in purposeful activity and therefore not consciously aware of their mood. This supports Mihaly Csikszentmihalyi's observations about the quality of absorption characteristic of people in a state of 'flow', a privileged condition in which action and awareness are merged and self-consciousness is suspended. Show me someone who has an extensive personal development library and I will show you someone who spends a lot of time thinking about their life, and not necessarily in a very upbeat fashion. The books and tapes that we buy to make us happier may paradoxically be encouraging habits of introspection and self-evaluation that could actually be decreasing our chances of ever finding what we came looking for.

Those of us who want to be happier also have to contend with a process called 'hedonic adaptation'. This boils down to the fact that once we get used to something it can no longer deliver the same level of reward. Our brains are responsive to novel pleasures, but familiar ones cease to stimulate us in the same way. The new car we drooled over, saved for and finally managed to afford undoubtedly gives us an initial thrill. But as the smell of the new upholstery fades, the psychological reality is that we soon re-calibrate and get used to the purr of the V6 engine and that useful little shelf we can put our coffee cup in. Our enjoyment tails off and it is only a matter of time before we find ourselves fixated on the next big thing: that special purchase, experience, relationship, or job opportunity

I told you that you weren't coming with us, Nicole! Mom and Dad are using you as the control group. They want to see if taking kids on vacation makes them happier as adults.

Scientific research has shed new light on happiness in recent years ...

that *really* will make us happy. We find ourselves back on the so-called 'hedonic treadmill'. Despite what you may think (and I know we'd all be up for trying it out) research really has confirmed that winning the lottery doesn't improve your perceived quality of life in the long term. Winners seldom report greater levels of life satisfaction than they did before fortune smiled upon them.

Worse still, according to Lyubomirsky and colleagues, it appears that we also have a personal happiness set-point to which we have a tendency to return, regardless of what may be going on in our lives, good or ill. With twin studies suggesting that as much as 50 per cent of an individual's happiness is down to their genetic make-up, it would appear some of us are just dispositionally inclined to be more miserable than others. Part of this may be down to inherited personality traits like extroversion, since there are some fairly robust findings suggesting that extroverts tend to experience more positive emotional states than introverts. If you are an introvert please don't despair (let's face it people: you probably feel bad enough already ...) because a recent body of work is rediscovering the strengths and advantages of being an introvert. However, I have to tell you that being bubbly, carefree and happy-go-lucky are not among them.

The historian Jennifer Hecht also makes the point that happiness comes in different flavours and that some forms of happiness may actually get in the way of us experiencing others. Hecht distinguishes between three types of happiness: the relatively mundane 'good day' type of happiness filled with repeatable, low-level pleasures; the intermittent emotional fireworks of intense euphoria; and finally the grounded satis-factions associated with a 'happy life'. This, Hecht points out, 'requires a lot of difficult work (studying, striving, nurturing, maintaining, negotiating, mourning, birthing), sometimes seriously cutting into time for a good day or for euphoria'. Along these lines she offers the helpful suggestion that if we find ourselves unhappy we might want to consider if we are focusing on certain domains at the expense of others. Perhaps you need time off from your conscientious life-building activities for a quick blast of euphoria, or alternatively to rein in the roller-coaster highs of your rock-star lifestyle in order to enjoy the calmer waters of a few 'good days'. However, if some forms of happiness actually undermine and compromise others, we can appreciate that there is going to be a strong chance that our lives will always feel less optimal than they could be.

Happiness defined simply as the experience of positive emotions, would therefore appear to be something that we might want only in moderation. But is this how we should be defining it anyway? Is popular psychology's frequent assumption that happiness is merely about 'hedonic flow' or 'feeling good' selling us short? Think about it for a moment. If it were indeed possible to hook yourself up to a virtual-reality machine that allowed you to experience the most pleasurable reality you could possibly imagine for the rest of your natural life, would you actually sign up for it? The philosopher Robert Nozick designed just such a thought experiment to make the point that some things are apparently more important to us than pleasure alone. When push comes to shove, most of us would rather endure the tribulations, disappointments and patchy satisfactions of real life than settle for virtual nirvana. Cultures older and more astute than our own understood this. In ancient Athens, Aristotle argued that *eudaimonia*, often mistranslated as 'happiness', was recognised as the highest good by educated and uneducated classes alike. However, the word really means 'human flourishing' and Aristotle certainly isn't just talking about feeling good. In the classic *Nicomachean Ethics,* Aristotle explains that *eudaimonia* really means 'doing and living well', and may well encompass events and experiences that don't necessarily contribute to one's sense of 'feeling good' at the time.

Emotions are useful things and valid sources of information in lots of ways. But when we use them as the primary compass to steer us through life we shouldn't be surprised if we end up taking wrong turns. Our feelings are not always a reliable gauge of how things are going, and if we err in making feeling happy the touchstone of our well-being, we are likely to live limited lives. If feeling happy is our main agenda and prime directive, how easily we can become preoccupied with soothing and comforting ourselves. The Psychobabble generation finds it hard to grow up because it believes (mistakenly) that we ought to feel okay all the time and, if we don't, that something is seriously wrong. We sometimes forget that we need the lows to appreciate the highs.

For the ancients, happiness necessitated striving after the Good, or trying to live a noble life. John F. Kennedy summarised the Greek position as 'the full use of your powers along lines of excellence'. It was accepted that this sometimes involved effort and pain but it seemed obvious to the Greeks that morality, values and well-being were closely intertwined. However, modern psychology often shuffles uncomfortably in its seat when moral considerations are raised. In the universe of Psychobabble, far from being the guardians of our happiness, ethical directives are often obstacles in its way. Thanks to Freud, emotions such as guilt are often dismissed as unhelpful grumblings from the superego – the psychological repository of 'Dos' and 'Don'ts' he claims we all import from childhood. In this model, therapy is tantamount to a mission to liberate the patient from the superego's unreasonable, moralistic demands, so that feelings of happiness can flow freely once more. Now therapists certainly can't afford to be overtly moralistic. It's a mighty tall order to be expected to explore the darkest and dankest parts of one's psyche if you don't feel you can do so safely without fear of censure. In the humanistic counselling tradition the therapist's chief job is to emit what Carl Rogers famously described as 'unconditional positive regard'. Judgmental therapists help no one and that compassion is a genuinely powerful and healing force. However, there is a real problem with Psychology always trying to act like Switzerland in this matter. It is pretty bizarre that, with the notable exception of pioneers like Jonathan Haidt, modern Psychology is only beginning to address moral reasoning. Its insistence that value judgments lie firmly outside its catchment area, when the daily mental lives of real people are so caught up with them, strikes me as odd. Perhaps Psychology should be paying less attention to trying to augment our cache of positive feelings and paying greater attention to the novelist Ayn Rand's vision of happiness as 'that state of consciousness which proceeds from the achievement of one's values'.

We are learning more about happiness and the conditions under which it is to be cultivated or, to be more accurate, we know more about the mental habits and behaviours of happy people. Optimism, gratitude, the ability to be satisfied with 'good enough' rather than insisting on the best, being kind to others, not dwelling on past mistakes and imagining yourself as the best version of yourself you can be – all these attitudes characterise those of us who report greater levels of subjective well-being. There is clearly much to learn from such research that could potentially improve the quality of all our lives, whatever our genes have bequeathed us. However, what is also clear is that we need to stop trying to equate happiness with merely feeling good. Aiming for targets like 'happiness', 'success' and 'fulfilment' is a recipe for disaster, because all the evidence suggests such states are the felicitous by-products of a life well lived, rather than prizes that can be grabbed hold of in their own right. I suspect the nineteenth-century author Nathaniel Hawthorne gave us a poetic but fairly accurate summary of the situation when he wrote: 'Happiness is as a butterfly which, when pursued, is always beyond our grasp, but which if you will sit down quietly, may alight upon you.'

Aiming for targets like 'happiness', 'success' and 'fulfilment' is a recipe for disaster, because all the evidence suggests such states are the felicitous by-products of a life well lived.

Epilogue

What is it about human beings that makes us so eager to have someone else tell us what to do? Consider the unfortunate lorry driver Steven Abbot, who had to spend his son's 18th birthday in the cab of a 17.5 tonne lorry he had managed to wedge between two walls. Or the cabbie (not, one suspects, the owner of a particularly awesome hippocampus)[1] who drove 180 metres up a river before the muddy riverbed brought his taxi to an ignominious halt. Or the Belgian truck driver who caused £20,000 of damage after panicking in a cul-de-sac, ploughing over a mini-roundabout, and taking out six other vehicles in the process.

What each of these tales has in common is that the drivers concerned all subsequently blamed their satellite navigation systems for misdirecting them. And there, but for the grace of God, go all of us. According to a recent poll, the average motorist will travel 1,292 additional miles in the wrong direction, purely out of deference to the wisdom of satellite navigation technology. Most of us will choose to follow the instructions of the severe American (or slightly more upbeat Australian) lady who resides on our dashboards, even when the evidence of our eyes, ears and several traffic signs are all strongly suggesting we should reconsider. Like the children of Hamelin we will cheerfully follow the electronic Pied Piper to our doom, with all too little heed as to where we might be headed.

It's a modern parable that all Psychobabble-speaking natives should take to heart. Life can be rich and wonderful at times but it is also extremely complicated. Consequently, few of us really know what we are doing, and it takes a particularly brave (or

---

[1] See Myth 12, 'You can learn to do anything you want', p. 99.

foolish) man or woman to stick their head above the parapet and cry: 'Follow me! I know the way.' Perhaps it is precisely because the very nature of human lives, made up as they are of a myriad of intersecting variables, endless choices and mysteriously branching pathways, makes them so very hard to fathom that we crave confident voices to direct us through the maze. However, as Voltaire cautioned, while doubt may not always be a pleasant condition, 'certainty is absurd …'.

Today's wisdom is tomorrow's folly. As I have gently hinted, much of what we take on good authority turns out to be fairly flimsy if you poke it with even a moderately sharp stick. We may comfort ourselves that as sensible moderns we are starting to evolve models of the world, and even our own minds, that are based on reliable scientific methods and hard data. However, the more solid and substantial our findings, the more nervous we ought to be. The biological anthropologist Matt Cartmill once compared looking to science to deliver factual certainty with becoming an archbishop in order to meet girls. Everything changes. The next Copernican revolution is just round the corner. The true value of science is not in providing us with answers but instead in reminding us just how hard it is to know anything for sure.

One thing does seem clear: most of us are flawed, imperfect creatures. Perhaps rather than striving to perfect ourselves with such ardour we should acknowledge this fact, offer ourselves a little compassion and risk letting ourselves off the hook. Who knows, a life that we are not trying to improve all the time might even have room in it for a bit more fun. A bit more time spent in the company of those we love. Time to kick back, shoot the breeze and simply enjoy the ride. Or, if you

Much of what we take on good authority turns out to be fairly flimsy if you poke it with even a moderately sharp stick.

fancy something a bit more highfalutin, time simply to 'drift forward into a splendid mystery'. Perhaps life is happy for us to 'come as we are' rather than insisting we have to upgrade and refine every aspect of ourselves before we will be sufficiently presentable?

I don't know. I definitely don't have all the answers. But I am not convinced that the self-help section of your local bookstore necessarily has them either. It's only natural that we want solutions to our problems, strategies to ease our pain, and guidance when we don't know where to turn. How easy it is to be seduced by the prospect of transforming yourself from an ugly duckling to a magnificent swan! But let's not forget: sometimes getting by as an adult duck (even a moderately ugly one) can work out okay too. Sometimes even our potential can be a burden. And sometimes we might do better to endure the bad times with as much good grace as we can muster, without the additional responsibility of wrestling them into submission or having to rise phoenix-like from the ashes.

Psychology may be able to offer suggestions about what works for some of the people some of the time, but only you are the expert on how to be you; after all, no one else has ever tried it before or will do again. And those of us who dish out the advice, whether we are paid for it or not, need to respect that fact. This book has been quote-heavy enough, but I will leave you with one final uplifting insight from one of our greatest contemporary philosophers, the comedienne Ellen DeGeneres. She summed up the message of this book in a commencement speech given at Tulane University, New Orleans in 2009. 'Don't give advice,' she told the assembled graduands, 'It will come

> *Psychology may be able to offer suggestions about what works for some of the people some of the time, but only you are the expert on how to be you.*

back and bite you in the butt … So my advice to you is to be true to yourself and everything will be fine.' I don't know whether this is true either. However, I like to hope that it might be.

Take a...
CLOSER LOOK
...at your life!

References

Introduction

P.xii '... *Richard Dawkins introduced us to the* meme, *defined as ...*' See *Merriam Webster Dictionary*: www.merriam-webster.com.

P.xv '... *The truth is rarely pure and never simple ...*' See Oscar Wilde, *The Importance of Being Earnest*, 1985, Act I.

P.xv 'As *David Rogers explains ...*' See Rogers (1990).

P.xvi '... "*For every problem ...*"' H. L. Mencken, 'The divine afflatus' in *New York Evening Mail*, 16 November 1917.

P.xvi '... *Follow your bliss ...*' See Campbell and Moyers (1989), 120, 149.

P.xvii Orwell, G. (2008) *Nineteen Eighty-four*. Penguin.

P.xix '... *The deepest sin against the human mind ...*' See Thomas Huxley, *Evolution and Ethics*, 1893.

P.xxii '*Let's just say that if I have to read ... Heisenberg's uncertainty principle ...*' See Heisenberg, Eckart and Hoyt (2003).

Myth 1 The root of all your problems is low self-esteem

P.1 '*High self-esteem isn't a luxury ...*' See Canfield (1989).

P.1 '*The catalogue of personal and societal ills now laid at the door of low self-esteem is extensive ...*' See, for example, Kermis et al. (1989); Jang and Thornberry (1998); Covington (1989); DeWit et al. (2000); Pottebaum and Ehly (1986); Tharenou (1979); Berry et al. (2000); Crockenberg and Soby (1989); Bruch (1975); Branden (1994).

P.3–4 '*Their self-ratings simply aren't upheld by the independent evaluations of their peers or by objective tests of their attributes and abilities ...*' See Martin et al. (1984); Baumeister et al. (2003); Gabriel et al. (1994); Diener et al. (1995); Buhrmester et al. (1988).

P.4 '... *there are indeed reasonable correlations between higher self-esteem and academic performance ...*' See, for example, Hansford and Hattie (1982).

P.4 '... *the most comprehensive objective review of the self-esteem literature so far conducted ...*' See Baumeister et al. (2003).

P.4 '... *Dan Olweus ... could find no evidence that male playground bullies were particularly anxious or insecure ...*' See Olweus (1993).

P.4–5 'A *crucial influence on our thinking ... high self-esteem, not low, is indeed an important cause of aggression.*' Quoted in Baumeister (August 2006).

P.5 '*Your self-esteem rating does* not *predict ...*' For discussion of all of the issues mentioned see Baumeister et al. (2003).

P.5 '... *If we really love ourselves, everything in our lives works ...*' Louise Hay quoted on ThinkExist.com.

P.5 '... *Do you desire to construct a vast and lofty fabric? ...*' St Augustine of Hippo quoted in Hotchkiss (1895).

P.6 '*... A voice of contemporary concern ... Professor Jean Twenge ...*' See Twenge, J. M. (2007).

P.6 '*... In many cases, the suggested cure for narcissistic behaviour is "feeling good about yourself." ...*' Quoted in Twenge and Campbell (2009).

P.6 '*... Wouldn't it be powerful if you fell in love with yourself so deeply ... ?*' Alan Cohen quoted at spiritwire.com.

Myth 2   Let your feelings out!

P.11 '*... Dr George Solomon ... people who repress their feelings are more at risk of rheumatoid arthritis, infections and certain types of cancer ...*' See Solomon et al. (1974); Dattore et al. (1980).

P.11 '*... a team from the University of Buffalo ...*' See Seery et al. (2008).

P.12 '*... a study of heart attack survivors conducted by Dr Karni Ginzburg and colleagues ...*' See Ginzburg et al. (2002).

P.12 '*... Expressing anger does not reduce aggressive tendencies ...*' Lohr (2006), in Cavell and Malcolm.

P.12 '*... an observation made by Charles Darwin ...*' See Darwin (1872).

P.13 '*... a study in which moderately painful heat was applied ...*' Salomons et al. (2008).

P.13–14 '*... Arlie Hochschild ... claims that the spontaneity of our feelings is often an illusion ...*' See Hochschild (1983).

Myth 3   Emotional intelligence is what really counts

P.17 '*... What really matters for success, character, happiness and life long achievements is a definite set of emotional skills ...*' Daniel Goleman (1996).

P.17 '*... psychologists Peter Salovey and John Mayer's original concept ...*' See Salovey and Mayer (1990).

P.17 '*... The strapline on the cover of Goleman's most famous book reassures us that emotional intelligence "can matter more than IQ" ...*' See Goleman (1996).

P.18 '*... emotional competencies were found to be twice as important as conventional intellect or expertise ...*' See Goleman (2009), 31.

P.18 '*... One of the most authoritative reviews of the evidence to date ...*' See Van Rooy and Viswesvaran (2004).

P.18–19 '*... Having had Lyle and Signe Spencer's original competence framework studies reanalysed ...*' See Spencer and Spencer (1993).

P.19 '*... On average close to 90 per cent of their success in leadership was attributable to emotional intelligence ... emotional competence accounts for virtually the entire advantage ...*' See Goleman (2009), 34.

P.19 '*my search for a full account of this research in any peer-reviewed, academic journal has so far come up empty-handed.*' I have contacted the Hay Group about this and, at time of writing, am awaiting their response.

P.19 '*... in interviews both Gates and Jobs have freely admitted to a pretty "robust", confrontational, management style ...*' For example, Gregory Ferenstein recounts how Walter Isaacson (Steve Jobs' biographer) recalled Jobs explaining to him:

> '*I can tell people in a meeting that they're full of shit, but they can bark back at me and tell me I'm full of shit. And then we have the most rip-roaring arguments and that's why we work together well.*'

Posted on *Fast Company* 26th October 2011 (www.fastcompany.com/1790791/ steve-jobs-biography-walter-isaacson).

Similarly Bill Gates, interviewed by *Playboy* magazine in 1994 regarding his 'brusque' management style responded:

> *'I don't know anything about employees in tears. I do know that if people say things that are wrong, others shouldn't just sit there silently. They should speak. Great organizations demand a high level of commitment by the people involved. That's true in any endeavor. I've never criticized a person. I have criticized ideas. If I think something's a waste of time or inappropriate I don't wait to point it out. I say it right away. It's real time. So you might hear me say, "That's the dumbest idea I have ever heard" many times during a meeting … . So, how do you have a successful software company? Well, you get me and Microsoft executive vice president Steve Ballmer and we just start yelling.'*

Accessed on http://beginnersinvest.about.com/od/billgates/l/blbillgatesint.htm.

P.19 '… *the emotionally intelligent individual portrayed by Goleman:* … *"poised and outgoing, committed to people and causes …"'* Goleman quoted in *Utne* magazine, Nov–Dec 1995. Published online at www.utne.com/Science-Technology/ Emotional-Intelligence-Quotient-Test.aspx.

P.21 '… *Critics have been left despairing of ever being able to identify a coherent common factor or unifying principle …'* See Murphy (2006); Matthews et al. (2004); Eysenck (2000).

P.22 '… *Hans Eysenck observed:* … *"if these five 'abilities' define 'emotional intelligence', we would expect some evidence that they are highly correlated …"'* See Eysenck (2000).

P.24 '… *Even in the fifteenth century Niccolo Machiavelli understood the psychology of power … .'* See Machiavelli.

Myth 4 Let your goals power you towards success!

P.27 '… *We're going on a bear hunt …'* See Rosen and Oxenbury (1993).

P.27–8 '… *according to Harvard psychologist Daniel Gilbert, we are often very poor at knowing what we want …'* See Gilbert (2006).

P.29 '… *"stretch goals" … can be crushing and disheartening …'* See Ordóñez et al. (2009).

P.29 '… *people apparently only achieve stretch goals about ten per cent of the time …'* See Daniels (2009).

P.29 '… *Push too far and your higher centres will shut off …'* See Arnsten et al. (2012).

P.30 '… *Goals Gone Wild … the authors …'* Who are: L. D. Ordóñez, M. E. Schweitzer, A. D. Galinsky and M. H. Bazerman.

P.31 '… *contentment is one of a group of positive emotions that … Barbara Fredrickson believes actively expands our field of attention …'* See Fredrickson and Branigan (2005).

P.31 '… *The yogi T. K. V. Desikachar says …'* Desikachar quoted by Miriam Ufberg on *Positive Psychology News Daily* (positivepsychologynews.com/news/ miriamufberg/20070329181).

P.32 '… *Dr Robert Emmons … discovered experimentally that people encouraged to cultivate gratitude were up to 25 per cent happier …'* See Emmons and McCullough (2003).

P.32–3 '... *Happiness in Taoism is the personal liberation from all human desires ...*' From Lu (2001).

Myth 5 No one can *make* you feel anything

P.35 '... *Just as money can't make you happy, other people can't make you happy either ...* See Kate Wachs (2002).

P.36 '... *Cognitive Behavioural Therapy has successfully demonstrated over numerous clinical trials ...*' See Roth et al. (2006) for an overview of such studies.

P.36 '... *Ahmad Hariri and colleagues found that when people were simply asked to label the expressions on faces ...*' See Hariri et al. (2000).

P.38 '... *Barry Ruback and Daniel Juieng conducted a series of experiments demonstrating precisely this phenomenon in 1997 ...*' For example, Ruback and Juieng (1997).

P.38 '... *men were found to linger longer in library aisles ...*' See Ruback (1987).

P.38 '... *In 1977 at the University of Minnesota Dr Mark Snyder and colleagues conducted an ingenious experiment ...*' See Snyder et al. (1977).

P.38–9 '... *What had initially been reality in the minds of the men had now become reality in the behaviour of the women ...*"' Snyder et al. (1977), 661.

P.39 '... *the behaviour of the subjects in Stanley Milgram's experiments ...*' See Milgram (1963).

P.39 '... *Or what about the behaviour of the students randomly allocated to play the role of guards in the infamous Stanford prison experiment ...?*' See Zimbardo (1971).

P.39 '... *people are reluctant to recognise how much of their everyday experience "is determined not by their conscious intentions and deliberate choices ..."*' John Bargh quoted in Buchanan (2009).

P.40 '... *Dr Robert Rosenthal reports on an experiment in which students were allocated to two classes ...*' See Rosenthal and Jacobson (1968).

P.40 '... *As Pentland explains, "honest cues are also unusual ..."*' From Pentland (2010).

P.41–2 '... *women whose ability to frown was inhibited after receiving botox injections reported feeling much happier ...*' See Lewis and Bowler (2009).

P.42 '... *In fact, research has established that even feelings like loneliness can be catching ...*' See Cacioppo et al. (2009).

P.42 '... *events that took place in another Massachusetts town, Salem, in 1662 ...*' For a summary see Linder, D.

P.42 '... *In recent years scientists have discovered specialised mirror neurones in the brain ...*' See Wicker et al. (2003); Morrison et al. (2004).

Myth 6 Think positive and be a winner!

P.46 '... *Professor Martin Seligman ... has done a great deal of methodical research demonstrating how important an optimistic explanatory style may be in warding off depression ...*' Results summarised in his 2003 book, *Authentic Happiness*.

P.46 '... *They found that ... if you suffer from low self-esteem then these affirmations can actually make you feel worse ...*' See Wood et al. (2009).

P.47 '... *Similarly, independent studies have shown that ... for depressed people the opposite effect is produced ...*' See Davey et al. (2011).

P.47 '... *To accomplish great things we must dream as well as act ...*' Anatole France: Discours de Réception, Séance De L'académie Française 24th December 1986.

P.47 '… Joseph Forgas, a professor of social psychology, reports …' Joseph Forgas quoted in 'Workers in bad moods perform better' in *The Telegraph*, 3 November 2009.

P.48 '… In 2011, Bettina von Helverson and colleagues conducted a research study that indicates depressed people are also better at sequential decision-making …' See Von Helverson et al. (2011).

P.48 '… Ronda Muir, who runs a consultancy firm to the legal profession …' See Ronda Muir, Law People (www.lawpeopleblog.com).

P.48 '… Research conducted at the University of Seattle …' See Leu et al. (2011).

P.50 '… As Yochelson and Samenow explain …' See Yochelson and Samenow (1976).

P.50 '… "The Psychological Inventory of Criminal Thinking Styles" …' See Walters (1995) for detail.

P.50 '… The most extreme version of positive thinking presented in "mind over matter" books like The Secret *…'* See Byrne, R. (2006).

Myth 7 We need to talk …

P.55 '… We have already seen how influential Alex Pentland's so-called "second channel" of communication can be …' See Myth 5, 'No one can *make* you feel anything'.

P.55 '… As psychologist Elaine Hatfield points out …' See Hatfield, Rapson and Yen-Chi (2009).

P.55 '… as relationship expert John Gottmann has shown in the lab, any signs of contempt may well prove fatal …' See Gottmann (2007).

P.57 'Author Alexander Penney reminds us …' Quoted by Penney in *Self* magazine.

P.58 '… Research into friendship conducted by Carolyn Weisz and Lisa F. Wood …' See Weisz and Wood (2005).

P.59 '… "an intentional response to promote well-being when responding to that which has generated ill-being" …' Oord (2010).

P.60 '… When we honestly examined our deepest feelings, we realised that our perception of him was that he was basically inadequate …' Covey (2004), 17.

P.61 '… This was the discovery of Sandra Murray and her colleagues …' See Murray et al. (2011).

P.62 '… "She did not talk to people as if they were strange hard shells …"' Bonner (November 1926).

Myth 8 Whatever your problem, CBT is the answer

P.64 '… in the spring of 2008 Stefan Hofmann and Jasper Smits performed a meta-analysis of CBT treatment outcomes …' See Hofmann and Smits (2008).

P.64 '… However, Dr Peter Kramer rather puts this result into perspective …' See Kramer (2008).

P.64–5 '… In a post on the website for the British Psychoanalytic Council …' See McQueen (2009).

P.65 '… Based on a careful literature review conducted in 1992 …' See Lambert (1992).

P.65 '… In 2001 Bruce Wampold … supported Lambert's conclusions …' See Wampold (2001).

P.65 'More recently the American Psychological Association …' See Norcross (2011).

P.67 '… A fascinating and well-known finding by Benjamin Libet …' See Libet et al. (1983).

P.68 '... *Susan Blackmore believes that these experiments indicate that "conscious experience takes time to build up ..."'* Blackmore (1998).

P.72 '... *Shakespeare was right when he said that "Love and reason keep little company together" ...'* William Shakespeare: *A Midsummer Night's Dream*, Act 3, Scene 1.

P.74 '... *Lowell was a brilliant man but he got carried away and assumed too much ...'* See Lowell (1906). For an analysis try Strauss (2001).

Myth 9 You can never be too assertive

P.78–9 '... *One commentator – clearly not a fan of the oriental way – parodies the ethos of* sonkeigo *as follows ...'* See 'Things that irk me about Japan 1: Keigo,' posted on: *A Foreigner's Tale in Japan: a certain type of Ninja Bread* (aaroninjapan09.wordpress.com/2009/03/06/things-that-irk-me-about-japan-1-keigo).

P.80 '"... *Assertive people tend to be seen as less likeable and less friendly than unassertive people ... even kinder and gentler versions of assertiveness are seen as leading to worse impressions ..."'* See Ames and Flynn (2007).

P.80 '... *These leaders were markedly unassuming in a way that contradicts the stereotype of what an assertive person should look like ...'* See Collins (2001).

Myth 10 Men and women live on different planets

P.83 '... *Gray says that a lot of what goes wrong in relationships between men and women stems from our failure to appreciate just how different they are ...'* See Gray (2012), 1: 14.

P.84 '... *There are a number of studies that claim to show contrasts ...'* See, for example, Cahill et al. (2004); Zaidi (2010); Frodi et al. (1977).

P.84 '... *Cordelia Fine argues that the scientific evidence is ultimately far from convincing ...'* See Fine (2011).

P.84 '... *Well, not according to researchers Ann Kring and Albert Gordon ...'* See Kring and Gordon (1998).

P.85 '... *Some additional evidence is provided by another study in which boys were much quicker than girls to turn off the sound of a baby crying ...'* See Fabes et al. (1994).

P.85 '... *Intriguingly, in one of the most comprehensive reviews of the gender research ...'* See Hyde (2005).

P.86 '... *As the anthropologist Victor Turner pointed out, culture is a big theatrical production ...'* See Turner (1975).

P.86 '... *Even the finding that women have a thicker corpus callosum ... has been called into question ...'* See Bishop and Wahlstein (1998).

P.88 '... *Carl Jung believed that ... within the psyche of every human being there is a masculine and feminine dimension ...'* See Jung (1991).

P.89 '... *Male and female represent the two sides of the great radical dualism ...'* In Fuller (1845).

Myth 11 Your inner child needs a hug

P.91 '... *as Cathryn Taylor's mystical* Seven Layers of Healing *technique recommends ...'* See Taylor (1991).

P.92 '... *Shades of the prison house begin to close/Upon the growing Boy* ...' William Wordsworth, 'Intimations of Immortality from Recollections of Early Childhood', in Quiller-Couch (1919).

P.93 '... *of the 65 per cent that fell neatly into Thomas and Chess's four proposed categories, only 40 per cent were "easy" babies* ...' See Thomas, Chess and Birch (1968).

P.93 '... *The child psychiatrist Jerome Kagan observed that children varied greatly in their level of arousal* ...' See Kagan (1997).

P.94 '... *Several critics have pointed out* ...' See Yapko (1994).

P.94–5 '... *With that, the little person dies, looking peaceful and serene* ...' See Tipping (2010), 339.

P.95 '... *Hence one inner-child guru recommends that in order to heal the child within you must "temporarily or permanently end all relationships in which you are being hurt"* ...' Attributed to DeFoore (undated).

P.95 '... *Many readers will associate the notion of the Child as a distinct persona with Transactional Analysis* ...' See Berne (2009) or Harris (1995) for a more accessible summary.

P.96 '... *Neurologist Oliver Sacks presents a more recent case of Mrs O'C* ...' In Sacks (2008).

P.96 '... *A recent study conducted at Hull University demonstrated that many of us have clear "memories" of childhood events that never actually happened* ...' See Mazzoni, Scoboria and Harvey (2010).

P.97 '... *In a very comprehensive review conducted in 1987* ...' See Nash (1987).

P.97 '... *The researchers concluded that while hypnosis seemed to activate some of the emotional responses of children, they certainly weren't reliving specific events* ...' See Nash et al. (1986).

Myth 12 You can learn to do anything you want

P.99 '... *As one NLP website enthuses: If one human can do something then, potentially anyone can* ...' Quoted for example in the 'Fundamental principles of NLP' on the pegasus NLP website: www.nlp-now.co.uk.

P.99 '... *As blogger Diana Hartman points out* ...' Hartman (January 2008).

P.100 '... *This was the rationale behind Bandler and Grinder's original analysis of the communication style of three eminent therapists ... and later Milton Erickson* ...' See Bandler and Grinder (1975); Grinder and Bandler (1976).

P.100–101 '... *'If one asks an expert for the rules he or she is using, one will, in effect, force the expert to regress to the level of a beginner* ...' From Dreyfus and Dreyfus (2005).

P.102 '... *Mice who have their RGS14 gene disabled remember objects better* ...' See Eastman (2010).

P.102 '*A team from the Cognitive Neuroscience Research Group in Barcelona* ...' See Díaz et al. (2008).

P.102 '... *Dr Melissa Libertus found that pre-schoolers whose superior "number sense" allowed them to judge more accurately* ...' See Libertus, Feigenson and Halberda (2011).

P.104 '... *Thus Dr Sara Lazar and colleagues found that the brains of regular meditators demonstrated thickening in the cortex* ...' See Hölzela et al. (2010).

P.104 '... *Similarly, the brains of London taxi drivers generally have larger than average hippocampi* ...' See Maguire (2000).

Myth 13 You'd better get yourself sorted

P.110 '... Albert Rothenberg studied the creative processes of 22 Nobel prize-winning scientists ...' See Rothenberg (1996).

P.110 '... [Andreasen] speculates: 'It is as if the association cortices are working actively, throwing out feelers for possible connections between unrelated capacities ...' Andreasen (2010).

P.111 '... One evening, contrary to my custom, I drank black coffee and could not sleep. Ideas rose in crowds ...' Poincaré (2001), 220 (cited by Andreasen 2010).

P.111 '... creates an extension of your thinking space and means that "you are using the environment to think as well" ...' Dr Jay Brand quoted by Carol Smith for the *Seattle Post-Intelligencer,* 8 November 1999.

P.111 '... An alternative recent take on the potential virtues of a messy desk comes from a German research team ...' See Liu, Smeesters and Trampe (in press).

P.112 '... One journalist remarked ...' Green (2006).

P.112 '... in psychoanalyst Karen Horney's book ...' See Horney (1991).

P.113 '... However, recently researchers at Cambridge University have produced evidence that makes it look as if it may be possible for compulsive behaviours to cause obsessional thoughts ...' See Gillan et al. (2011).

P.114 '... My new desk was beginning to take on the characteristics of a shrine ...' Gould (2010).

P.114 '... Suddenly the breeze started picking up and blowing my papers about ...' Covey (2004), 253.

P.115 '... If neuropsychologist Jerrold Pollak is right ...' See Green (2006).

P.115 '... As David Freedman and Eric Abrahamson ... explain, "It takes extra effort to neaten up a system ..."' Abrahamson and Freedman (2006).

P.116 '... Nothing seems more brutalizing ...' Hirschhorn (1984), 13.

P.116 '... As the sociologist Max Weber warned us, in a world where the principles of instrumental rationality prevail, life is soon reduced to an endless cascade of means and ends ...' See Gerth and Wright Mills (1970).

P.117 '... icy waves of egotistical calculation ...' See 'The Communist Manifesto' (1847) 475 in The Marx-Engels reader edited by Richard Tucker (1978).

P.117–18 '... "Almost anything looks pretty neat," he told her, "if it's shuffled into a pile" ...' David Freedman interviewed by Penelope Green for *The New York Times* in December 2006.

P.118 '... It may be true that in space "... no one can hear you scream ..."' Film poster for *Alien* by Ridley Scott.

P.118 '... the will to system betrays a lack of integrity ...' Friedrich Nietzsche in *Twilight of Idols,* Maxims and Arrows, 33.

Myth 14 You are stronger than you know

P.119 '... "Most people have no idea of the giant capacity we can immediately command when we focus all of our resources on mastering a single area of our lives" ...' Anthony Robbins courtesy of quotationsbook.com.

P.122 '... In one of Shiv's more unnerving experiments ...' See Shiv and Fedorikhin (1999).

P.122 '... our level of will-power is surprisingly dependent upon our blood-sugar levels ...' See Gailliot et al. (2007).

P.122 '... "Control is a funny thing. It comes and goes ..."' See Ugel (2011).

P.123 '... Wolfgang Stroebe found skipping meals often predicts weight gain ...' See Stroebe (2008).

P.123 '... according to Daniel Wegner, efforts to banish all thoughts of certain foods ends up in more rather than less of them ...' See Wegner (1994).

P.123 '... life's greatest rewards are reserved for those who demonstrate a never-ending commitment to act until they achieve ...' Anthony Robbins quoted in Blaydes (2003), 57.

P.123 '... Then roll up your sleeves and start logging those 10,000 hours of deliberate practice Malcolm Gladwell says it's going to take ...' See Gladwell (2009), 38.

P.127 '... when we find what works for us, we are naturally drawn into a state of "flow" in which we become effortlessly attuned, absorbed and fascinated by the task in hand ...' See Csikszentmihalyi (2002).

P.128 '... This is surely what agony aunt Ann Landers was driving at when she wrote: "Some people believe holding on and hanging in there are signs of great strength ..."' Ann Landers quoted on www.goodreads.com.

Myth 15 **You are a master of the universe!**

P.129 '... as the author of the bestseller, The Secret *keeps reminding us ...'* See Byrne (2006).

P.130 '... 'It's like having the universe as your catalogue ...' Joe Vitale in Byrne (2006), 48.

P.133 '... "I think I can safely say nobody understands quantum mechanics ..."' Feynman (1992).

P.134 'At the heart of the research run at the PEAR ... lab was endless trials ...' For a summary of this research see Jahn and Dunne (2005).

P.136 '... Psychologist Daryl Bem used the technique of reverse priming to demonstrate what look like precognitive abilities ...' See Bem (2011).

P.137 '... I suggest you have a look at the Global Consciousness project website for yourself ...' Global Consciousness website: http://noosphere.princeton.edu.

P.138 '... This might fit quite well with data reported from Lynne McTaggart's Intention Experiments ...' See http://theintentionexperiment.com.

Myth 16 **There is no failure, only feedback**

P.141 '... "there is no failure, only feedback."' See www.mymotivational-nlp.com/nlp-presuppositions.

P.142 '... Walt Disney is a classic example ...' See Thomas (1994) for a comprehensive biography.

P.142 '... made such a pig's ear of running the family farm ...' See Gleik (2004) for a readable biography.

P.144 '... a recent comment from Jason Fried, the co-founder of 37 Signals ...' What Fried actually said at a keynote speech at SXSW 2006 (an annual music, film and interactive conference held in Austin) was: 'Obscurity is a good thing. You can fail in obscurity. It removes the fear of failure.'

Myth 17 **It's all your parents' fault**

P.148 '... Judith Rich Harris, for one, has little time for those who succumb to what she calls The Nurture Assumption *...'* Harris (1999).

P.148 '... "The classic case is the poet Philip Larkin, who famously griped ..."' Harris (2010) *No Two Alike* (Kindle edition) location 5272.

P.148 '... "the home environment and the parent's style of child-rearing are found to be ineffective in shaping children's personalities ..."' Harris (2010) ibid, location 818.

P.148 '... the direction of her findings very much agrees with those of other authors like David Cohen ...' See Cohen (1999).

P.149 '... an enigma explored by Harris in her latest book, No Two Alike ...' See Harris (2010).

P.150 '... For example, if we know, as psychologist Diana Baumrind reminds us, that children of dominating, authoritarian parents are prone to lower self-esteem, reactions of fear and aggression and tend to emulate their parents' coercive behaviours ...' See Baumrind, Lazelere and Owens (2010).

P.150 '... If you still need convincing, consider the salutary case of one study of adopted children ...' See Tehrani and Mednick (2000); DiLalla and Gottesman (1989).

P.151 '... I am also somewhat reassured by developmental psychologist Sandra Scarr's recent suggestion that it is perhaps only extreme environmental conditions that may tend to affect us, depending on our predisposing vulnerabilities ...' See Scarr (1992).

P.152 '... Reviewing the findings of over 130 studies ...' See Huang (2010).

P.152 '... We know, for example, from Susan Harter's work how powerfully peer relationships orchestrate the rise and fall of adolescent self-esteem ...' See Harter (1999); Adler and Adler (1998); Savin-Williams and Berndt (1990).

P.152 '... Satisfaction with physical appearance is another strong predictor of self-esteem levels within this age group ...' See Harter (1990) and (1999).

P.153 '... According to Oliver James, just the right blend of strictness and empathy from your folks produces a benign conscience ...' See James (2007), chapter 3.

P.153 '... "Of the large number of correlations the researchers calculated between maternal practices and child outcomes, only 6 per cent ... were statistically significant ..."' Harris (2010) ibid, location 1682.

P.153 '... "Freda Cohen is having a very torrid time with her teenage son ..."' As found on: www.jokebuddha.com

P.153–4 '... Evolutionary psychologists Martin Daly and Margo Wilson found little evidence of the Oedipus complex ...' See Daly and Wilson (1988).

P.154 '... Meanwhile Walter Mischel argued that the flexibility of our moral standards ... weighs against the likelihood that "a unitary moral agency like the superego" even exists ...' See Mischel (1968).

P.154 '... Alison Kirk found that while being a child of divorcees made people more anxious/realistic about the likelihood of relationship breakdown ...' See Kirk (2002).

P.154 '... A "securely" attached infant is confident that their parent will respond to their needs. They seek comfort when required, enjoy being close, but can also tolerate brief separations without undue distress ...' For an account of the 'Strange Situation' test see Bretherton (1992).

P.155 '... Cindy Hazan and Philip Shaver found evidence of equivalent attachment styles at work in adults' romantic relationships ...' See Hazan and Shaver (1987).

P.156 '... One study that followed the attachment behaviours of children from infancy through to maturity found only 17 per cent still demonstrated the same attachment style in their adult romantic relationships ...' See Steele et al. (1998).

P.156 '... Another found correlations of security ratings between parents and current romantic partners of under a third ...' See Crowell, Fraley and Shaver (1999).

P.156 '*... the attachment style of adults often wobbles quite dramatically in the wake of stressful life events ...*' See Waters et al. (2000).

P.156 '*... As Paula Pietromonaco and Lisa Barrett concede, "From this perspective, people do not hold a single set of working models of the self and others ..."*' See Pietromonaco and Barrett (2000).

P.156 '*... while Mark Baldwin acknowledges that "Within romantic relationships, expectations might then vary significantly ..."*' See Baldwin (1992).

P.157 '*... There is certainly little evidence to support popular-psychology authors Amir Levine and Rachel Heller's bold assertion ...*' Levine and Heller (2011).

P.157 '*... "A baby whose mother is depressed doesn't expect everyone to be depressed ..."*' See Harris (2010) ibid, location 2670.

P.157 '*... For example, infant attachment doesn't necessarily predict how we will relate to our friends ...*' See Saferstein, Neimeyer and Hagans (2005).

P.157 '*... and Dinero and colleagues discovered that even having a secure attachment style in your mid-twenties was no guarantee of the quality of your interactions with your romantic partner ...*' See Dinero et. al (2008).

P.157 '*... Crittenden's Dynamic-Maturational Model ...*' See Crittenden (2006).

P.158 '*... Bartholomew and Horowitz have managed to reformulate the whole taxonomy of adult attachment ...*' See Bartholomew and Horowitz (1991).

P.159 '*... In 2006 David Huh and colleagues tracked the behaviour of 500 teenage girls ...*' Huh et al. (2006).

P.160 '*... "Each parent treats each child so differently that they might as well have been raised in completely different families" ...*' James (2007), 186.

P.161 '*... Harris claims that differential treatment by their parents accounts for only two per cent of the variance shown between siblings ...*' Harris (2010) ibid, location 1826.

P.161 '*... What this indicates is that "the parents were reacting to the genetic differences between their children, rather than causing their children to be different ..."*' Harris (2010) ibid, location 1849.

P.161 '*... "All over the world, teenagers are choosing friends, and even mates, that their parents disapprove of ..."*' Miller (1999).

Myth 18 You can heal your body

P.163 '*... Guang Yue, an exercise psychologist from Ohio, reports that a group of volunteers who regularly pictured themselves flexing their biceps ...* See Ranganathan et. al (2004).

P.164 '*... There are some intriguing studies suggesting that hypnosis and visualisation can increase your bust size ...*' See, for example, Willard (1977); Williams (1974); Staib and Logan (1977).

P.164 '*... it appears that hypnosis can help with weight loss ...*' See Cochrane and Friesen (1986); Pittler and Ernst (2005).

P.164 '*... As the author Barbara Ehrenreich points out, it is all too easy for already sick people to be left feeling like utter failures ...*' See Ehrenreich (2010).

P.164 '*... "When cancer or any other illness returns, I don't believe it's because the doctor didn't 'get it all out', but rather, that the patient has made no mental changes and so just recreates the same illness" ...*' Hay (1984), *Heal Your Body*. Kindle edition. location 67.

P.165 '*... consequently she knows that if people are "willing to do the mental work of releasing and forgiving, almost anything can be healed ..."*' Hay (1984), ibid, location 85.

P.165 '... According to psychologist Johan Denollet, so-called Type D personalities ...' See Denollet, Vaes and Brutsaert (2000).

P.166 '... those who scored as the most angry and antagonistic in their dealings with others often demonstrated pronounced and ominous thickening of their neck arteries ...' See Sutin et al. (2010).

P.166 '... research conducted by Jenny Choi, Steven Fauce and Rita Effros demonstrated how cortisol inhibits immune cells ability to use telomerase ...' See Choi, Fauce and Effros (2008).

P.166 '... writing about life-enhancing, happy experiences seemed to make no difference ...' Rosenkranz et al. (2003).

P.167 '... placebos themselves tend to produce improvements in approximately 35 per cent of cases ...' See Hamilton (2008), chapter 2.

P.168 '...While it is the case that neuropeptides may indeed stimulate DNA synthesis in certain cell types...' See Nilsson and Edvinsson (2000) and Reid et al. (1993) for more details.

P.168 '... Having conducted a careful and comprehensive analysis of the relevant existing studies ...' Coyne and Tennen (2010).

Myth 19 You are in control of your life

P.171 '... Some ingenious experiments conducted in 2008 by Adam Galinsky and Jennifer Whitson discovered that people deprived of control are far more likely to see images in patterns of random dots ...' See Whitson and Galinsky (2008).

P.171 '... In recent experiments in which participants were asked to estimate the chances of various significant misfortunes befalling them ...' See Sharot, Korn and Dolan (2011).

P.172 '... Ellen Langer conducted a celebrated experiment ... in which she sold lottery tickets to two groups of people ...' See Langer (1975).

P.172 '... The economist Burton Malkiel explains ...' See Malkiel (1997).

P.173 '... Type A personality. This was based on a cluster of common chacteristics that Meyer Friedman and Mike Jordan identified ...' See Friedman and Rosenman (1959).

P.173 '... Now while it turned out that being a Type A per se doesn't inevitably put you at greater risk of heart disease ...' According to Haukkala et al. (2010).

P.173 '... In fact Richard Lazarus specifically defines stress as what occurs when "individuals perceive that they cannot adequately cope with the demands being made on them or with threats to their well-being" ...' See Lazarus (1966).

P.173 '... Life is difficult and complicated and beyond anyone's total control ...' J. K. Rowling at Harvard Commencement address given in 2008.

P.173 '... In the 1970s Jonathan Rotter discovered that all of us tend to fall into one of two camps ...' See Rotter (1975).

P.174 '... People with a really strong internal locus are consequently vulnerable to guilt, perfectionism, anxiety and self-recrimination ...' See 'The Disadvantages of Internal Locus of Control' by David Stewart, published on eHow (6 October 2011) (ehow.com/info_8603703_disadvantages-internal-locus-control.html).

P.174 '... as Daniel Gilbert has shown us, spectacularly bad at predicting which options will secure our happiness ...' See Gilbert (2006).

P.175 '... This is the essence of Mindfulness training, which is proving to be a very effective antidote for depression and many other psychological problems ...' See Segal, Williams and Teasdale (2002).

P.175 '... *As the actress Nicole Kidman has discovered* ...' Interviewed in *The Scotsman*.

P.175 '... *Researchers Evan Apfelbaum and Samuel Sommers found that when they deliberately depleted subjects' reserves of self-control* ...' See Apfelbaum and Sommers (2009).

P.176 '... *As Sandra Sanger stresses, flexibility at a behavioural and mental level is a hallmark of good mental health* ...' Dr Sandra Sanger, 'The Illusion of Control', psychcentral.com, 3 October 2011.

P.176 '*In his discussion of the "wisdom of spontaneity", Dr Leon Seltzer argues* ...' Dr Leon F. Seltzer, 'The Wisdom of Spontaneity', Psychology Today (www. psychology today.com).

P.176 '*As Ed Smith argues, chance plays a much bigger role* ...' See Smith (2012).

P.178 '... "*Think of life as a giant fat cat you're in charge of* ..."' Randy K. Milholland, *Something Positive*, 7 November 2011 (www.somethingpositive.net/ sp11072011.shtml).

Myth 20 Married bliss: a matter of give and take

P.179 '... "*Given all that we know about relationships," enthuses one of the many websites offering advice in this area* ...' Michael Myerscough quoted in *The Relationship Gym: Relationship Advice to Get You Fit for Love* (www. therelationshipgym.com).

P.179 '... *Men and women, women and men. It will never work* ...' So insists Isadora Wing, Erica Jong's narrator, in chapter 16 of her 1973 novel *Fear of Flying*.

P.179 '... *Why Men Love Bitches: From Doormat To Dreamgirl: A Woman's Guide to Holding Her Own in a Relationship* ...' Argov (2002).

P.180 '... *a book that bears the epic tag-line: "the love she most desires ... the respect he desperately needs"* ...' Eggerichs (2005).

P.180 '*We are not a million miles away from the utilitarian ethos of Social Exchange Theory* ...' See Roloff (1981).

P.183 '... "*Unfortunately, approaching a relationship to get your needs met tends to attract partners who require you to give up or alter some part of you* ..."' Paries, R.

P.183 '*In his famous book*, Games People Play, *the transactional analyst Eric Berne gives a number of illustrations* ...' See Berne (2010).

P.184 '... *As John Bowlby explained in 1969* ...' Bowlby (1969).

P.184 '... "*You have a responsibility to yourself to get your needs met in your love relationship*" ...' James (2006).

P.185 '... *In his great treatise on Nicomachean Ethics, Aristotle wrote: "Those who love because of utility love because of what is good for themselves* ..."' Aristotle, *Nicomachean Ethics*, VIII 3.1156a, 14–19.

P.185 '... *This kind of perception, he suggests, is "gentle, delicate, unintruding, undemanding, able to put itself passively into the nature of things as water gently soaks into crevices* ..."' Maslow (2011), 41.

P.185 '... *On the other hand, Needs-motivated perception, Maslow warns us, "shapes things in a blustering, over-riding, exploiting, purposeful fashion in the manner of a butcher chopping apart a carcass* ..."' Ibid.

P.186 '... *True togetherness requires a good dose of Being Cognition, because according to Abraham Maslow it is only under these conditions that empathic fusion becomes possible* ...' Maslow (2011), 105.

P.187 '... "The only reward of love is the experience of loving ..."' Le Carré (1999).

myth 21 **Discover the real you!**

P.190 '... The humanist psychologist Carl Rogers ... believed that given generous lashings of empathy and unconditional regard, our positive "true" selves will emerge spontaneously ...' See Rogers (2004).

P.191 '... If memory is reconstruction rather than accurate recall ...' See Loftus and Palmer (1974); Goff and Roediger (1998).

P.192 '... "The pastiche personality is a social chameleon ..."' Gergen (2000), 150.

P.192 '... Spare a thought for those brave pioneers of science recruited by Dan Ariely and George Loewenstein for their experiments into the impact of sexual arousal and decision-making ...' Ariely and Loewenstein (2006).

P.193 '... just one of a number indicating that people give different responses to personality questionnaires over time ...' Boyce, Wood and Powdthavee (2012); Ramírez-Esparza et al. (2004).

P.193 '... "I am large. I contain multitudes ..."' Walt Whitman, *Song of Myself.*

P.194 '... "We are made up of many selves, identifying with some and rejecting others ..."' Hal and Sidra Stone's website is: www.delos-inc.com.

P.194 '... You might want to try it for yourself. It could be a revelation ...' You can find a friendly American 'inner' family therapist who will tell you how at the following address: www.youtube.com/watch?v=b-vS_E-nY1w.

P.194 '... As Professor Edward Sampson of California State University points out ...' Edward Sampson quoted by Mitchell Stephens (1992).

P.195 '... in a recent TED talk the philosopher and journalist Julian Baggini drew on the idea of the brain as a self-evolving neural network ...' (www.ted.com/talks/lang/en/julian_baggini_is_there_a_real_you.html).

P.196 '... As he explained, "Each and every characteristic within the personality has a position, status and value in both organizations ..."' Angyal quoted in Frick (1984).

P.198 '... gave an example of one patient ...' Maureen O'Hara quoted by Mitchell Stephens (1992).

myth 22 **make every second count**

P.200 '... Psychobabble is encouraging us all to become "Type As" in our attitudes towards time ...' According to an anonymous article 'What is the Type A Personality?' posted on www.essortment.com.

P.200 '... Between 1998 and 2005 the number of people working over 48 hours a week doubled ...' See Gillan (2005).

P.201 '... Professor Carey Cooper points out that ... working over 45 hours a week has been consistently linked to all manner of physical and psychological ill effects ...' Carey Cooper, quoted in Gillan (2005).

P.202 '... They also happen to be those who, from a developmental point of view, have had most need of it ...' See: Ginsberg (2007); Pellegrini (2009).

P.202 '... According to a survey conducted by the University of Michigan, children have just half as much free time as they did 30 years ago ...' See Klevmarken and Stafford (1999).

P.202 '... Increasingly, kids from middle-income homes spend more and more time in adult-led activities ...' See Elkind (2008).

P.202 '... Sandra Hofferth sees them affected by the same "time crunch" as their parents ...' Quoted in 'The joy of doing nothing' published by Scholastic (www.scholastic.com/resources/article/the-joys-of-doing-nothing).

P.202 '... "As a society," claims Kathy Hirsh-Pasek, "we have talked ourselves into believing that we have to make every moment count ..."' Ibid.

P.202 '... Alvin Rosenfeld reports that: "... many overscheduled kids are anxious, angry and burned out ..."' Ibid.

P.202 '... A study which examined the performance of pre-schoolers who received extra reading tuition before starting school ...' See Smith (2001).

P.202 '... the opposite of play is not work. It's depression...' See Professor Brian Sutton-Smith in his book *The Ambiguity of Play* (2001).

P.203 '... Gary Chick's observation that: "Playfulness has been replaced by aggressiveness ..."' Gary Chick quoted in 'The Power of Play'. Interviewed by Hara Marano for *Psychology Today* (www.psychologytoday.com).

P.203 '... Self-confessed slacker Marc Allen claims ...' See Marc Allen: 'How being a laid-back Type Z can make you happy, healthy, wealthy and wise'. Blog published on New World Library (www.newworldlibrary.com/NewWorldLibraryUnshelved).

P.203 '... Psychologist Kathy Hirsh-Pasek concurs that doing nothing is far from being a "waste" of time ...' See Hirsh-Pasek et al. (2003).

P.204 '... Play has been linked to cognitive flexibility, better emotional processing, superior memory and the enhancement of problem-solving capacities ...' See *The American Journal of Play* for a number of articles on these subjects, as well as the extensive reference list provided on the National Institute for Play website (www.nifplay.org/biblio_fin.html).

The Art of Play by Adam and Alee Blatner also has useful material on the benefits of play for adults as well as children.

Dr Stuart Brown's TED talk on 'Serious Play' is also instructive (www.ted.com/talks/stuart_brown_says_play_is_more_than_fun_it_s_vital.html).

P.204 '... Play "refreshes and recharges us. It restores our optimism ..." claims Hara Marano ...' In 'The Power of Play', posted on *Psychology Today* (www.psychologytoday.com).

P.204 '... among Lewis Terman's cohort of gifted children born in the 1920s, those who played the most are more likely to be alive today ...' Cited by Hara Marano 'The Power of Play', *Psychology Today* (www.psychologytoday.com).

P.204 '... Cindy Aron detects a "deep ambivalence" towards play ...' Aron (2001).

P.205 '... This is precisely what Nadine Stair tried to stress in a poem written at the very end of her life, in her 85th year ...' See 'If I Had My Life to Live Over' by Nadine Stair.

P.206 '... The Greek historian Herodotus believed ...' Herodotus: *The Histories*. Book 2, chapter 173.

P.206 '... as the journalist Sydney Harris reminds us ...' Writing in his syndicated column *Strictly Personal* which ran between 1944 and 1986, Harris wrote: 'The time to relax is when you don't have time for it'.

Myth 23 We must all strive to be happy

P.208 '... happy people tend to be more selfish than their less happy but more even-handed peers ...' For studies exploring the 'dark side' of happiness see Tan and Forgas (2010); Forgas and East (2008); Deldin and Levin (1986); Johnson and Tversky (1983); Oishi, Diener and Lucas (2007).

P.209 '… *the journalist Marta Zaraska cites several studies* …' See Zaraska (2012).

P.209 '… *Being too happy, it turns out, may well make you more racist and sexist!* …' See Bodenhausen, Kramer and Süsser (1994) and Forgas (2011).

P.209 '*After the induction of a happy mood* …' See Bodenhausen, Kramer and Süsser (1994).

P.209 '… *the most disappointed were those who had invested the most emotionally and practically in their preparations* …' See Schooler, Ariely and Loewenstein (2003).

P.209 '… *Professor Iris Mauss* … *discovered that people who rated happiness as particularly important to them were likely to feel especially lonely after experiencing stressful life events* …' Mauss et al. (2011).

P.210 '… *Introspection and self-analysis is consistently associated with lower levels of self-reported happiness* …' Lyubomirsky and Lepper (1999); Schooler, Ariely and Loewenstein (2003).

P.210 '… *Ask yourself if you are happy, and you cease to be so* …' John Stewart Mill in chapter 5 of his autobiography entitled *A Crisis in My Mental History* (see Stewart Mill, 1960, 105.)

P.210 '… *This supports Mihaly Csikszentmihalyi's observations* …' Csikszentmihalyi (1990).

P.211 '… *we also have a personal happiness set-point to which we have a tendency to return* …' See Lyubomirsky (2010).

P.212 '… *This, Hecht points out, "requires a lot of difficult work* …"' See Hecht (2008), 10.

P.212 '… *The philosopher Robert Nozick designed just such a thought experiment* …' See 'The Experience Machine' in Nozick (1977).

P.213 '… *John F. Kennedy summarised the Greek position as "the full use of your powers along lines of excellence* …"' John F. Kennedy, Remarks to Student Participants in the White House Seminar in Government, 27 August 1963.

P.214 '… *with the notable exception of pioneers like Jonathan Haidt* …' For example, Haidt (2012).

P.214 '… *novelist Ayn Rand's vision of happiness as "that state of consciousness which proceeds from the achievement of one's values* …"' See *Atlas Shrugged*, part three, chapter seven: This is John Galt Speaking.

Epilogue

P.217 '… *Consider the unfortunate lorry driver* …' Sat Nav stories taken from 'Sat Nav Disasters: Mirror.co.uk Top 10' (25 March 2009) published on www.mirror.co.uk.

P.218 '… *as Voltaire cautioned* … *certainty is absurd* …' Voltaire in a letter to Frederick II of Prussia in 1767.

P.218 '… *The biological anthropologist Matt Cartmill once compared* …' Quoted on Matt Cartmill's page on the Boston University Anthropology Department website (www.bu.edu/anthrop/people/faculty/m-cartmill).

P.219 '… *"drift forward into a splendid mystery"*' Edwin Hubbell Chapin, www.quotationpark.com/topics/future%20state.html.

Bibilography

Abrahamson, E. and Freedman, D. H. (2006) *A Perfect Mess: The Hidden Benefits of Disorder*. Weidenfeld and Nicolson.

Adler, P. A. and Adler, P. (1998) *Peer Power: Preadolescent Culture and Identity*. Rutgers University Press.

Allen, D. (2002) *Getting Things Done: How To Achieve Stress-Free Productivity*. Piatkus.

Ames, D. R. and Flynn, F. J (2007) 'What breaks a leader: the curvilinear relation between assertiveness and leadership', *Journal of Personality and Social Psychology*, 92, 2: 307–324.

Andreasen, N. C. (January 2010) 'A Journey Into Chaos: Creativity and the Unconscious', Seminar on Mind, Brain and Consciousness. Keynote address.

Apfelbaum, E. P. and Sommers, S. R. (2009) 'Liberating effects of losing control: when regulatory strategies turn maladaptive', *Psychological Science*, 20, 139–143.

Argov, S. (2002) *Why Men Love Bitches: From Doormat To Dreamgirl: A Woman's Guide to Holding Her Own in a Relationship*. Adams Media Corporation.

Ariely, D. and Loewenstein, G. (2006) 'The heat of the moment: the effect of sexual arousal on sexual decision making', *Journal of Behavioral Decision Making*, 19: 87–98.

Aristotle. J. Barnes (ed.) (1984) *Aristotle: The Complete Works. The Revised Oxford Translation*. Princeton University Press.

Arnsten, A., Mazure, C. and Sinha, R. (April 2012) 'This is your brain in meltdown', *Scientific American*, 306: 48–53.

Aron, C. (2001) *Working at Play: A History of Vacations in the United States*. OUP, US.

Augustine of Hippo quoted in Hotchkiss, J. G. (1895) *Dictionary of Burning Words of Brilliant Writers*. W. B. Ketcham. Original at Harvard University.

Baldwin, M. W. (1992), 'Relational schemas and the processing of social information', *Psychological Bulletin*, 112: 461–484.

Bandler, R. and Grinder, J. (1975) *The Structure of Magic I: A Book About Language and Therapy*. Science and Behavior Books.

Bartholomew, K. and Horowitz, L. M. (1991) 'Attachment styles among young adults: a test of a four category model', *Journal of Personality and Social Psychology*, 61, 2: 226–244.

Baumeister, R. F. (August 2006) 'Violent pride', *Scientific American Mind*, 17, Issue 4.

Baumeister, R. F., Cambell, J. D., Krueger, J. I. and Vohs, K. D. (2003) 'Does self-esteem cause better performance, interpersonal success, happiness or healthier lifestyles?', *Psychological Science in the Public Interest*, 4, 1: 1–44.

Baumrind, D., Lazelere, R. E. and Owens, E. B. (2010) 'Effects of preschool parents' power assertive patterns and practices on adolescent development', *Parenting: Science and Practice*, 10: 157–201.

Bem, D. J. (2011) 'Feeling the future: experimental evidence for anomalous retroactive influences on cognition and affect', *Journal of Personality and Social Psychology*, 100, 3: 407–425.

Berne, E. (2009) *Transactional Analysis in Psychotherapy*. Eigal Meirovich.

Berne, E. (2010) *Games People Play: The Psychology of Human Relationships*. Penguin.

Berry, E. H., Shillington, A. M., Peak, T. and Hohman, M. M. (2000) 'Multi-ethnic comparison of risk and protective factors for adolescent pregnancy', *Child and Adolescent Social Work Journal*, 17: 79–96.

Bishop, K. M. and Wahlstein, D. (1998) 'Sex differences in the human corpus callosum: myth or reality?', *Neuroscience and Biobehavioral Reviews*, 21, 5: 581–601.

Blackmore, S. (1998) 'Why psi tells us nothing about consciousness', in S. R. Hameroff, A. W. Kaszniak and C. Scott (eds) (1998) *Toward a Science of Consciousness II*. MIT Press, 701–707.

Blatner, A. and Blatner, A. (1997) *The Art of Play: Helping Adults Reclaim Imagination and Spontaneity*. Brunner-Mazel Inc.

Blaydes, J. (2003) *The Educator's Book of Quotes*. Corwin Press.

Bodenhausen, G. V., Kramer, G. P. and Süsser, K. (1994) 'Happiness and stereotypic thinking in social judgment', *Journal of Personality and Social Psychology*, 66: 621–632.

Bonner, M. (November 1926) 'Nothing new', *Crisis* 33: 17–20.

Bowlby, J. (1969) *Attachment and Loss, Vol. 1: Attachment*. Basic Books.

Boyce, C. J., Wood, A. M. and Powdthavee, N. (2012) 'Is personality fixed? Personality changes as much as "variable" economic factors and more strongly predicts changes to life satisfaction', *Social Indicators Research*. Springerlink: online.

Branden, N. (1994) *The Six Pillars of Self-Esteem*. Bantam Books.

Brennan, K. A., Clark, C. L. and Shaver, P. R. (1998) 'Self-report measurement of adult romantic attachment: an integrative overview', in J. A. Simpson and W. S. Rholes (eds) *Attachment Theory and Close Relationships*. Guilford Press, 46–76.

Bretherton, I. (1992) 'The origins of attachment theory: John Bowlby and Mary Ainsworth', *Developmental Psychology*, 28, 5: 759.

Bruch, H. (1975) 'Obesity and anorexia nervosa: psycho-social aspects', *Australian and New Zealand Journal of Psychiatry*, 9: 159–161.

Buchanan, M. (2009) 'Secret signals', *Nature,* 457: 528–530.

Buhrmester, D., Furman, W., Wittenberg, M. T. and Reiss, H. T. (1988) 'Five domains of interpersonal competence in peer relationships', *Journal of Personality and Social Psychology*, 55: 991–1008.

Byrne, R. (2006) *The Secret*. Simon and Schuster.

Cacioppo, J. T., Fowler, J. H. and Christakis, N. A. (2009) 'Alone in the crowd: the structure and spread of loneliness in a large social network', *Journal of Personality and Social Psychology*, 97, 6: 977–991.

Cahill, L., Uncapher, M., Kilpatrick, L., Alkire, M. T. and Turner, J. (2004) 'Sex-related hemispheric lateralization of amygdala function in emotionally influenced memory: an fMRI investigation', *Learning and Memory*, 11: 261–266.

Campbell, J. and Moyers, B. (1989) *The Power of Myth*. Bantam, Doubleday, Dell.

Canfield, J. (1989) *How to Build High Self-Esteem – A Practical Process for your Personal Growth*: audio course. Nightingale Conant Corporation.

Chapman, G. (27 June 2008) 'Bill Gates signs off', *Agence-France-Presse*.

Choi J., Fauce, S. R. and Effros, R. B. (2008) 'Reduced telomerase activity in human T lymphocytes exposed to cortisol', *Brain Behaviour Immunology*, 22, 4: 600–605.

Clark, L. V. (1960) 'Effect of mental practice on the development of a certain motor skill', *Research Quarterly*, 31, 4: 560–569.

Cochrane, G. and Friesen, J. (1986) 'Hypnotherapy in weight loss treatment', *Journal of Consulting and Clinical Psychology*, 54: 489–492.

Cohen, D. B. (1999) *Stranger in the Nest: Do Parents Really Shape Their Child's Personality, Intelligence or Character?* John Wiley and Sons.

Collins, J. (2001) 'Level five leadership: the triumph of humility and fierce resolve', in *Best of HBR 2001, Harvard Business Review*, July–August 2005: 1–11.

Covey, S. R. (2004) *The Seven Habits of Highly Effective People*. Simon and Schuster.

Covington, M. J. (1989) 'Self-esteem and failure in schools: analysis and policy implications', in A. M. Mecca, N. J. Smelser and J. Vasconcellos (eds) *The Social Importance of Self-Esteem*. University of California Press, Berkeley, 72–124.

Coyne, J. C. and Tennen, H. (2010) 'Positive psychology in cancer care: bad science, exaggerated claims, and unproven medicine', *Annals of Behavioural Medicine*, 39, 1: 16–26.

Crittenden, P. M. (2006) 'A dynamic-maturational model of attachment', *Australian and New Zealand Journal of Family Therapy*, 27, 2: 105–115.

Crockenberg S. and Soby, B. (1989) 'Self-esteem and teenage pregnancy', in A. M. Mecca, N. J. Smelser and J. Vasconcellos (eds) *The Social Importance of Self-Esteem*. University of California Press, Berkeley.

Crowell, J. A., Fraley, R. C. and Shaver, P. R. (1999) 'Measures of individual differences in adolescent and adult attachment', in J. Cassidy and P. R. Shaver (eds) *Handbook of Attachment: Theory, Research, and Clinical Applications*, Guilford. 434–465.

Csikszentmihalyi, M. (1990). *Flow: The Psychology of Optimal Experience*. Harper and Row.

Csikszentmihalyi, M. (2002) *Flow: The Classic Work on How to Achieve Happiness*. Rider.

Daly, M. and Wilson, M. (1988) *Homicide*. Aldine de Gruyter.

Daniels, A. C. (2009) *Oops! 13 Management Practices that Waste Time and Money (and What to Do Instead)*. Performance Management Pub.

Darwin, C. (1872) *The Expression of the Emotions in Man and Animals*. University of Chicago Press: Chicago.

Dattore, P. J., Shontz, F. C. and Coyne, L. (1980) 'Premorbid personality differentiation of cancer and non-cancer groups: a test of the hypothesis of cancer proneness', *Journal of Consulting and Clinical Psychology*, 48: 388–394.

Davey, C. G., Allen, N. B., Harrison, B. J. and Yücel, M. (2011) 'Increased amygdala response to positive social feedback in young people with major depressive disorder', *Biological Psychiatry*, 69, 8: 734–741.

DeFoore, W. G. (undated) 'Nurturing and caring for your inner child: how to heal emotionally and master the art of self-love', posted on: *SelfGrowth.com – the online self improvement community*.

Deldin, P. J. and Levin, I. P. (1986) 'The effect of mood induction in a risky decision-making task', *Bulletin of the Psychonomic Society*, 24.

Denollet, J., Vaes, J. and Brutsaert, D. L. (2000) 'Inadequate response to treatment in coronary heart disease adverse effects of type D personality and younger age on 5-year prognosis and quality of life', *Circulation*, 102, 6: 630–635.

DeWit, D. J., Offord, D. R., Sanford, M., Rye, B. J., Shain, M. and Wright, R. (2000) 'The effect of school culture on adolescent behavioural problems: self-esteem, attachment to learning, and peer approval of deviance as mediating mechanisms', *Canadian Journal of School Psychology*, 16: 15–38.

Díaz, B., Baus, C., Escera, C., Costa, A. and Sebastián-Gallés, N. (2008) 'Brain potentials to native phoneme discrimination reveal the origin of individual differences in learning the sounds of a second language', *Proceedings of the National Academy of Sciences*, 105, 42: 16083–16088.

Diener, E., Wolsic, B. and Fujita, F. (1995) 'Physical attractiveness and subjective wellbeing', *Journal of Personality and Social Psychology*, 69: 120–129.

DiLalla, L. F. and Gottesman, I. I. (1989) 'Heterogeneity of causes for delinquency and criminality: lifetime perspectives', *Development and Psychopathology*, 1: 339–349.

Dinero, R., Conger, R. D., Shaver, P. R., Widaman, K. F. and Larsen-Rife, D. (2008) 'Influence of family of origin and adult romantic partners on romantic attachment security', *Journal of Family Psychology*, 22, 4: 622–632.

Dreyfus, H. and Dreyfus, S. (2005) 'Expertise in real world contexts', *Organization Studies*, 26, 5: 779–792.

Eastman, Q. (September 2010) 'Gene limits learning and memories in mice', posted by Emory: Woodruff Health Sciences Center. News release online (http://shared.web. emory.edu/whsc/news/releases/2010/09/gene-limits-learning-and-memory-in-mice. html).

Eggerichs, E. (2005) *Love and Respect*. Thomas Nelson.

Ehrenreich, B. (2010) *Smile or Die: How Positive Thinking Fooled America and the World*. Granta Books.

Elkind, D. (spring 2008) 'Can we play?' published on *Greater Good: the Science of a Meaningful Life* (greatergood.berkeley.edu).

Emmons, R. A. and McCullough, M. E. (2003) 'Counting blessings versus burdens: experimental studies of gratitude and subjective well-being in daily life', *Journal of Personality and Social Psychology*, 84: 377–389.

Eysenck, H. J. (2000) *Intelligence: A New Look*. Transaction Publishers.

Fabes, R. A., Eisenberg, N., Karbon, M., Troyer, D. and Switzer, G. (1994) 'The relations of children's emotion regulation to their vicarious emotional responses and comforting behaviours', *Child Development*, 65: 1678–1693.

Fey, T. (2012) *Bossypants*. Sphere.

Feynman, R. P. (1992) *The Character of Physical Law*. Penguin.

Fine, C. (2011) *Delusions of Gender: How Our Minds, Society and Neurosexism Create Difference*. W. W. Norton.

Forgas, J. P. (2011) 'She just doesn't look like a philosopher … ? Affective influences on the halo effect in impression formation', *European Journal of Social Psychology*, 41, 7: 812–817.

Forgas, J. P. and East, R. (2008) 'On being happy and gullible: mood effects on scepticism and the detection of deception', *Journal of Experimental Social Psychology*, 44: 1362–1367.

Fox, E. (1932) *The Wonder Child*. Harper.

Fredrickson, B. and Branigan, C. (2005) 'Positive emotions broaden the scope of attention and thought-action repertoires', *Cognition and Emotion*, 19, 3: 313–332.

Freud, S. (1991 edition) *On Sexuality: Three Essays on the Theory of Sexuality and Other Works*. Penguin.

Frick, W. B. (1984) 'Angyal's theory of the ambiguous gestalt: its implications for psychotherapy', *Psychotherapy: Theory, Research, Practice, Training*, 21, 2: 226–231.

Friedman, M. and Rosenman, R. (1959) 'Association of specific overt behaviour pattern with blood and cardiovascular findings'. *Journal of the American Medical Association*, 169: 1286–1296.

Frodi, A., Macaulay, J. and Thorne, P. R. (1977) 'Are women always less aggressive than men? A review of the experimental literature', *Psychological Bulletin*, 84: 634–660.

Fuller, M. (1845) *Woman in the Nineteenth Century*, Girlebooks.

Gabriel, M. T., Critelli, J. W. and Ee, J. S. (1994) 'Narcissistic illusions in self-evaluations of intelligence and attractiveness', *Journal of Personality*, 62: 143–155.

Gailliot, M., Baumeister, R., DeWall, C., Maner, J., Plant, E., Tice, D., Brewer, L. E. and Schmeichel, B. (2007) 'Self-control relies on glucose as a limited energy source: willpower is more than a metaphor', *Journal of Personality and Social Psychology*, 92, 2: 325–336.

Gergen, K. J. (2000) *The Saturated Self: Dilemmas of Identity in Contemporary Life*. Basic Books, 150.

Gerhardt, S. (2004) *Why Love Matters: How Affection Shapes a Baby's Brain*. Routledge.

Gerth, H. H. and Wright Mills, C. (1970) *From Max Weber: Essays in Sociology*. Routledge.

Gilbert, D. (2006) *Stumbling on Happiness*. Knopf.

Gilbert, P. (2010) *The Compassionate Mind*. Constable.

Gillan, A. (20 August 2005) 'Work until you drop: how the long-hours culture is killing us', *The Guardian*.

Gillan, C. M., Papmeyer, M., Morein-Zamir, S., Sahakian, B. J., Fineberg, N. A., Robbins, T. W. and de Wit, S. (2011) 'Disruption in the balance between goal-directed behavior and habit learning in obsessive-compulsive disorder', *American Journal of Psychiatry*, 168, 7: 718–726.

Ginsburg, K. R., Committee on Communications and Committee on Psychosocial Aspects of Child and Family Health (2007) 'The importance of play in promoting healthy child development and maintaining strong parent-child bonds', *Pediatrics*, 119, 1: 182–191.

Ginzburg, K., Solomon, Z. and Bleich, A. (2002) 'Repressive coping style, acute stress disorder, and post-traumatic stress disorder after myocardial infarction, *Psychosomatic Medicine* 64: 748–757.

Gladwell, M. (2009) *The Outliers: The Story of Success*. Penguin.

Gleik, J. (2004) *Isaac Newton*. Harper Perennial.

Goff, L. M. and Roediger, H. L. (1998) 'Imagination inflation for action events: repeated imaginings lead to illusory recollections', *Memory and Cognition* 26: 20–33.

Goleman, D. (1996) *Emotional Intelligence: Why It Can Matter More than IQ*. Bloomsbury.

Goleman, D. (2009) *Working with Emotional Intelligence*. Bloomsbury. Electronic version: available in paperback edition (1999).

Gottmann, J. (2007) *The Seven Principles for Making Marriage Work*. Orion.

Gould, A. (October 2010) 'Well-maintained chaos and signs you are too organized', published on: *Learn This: A productivity site for self-learning, career, leadership and life improvement tips* (http://learnthis.ca/2010/10/well-maintained-chaos-and-signs-you-are-too-organized).

Gray, J. (2012) *Men are from Mars, Women are from Venus*. Reissue. Harper Element, chapter 1: 14.

Gray, J. (2005) *Mars and Venus Together Forever: Relationship Skills for Lasting Love*. Harper Perennial.

Green, P. (December 2006) 'Saying yes to mess', *The New York Times*.

Greene, B. (2005) *The Elegant Universe: Superstrings, Hidden Dimensions and the Quest for the Ultimate Theory*. Vintage.

Grinder, J. and Bandler, R. (1976) *Patterns of the Hypnotic Techniques of Milton H. Erickson, M.D. Volume I.* Meta Publications.

Haidt, J. (2012) *The Righteous Mind: Why Good People Are Divided By Politics and Religion.* Allen Lane.

Hamilton, D. R. (2008) *How Your Mind Can Heal your Body.* Hay House UK, chapter 2.

Hansford, B. C. and Hattie, J. A. (1982) 'The relationship between self and achievement/performance measures', *Review of Educational Research*, 52: 123–142.

Hariri, A, Bookheimer, S. Y. and Mazziotta, J. (2000) 'A neural network for modulating the emotional response to faces', *Neuroreport*, 11, 1: 43–48.

Harris, J. R. (1999) *The Nurture Assumption.* Bloomsbury Publishing PLC.

Harris, J. R. (2010) *No Two Alike: Human Nature and Human Individuality.* W. W. Norton & Co.

Harris, T. A. (1995) *I'm OK, You're OK.* Arrow.

Harter, S. (1990) 'Identity and self development', in S. S. Feldman and G. R. Elliott (eds) *At the Threshold: The Developing Adolescent.* Harvard University Press 352–387.

Harter, S. (1999) *The Construction of the Self: A Developmental Perspective.* Guilford Press, New York.

Hartman, D. (January 2008) 'Life's lie: you can be anything you want to be', published online: *Blogcritics* (http://blogcritics.org/culture/article/lifes-lie-you-can-be-anything).

Hatfield E., Rapson, R. L. and Yen-Chi, L. L. (2009) 'Primitive emotional contagion: recent research,' in J. Decety and W. Ickes (eds) *The Social Neuroscience of Empathy.* MIT Press.

Haukkala, A., Konttinen, H., Laatikainen, T., Kawachi, I. and Uutela, A. (2010) 'Hostility, anger control, and anger expression as predictors of cardiovascular disease', *Psychosomatic Medicine*, 72, 6: 556–562.

Hay, L. (1984) *Heal Your Body.* Hay House.

Hazan, C. and Shaver, P. R. (1987) 'Romantic love conceptualized as an attachment process', *Journal of Personality and Social Psychology*, 52, 3: 511–524.

Hecht, J. M. (2008) *The Happiness Myth: Why What We Think is Right is Wrong.* Harper Collins.

Heisenberg, W. (2003). Translators C. Eckart and F. C. Hoyt *The Physical Principles of the Quantum Theory.* Dover Publications Inc.

Herodotus, C. Dewald (ed.) and R. Waterfield (trans) (2008) *The Histories.* Oxford World's Classics.

Hirschhorn, L. (1984) *Beyond Mechanization: Work and Technology in a Post-Industrial Age.* MIT Press.

Hirsh-Pasek, K., Golinkoff R. M. and Eyer, D. E. (2003) *Einstein never used flash cards: how our children really learn – and why they need to play more and memorize less.* Rodale.

Hochschild, A. (1983) *The Managed Heart: Commercialization of Human Feeling.* University of California Press, Berkeley.

Hofmann, S. G. and Smits, J. A. (2008) 'Cognitive-behavioural therapy for adult anxiety disorders: analysis of randomized placebo-controlled trials', *Journal of Clinical Psychiatry* 69, 4: 621–632.

Hölzela, B. K., Carmodyc, J., Vangela, M., Congletona, C., Yerramsettia, S. M., Garda, T. and Lazar, S. W. (2010) 'Mindfulness practice leads to increases in regional brain gray matter density', *Psychiatry Research: Neuroimaging*, 191: 36–43.

Horney, K. (1991) *Neurosis and Human Growth: The Struggle Towards Self-realisation* (new edition). W. W. Norton and Co.

Huang, C. (2010) 'Mean-level change in self-esteem from childhood through adulthood: meta-analysis of longitudinal studies', *Review of General Psychology*, 14, 3: 251–260.

Huh, D., Tristan, J., Wade, E. and Stice, E. (2006) 'Does problem behavior elicit poor parenting? A prospective study of adolescent girls', *Journal of Adolescent Research*, 21, 2: 185–204.

Hyde, J. S. (2005) 'The gender similarities hypothesis', *American Psychologist*, 60: 581–592.

Isaacson, W. (13 January 1997) 'The Gates operating system', *Time Magazine*.

Isaacson, W. (2011) *Steve Jobs: The Exclusive Biography*. Little, Brown.

Isen, A. (1985) 'The influence of positive affect on acceptable level of risk: the person with a large canoe has a large worry', *Organizational Behavior and Human Decision Processes*, 39, 2: 145–154.

Jahn, R. G. and Dunne, B. J. (2005) 'The PEAR proposition', *Journal of Scientific Exploration*, 19, 2: 195–245.

James, L. (30 April 2006) 'Getting your needs met must be a high priority' posted on: *Celebrate Love* (www.celebratelove.com/blog.htm).

James, O. (2007) *They F*** You Up: How To Survive Family Life*. Bloomsbury, chapter 3.

James, U. (2008) *You Can Think Yourself Thin*. Century.

Jang, S. J. and Thornberry, T. P. (1998) 'Self-esteem, delinquent peers and delinquency: a test of the self-enhancement hypothesis', *American Sociological Review*, 63: 586–598.

Johnson, E. J. and Tversky, A. (1983) 'Affect, generalization, and the perception of risk', *Journal of Personality and Social Psychology*, 45, 1: 20–31.

Jong, E. (1994) *Fear of Flying*. Vintage.

Jung, C. G. (1991 edition) *The Archetypes and the Collective Unconscious*. Collected works of C. G. Jung. Routledge.

Kagan, J. (1997) *Galen's Prophecy:Temperament in Human Nature*. Perseus.

Kermis, M. H., Grannemann, B. D. and Barclay, L. C. (1989) 'Stability and level of self-esteem as predictors of anger arousal and hostility', *Journal of Personality and Social Psychology*, 56: 1013–1022.

Kirk, A. (2002) 'The effect of divorce on young adults' relationship competence', *Journal of Divorce and Remarriage*, 38, 1–2: 61–89.

Klein, M. (1997) *The Psycho-Analysis of Children*. Vintage.

Klevmarken, A. and Stafford, F. (1999) 'Measuring investment in young children with time diaries', in J. P. Smith and R. J. Willis (eds) *Wealth, Work and Health. Innovations in Measurement in Social Sciences*. University of Michigan Press.

Kramer, P. D. (17 July 2008) 'Debunking CBT: just how effective is cognitive behavioral therapy?', posted on: *Psychology Today* (www.psychologytoday.com/blog/in-practice/200807/debunking-cbt).

Kring, A. and Gordon, A. (1998) 'Sex differences in emotion: expression, experience and physiology', *Journal of Personality and Social Psychology*, 74: 686–703.

Lambert, M. J. (1992) 'Implications of outcome research for psychotherapy integration', in J. C. Norcross and M. R. Goldstein (eds) *Handbook of Psychotherapy Integration*. Basic Books, 94–129.

Langer, E. (1975) 'The illusion of control', *Journal of Personality and Social Psychology*, 32: 311–328.

Lashinsky, A. (2012) *Inside Apple: The Secrets Behind the Past and Future Success of Steve Job's Iconic Brand*. John Murray.

Lazarus, R. S. (1966) *Psychological Stress and The Coping Process*. McGraw-Hill.

Le Carré, J. (1999) *The Secret Pilgrim*. Sceptre.

Lester, D. (1992) 'The disunity of the self: a systems theory of personality', *Personality and Individual Differences*, 8: 947–948.

Leu J., Wang, J. and Koo, K. (2011) 'Are positive emotions just as "positive" across cultures?' *Emotion*, 11: 4, 994–999.

Levine, A. and Heller, R. (2011) *Attached: Identify Your Attachment Style and Find Your Perfect Match*. Rodale.

Lewis, M. B. and Bowler, P. J. (2009) 'Botulinum toxin cosmetic therapy correlates with a more positive mood', *Journal of Cosmetic Dermatology*, 8: 24–26.

Libertus, M., Feigenson, L. and Halberda, J. (2011) 'Preschool acuity of the approximate number system correlates with school math ability', *Developmental Science*, 14, 6: 1292–1300.

Libet, B., Gleason, C. A., Wright, E. W and Pearl, D. K. (1983) 'Time of conscious intention to act in relation to onset of cerebral activity (readiness-potential). The unconscious initiation of a freely voluntary act', *Brain*, 106: 623–642.

Linder, D. 'The witchcraft trials in Salem: a commentary'. University of Missouri-Kansas City Law School website (http://law2.umkc.edu/faculty/projects/trials/salem/SAL_ACCT.HTM).

Liu, J. E., Smeesters, D. and Trampe, D. (in press) 'Effects of messiness on preferences for simplicity', *Journal of Consumer Research*.

Lodi-Smith, J., Jackson, J., Bogg, T., Walton, K., Wood, D., Harms, T. and Roberts, B. W. (2010) 'Mechanisms of health: education and health-related behaviours partially mediate the relationship between conscientiousness and self-reported physical health', *Psychology and Health*, 25, 3: 305–319.

Loftus, E. F. and Palmer, J. C. (1974) 'Reconstruction of automobile destruction: an example of the interaction between language and memory', *Journal of Verbal Learning and Verbal Behavior*, 13: 585–589.

Lohr, J. M. (2006) 'The pseudopsychology of venting in the treatment of anger: implications and alternatives for mental health practice', in T. A. Cavell and K. T. Malcolm (eds) *Anger, Aggression, and Interventions for Interpersonal Violence*. Routledge.

Lowell, P. (1906) *Mars and its Canals*. Macmillan.

Lu, L. (2001) 'Understanding happiness: a look into Chinese folk psychology', *Journal of Happiness Studies*, 2: 407–432.

Lyubomirsky, S. (2010) *The How of Happiness: A Practical Guide to Getting the Life You Want*. Piatkus.

Lyubomirsky, S. and Lepper, H. S. (1999) 'A measure of subjective happiness: preliminary reliability and construct validation', *Social Indicators Research*, 46: 137–155.

Machiavelli, N. (2003 edition) *The Prince*. Longman, chapter 15.

Maguire, E. (2000) 'Navigation-related structural change in the hippocampi of taxi drivers', *Proceedings of the National Academy of Sciences*, 97, 8: 4398–4403.

Malkiel, B. G. (1997) *A Random Walk Down Wall Street*. W. W. Norton & Co.

Martin, D. J., Abramson, L. Y. and Alloy, L. B. (1984) 'Illusion of control for self and others in depressed and non-depressed college students', *Journal of Personality and Social Psychology*, 46: 126–136.

Maslach, C., Jackson, S. E. and Leiter, M. P. (1997) In C. P. Zalaquett and R. J. Wood (eds) *Evaluating Stress: A Book of Resources*. The Scarecrow Press Inc., 191–218.

Maslow, A. (2011) *Toward a Psychology of Being*. Wilder Publications Ltd.

Masters, W. H. and Johnson, V. E. (1966) *Human Sexual Response*. Bantam Books.

Matthews, G., Roberts, R. D. and Zidner, M. (2004) *Emotional Intelligence: Science and Myth*. MIT Press.

Mauss, I. B., Savino, N. S., Anderson, C. L., Weisbuch, M., Tamir, M. and Laudenslager, M. L. (2011) 'The pursuit of happiness can be lonely', *Emotion* [epub ahead of print] PMID: 21910542.

Mazzoni, G., Scoboria, A. and Harvey, L. (2010) 'Nonbelieved memories', *Psychological Science*, 21, 9: 1334–1340.

McKenna, P. (2007) *I Can Make You Thin*. Bantam Press.

McQueen, D. (2009) 'NICE depression guidelines: are patients losing out?' posted on: *New Associations: News, Analysis, Opinion for the Psychoanalytic Community*. British Psychoanalytic Council (www.psychoanalytic-council.org/main/index. php?page=15347).

Mencken, H. L. (16 November 1917) 'The divine afflatus' in *New York Evening Mail*.

Milgram, S. (1963) 'Behavioural study of obedience', *Journal of Abnormal and Social Psychology*, 67, 4: 371–378.

Miller, E. M. (January 1999) Review of 'Stranger in the nest' published on *Stalking the Wild Taboo* (www.lrainc.com/swtaboo/stalkers/em_strangers.html).

Mischel, W. (1968) *Personality and Assessment*. Wiley.

Morrison, I., Lloyd, D., di Pellegrino, G. and Roberts, N. (2004) 'Vicarious responses to pain in anterior cingulate cortex: is empathy a multisensory issue?', *Cognitive and Affective Behavioral Neuroscience*, 4: 270–278.

Murphy, K. R. (2006) *A Critique of Emotional Intelligence: What are the Problems and How Can They be Fixed?* Psychology Press.

Murray, S. L., Griffin, D. W., Derrick, J. L., Harris, B., Aloni, M. and Leder, S. (2011) 'Tempting fate or inviting happiness? Unrealistic idealization prevents the decline of marital satisfaction' *Psychological Science*, 22, 5: 619–626.

Nash, M. (1987) 'What, if anything, is regressed about hypnotic age regression?', *Psychological Bulletin*, 102, 1: 42–52.

Nash, M. R., Drake, S. D., Wiley, S., Khalsa, S. and Lynn, S. J. (1986) 'The accuracy of recall by hypnotically age regressed subjects', *Journal of Abnormal Psychology*, 95: 298–300.

Nietzsche, F., Tanner, M. and Hollingdale R. J. (1990) *Twilight of Idols and Anti-Christ*. Penguin Classics.

Nilsson, T. and Edvinsson, L. (2000) 'Neuropeptide Y stimulates DNA synthesis in human vascular smooth muscle cells through neuropeptide Y Y1 receptors' in the *Canadian Journal of Physiology and Pharmacology* 78, 3, 256–9.

Norcross, J. C. (ed.) (2011) *Psychotherapy Relationships that Work* (2nd edition). OUP.

Nozick, R. (1977) *Anarchy, State and Utopia*. Basic Books.

Oishi, S., Diener, E. and Lucas, R. E. (2007) 'The optimum level of well-being: can people be too happy?', *Perspectives on Psychological Science*, 2, 4: 346–360.

Olweus, D. (1993) *Bullying at school: what we know and what we can do*. Blackwell.

Oord, T. J. (2010) *The Nature of Love: A Theology*. Chalice Press.

Ordóñez, L. D., Schweitzer, M. E., Galinsky, A. D. and Bazerman, M. H. (2009) 'Goals gone wild: the systematic effects of over-prescribing goal setting', Harvard Business School Working Paper, No. 09–083.

Paries, R. (undated) 'Leave your needs at the door', posted on E-nterests. Com. (www.e-nterests.com/familyhtml/leaveyourneeds.php).

Pease, A. and Pease, B. (2010) *The Mating Game: Why Men Want Sex and Women Need Love*. Orion.

Pellegrini, A. (2009) *The Role of Play in Human Development*. OUP, US.

Pentland, A. (2010) 'To signal is human. Real-time data-mining unmasks the power of imitation, kith and charisma in our face-to-face social networks', *American Scientist*, 98: 204–211.

Peter, L. J. and Hull, R. (1994) *The Peter Principle: Why Things Always Go Wrong*. Souvenir Press Ltd.

Pietromonaco, P. R. and Barrett, L. F. (2000) 'The internal working models concept: what do we really know about the self in relation to others?', *Review of General Psychology*, 4: 155–175.

Pittler, M. H. and Ernst, E. (2005) 'Complementary therapies for reducing body weight: a systematic review', *International Journal of Obesity*, 29: 1030–1038.

Poincaré, H. (2001) *The Value of Science. Essential Writings of Henri Poincaré*. Random House, 220 (cited in Andreasen, 2010).

Pottebaum, S. M., Keith, T. Z. and Ehly, S. W. (1986) 'Is there a causal relation between self-concept and academic achievement?', *Journal of Educational Research*, 79: 140–144.

Quiller-Couch, A. T. (ed.) (1919) *The Oxford Book of English Verse: 1250–1900*. Clarendon.

Ramírez-Esparza, N., Gosling, S. D., Benet-Martínez, V., Potter, J. P. and Pennebaker, J. W. (2004) 'Do bilinguals have two personalities? A special case of cultural frame switching', *Journal of Research in Personality*, 40: 99–120.

Rand, A. (2007) *Atlas Shrugged*. Penguin Classics.

Ranganathan, V. K., Siemionow, V., Liu, J. Z., Sahgal, V. and Yue, G. H. (2004) 'From mental power to muscle power: gaining strength by using the mind', *Neuropsychologia*, 42: 944–956.

Reid, T. W., Murphy, C. J., Iwahasi, C. K. and Mannis, M. J. (1993) 'Stimulation of epithelial cell growth by the neuropeptide substance P.' *Journal of Cellular Biochemistry* 52, 4, 476–85.

Robbins, A. (2001) *Awaken the Giant Within: How to Take Immediate Control of Your Mental, Emotional, Physical and Financial Life*. Pocket Books.

Robbins, A. (2001) *Unlimited Power: The New Science of Personal Achievement*. Pocket Books.

Rogers, C. R. (2004) *On Becoming a Person: A Therapist's View of Psychotherapy*. Constable.

Rogers, D. (1990) *Weather Prediction Using a Genetic Memory*. Research Institute for Advanced Computer Science. NASA Ames Research Centre. Technical Report 90.6.

Roloff, M. E (1981) *Interpersonal Communication: The Social Exchange Approach*. Sage.

Rosen, M. and Oxenbury, H. (1993) *We're Going on a Bear Hunt*. Walker Books Ltd.

Rosenthal, R. and Jacobson, L. (1968) *Pygmalion in the Classroom: Teacher Expectation and Pupil's Intellectual Development*. Holt, Rinehart and Winston.

Roth, A., Fonagy, P., Parry, G., Target, M. and Woods, R. (eds) (2006) *What Works for Whom? A Critical Review of Psychotherapy Research*, 2nd edition. Guilford Press.

Rothenberg, A. (1996) 'The Janusian process in scientific creativity', *Creativity Research Journal*, 9: 2–3; 207–231.

Rotter, J. B. (1975) 'Some problems and misconceptions related to the construct of internal versus external control of reinforcement', *Journal of Consulting and Clinical Psychology*, 43: 56–67.

Rosenkranz, M. A., Jackson, D. C., Dalton, K. M., Dolski, I., Ryff, C. D., Singer, B. H., Muller, D., Kalin, N. H. and Davidson, R. J. (2003) 'Affective style and *in vivo* immune response: neurobehavioral mechanisms', *Proceedings of the National Academy of Sciences*, 100: 1148–1152.

Rowan, J. (1990) *Subpersonalities: The People Inside Us*. Routledge.

Ruback, R. B. (1987) 'Deserted (and non-deserted) aisles: territorial intrusion can produce persistence, not flight', *Social Psychology Quarterly*, 50: 270–276.

Ruback, R. B. and Juieng, D. (1997) 'Territorial defense in parking lots: retaliation against waiting drivers', *Journal of Applied Social Psychology*, 27, 9: 821–834.

Sacks, O. (2008) *Musicophilia: Tales of Music and The Brain*. Picador.

Saferstein, J., Neimeyer, G. J. and Hagans, C. (2005) 'Attachment as a predictor of friendship qualities in college youth', *Social Behaviour and Personality*, 33, 8: 767–776.

Salomons, T. V., Coan, J. A., Hunt, S. M., Backonja, M. M. and Davidson, R. J. (2008) 'Voluntary facial displays of pain increase suffering in response to nociceptive stimulation', *Journal of Pain*, 9, 5: 443–448.

Salovey, P. and Mayer, J. D. (1990) 'Emotional intelligence', *Imagination, Cognition, and Personality*, 9: 185–211.

Savin-Williams, R. C. and Berndt, T. J. (1990) 'Friendship and peer relations', in S. S. Feldman and G. R. Elliott (eds) *At the Threshold: The Developing Adolescent*. Harvard University Press, 277–307.

Scarr, S. (1992) 'Developmental theories for the 1990s: development and individual differences', *Child Development*, 63: 1–19.

Schooler, J. W., Ariely, D. and Loewenstein, G. (2003) 'The pursuit and assessment of happiness may be self-defeating', in I. Brocas and J. D. Carillo (eds) *The Psychology of Economic Decisions*. OUP.

Seery, M., Silver, R. C., Holman, E. A., Ence, W. A. and Thai, Q. C. (2008) 'Expressing thoughts and feelings following a collective trauma: immediate responses to 9/11 predict negative outcomes in a national sample', *Journal of Consulting and Clinical Psychology*, 76, 4: 657–667.

Segal, Z. V., Williams, J. M. and Teasdale, J. D. (2002) *Mindfulness-based Cognitive Therapy for Depression*. Guilford Press.

Seligman, M. E. P. (2003) *Authentic Happiness: Using the New Positive Psychology to Realise your Potential for Lasting Fulfilment*. Nicholas Brealey Publishing.

Shakespeare, W., Holland, P. (ed.) (2008) *A Midsummer Night's Dream*. Oxford Paperbacks.

Sharot, T., Korn, C. W. and Dolan, R. J. (2011) 'How unrealistic optimism is maintained in the face of reality', *Nature Neuroscience*, 14: 1475–1479.

Shiv, B. and Fedorikhin, A. (1999) 'Heart and mind in conflict: the interplay of affect and cognition in consumer decision making,' *Journal of Consumer Research*, 26: 278–292.

Simons, D. J. and Chabris, C. F. (1999) 'Gorillas in our midst: sustained inattentional blindness for dynamic events', *Perception*, 28: 1059–1074.

Smith, B. S. (2001) *The Ambiguity of Play*. Harvard University Press.

Smith, C. (8 November 1999) 'Messy desk = ordered mind, expert says', *Seattle Post-Intelligencer*.

Smith, E. (2012) *Luck: What it Means and Why it Matters*. Bloomsbury plc.

Smith, M. J. (1975) *When I Say No I Feel Guilty: How to Cope, Using the Skills of Systematic Assertive Therapy*. Bantam.

Snyder, M., Tanke, E. D., Berscheid, E. (1977) 'Social perception and interpersonal behaviour: on the self-fulfilling nature of social stereotypes', *Journal of Personality and Social Psychology*, 35, 9: 656–666.

Solomon, G. F., Amkraut, A. A. and Kasper, P. (1974) 'Immunity, emotions and stress', *Psychotherapy and Psychosomatics*, 23: 209–217.

Spencer, L. M. and Spencer, S. M. (1993) *Competence at Work: Models for Superior Performance*. John Wiley and Sons.

Staib, A. R. and Logan, D. R. (1977) 'Hypnotic stimulation of breast growth', *The American Journal of Clinical Hypnosis*, 4: 201–208.

Steele, J., Waters, E., Crowell, J. and Treboux, D. (1998) 'Self-report measures of attachment: secure bonds to other attachment measures and attachment theory?', paper presented at the biennial meeting of the International Society for the Study of Personal Relationships, Saratoga Springs, NY.

Stephens, M. (23 August 1992) quoting Edward Sampson, 'To thine own selves be true', *Los Angeles Time Magazine*.

Stewart-Mill, J. (1960) *Autobiography of John Stewart-Mill*. Columbia University Press.

Strauss, D. (2001) *Percival Lowell: The Culture and Science of a Boston Brahmin*. Harvard University Press.

Struebe, W. (2008) *Dieting, Overweight and Obesity: Self-Regulation in a Food-Rich Environment*. American Psychological Association.

Sutin, A. R., Scuteri, A., Lakatta, E. G., Tarasov, K. V., Ferrucci, L., Costa, P. T., Schlessinger, D., Uda, M. and Terracciano, A. (2010) 'Trait antagonism and the progression of arterial thickening: women with antagonistic traits have similar carotid arterial thickness as men', *Hypertension*, 56: 617–622.

Sutton-Smith, B. (2001) *The Ambiguity of Play*. Harvard University Press.

Tan, H. B. and Forgas, J. P. (2010) 'When happiness makes us selfish, but sadness makes us fair: affective influences on interpersonal strategies in the dictator game', *Journal of Experimental Social Psychology*, 46, 3: 571–576.

Taylor, C. (1991) *The Inner Child Workbook*. Tarcher.

Tehrani, J. A. and Mednick, S. A. (December 2000) 'Genetic factors and criminal behaviour', *Federal Probation*, 24–27.

Tharenou, P. (1979) 'Employee self-esteem: a review of the literature', *Journal of Vocational Behaviour*, 15: 316–346.

Thomas, A., Chess, S. and Birch, H. G. (1968) *Temperament and Behavior Disorders in Children*. New York University Press.

Thomas, B. (1994) *Walt Disney*. Little, Brown & Company.

Tipping, C. (2010) *Radical Forgiveness: A Revolutionary Five Stage Process*. Sounds True Inc., 339.

Tucker, R. (1978) *The Marx-Engels Reader*. Norton.

Turner, V. (1975) *Dramas, Fields, and Metaphors: Symbolic Action in Human Society*. Cornell University Press.

Twenge, J. M. (2007) *Generation Me: Why Today's Youth Are More Confident, Assertive, Entitled – And More Miserable Than Ever Before*. Free Press.

Twenge, J. M. and Campbell, W. K. (2009) *The Narcissism Epidemic. Living in the Age of Entitlement*. Free Press.

Ugel, E. (2011) *'I'm With Fatty: Losing Fifty Pounds in Fifty Miserable Weeks*. Weinstein Books.

Van Rooy, D. L. and Viswesvaran, C. (2004) 'Emotional intelligence: a meta-analytic investigation of predictive validity and nomological net', *Journal of Vocational Behavior*, 65: 71–95.

Von Helverson, B., Wilke, A., Johnson, T., Schmid, G. and Klapp, B. (2011) 'Performance benefits of depression: sequential decision making in a healthy sample and a clinically depressed sample', *Journal of Abnormal Psychology*, 120, 4: 962–968.

Wachs, K. M. (2002) *Relationships for Dummies*. John Wiley & Sons.

Walters, G. D. (1995) 'The psychological inventory of criminal thinking styles', *Criminal Justice and Behavior*, 22, 3: 307–325.

Wampold, B. (2001) *The Great Psychotherapy Debate: Models, Methods and Findings*. Erlbaum.

Waters, E., Merrick, S., Treboux, D., Crowell, J. and Albersheim, L. (2000) 'Attachment security in infancy and early adulthood: a twenty-year longitudinal study', *Child Development*, 3: 684–689.

Weber, M. (2001) *The Protestant Ethic and the Spirit of Capitalism*. Routledge.

Wegner, D. M. (1994) 'Ironic processes of mental control', *Psychological Review*, 101, 1: 34–52.

Weisz, C. and Wood, L. F. (2005) 'Social identity support and friendship outcomes: a longitudinal study predicting who will be friends and best friends four years later', *Journal of Personal and Social Relationships*, 22: 416–432.

Whitman, W. (1995) *The Complete Poems of Walt Whitman*. Wordsworth Poetry Editions Ltd.

Whitson, J. A and Galinsky, A. D. (2008) 'Lacking control increases illusory pattern perception', *Science*, 322, 5898: 115–117.

Wicker, B., Keysers, C., Plailly, J., Royet, J. P., Gallese, V. and Rizzolatti, G. (2003) 'Both of us disgusted in my insula: the common neural basis of seeing and feeling disgust', *Neuron*, 40: 655–664.

Willard, R. D. (1977) 'Breast enlargement through visual imagery and hypnosis', *The American Journal of Clinical Hypnosis*, 19, 4: 195–200.

Williams, J. E. (1974) 'Stimulation of breast growth by hypnosis', *Journal of Sex Research*, 10: 316.

Williamson, M. (1996) *A Return to Love: Reflections on the Principles of a 'Course in Miracles'*. Thorsons.

Willis, A. (29 January 2012) 'Inside Apple: one of the most secretive organisations in the world', *The Times*.

Wood, J. V., Perunovic, W. Q. E. and Lee, J. W. (2009) 'Positive self-statements: power for some, peril for others', *Psychological Science*, 20: 860–866.

Yapko, M. (1994) *Suggestions of Abuse: True and False memories of Childhood Sexual Trauma*. Simon and Schuster.

Yochelson, S. and Samenow, S. E. (1976) *The Criminal Personality, Volume I: A Profile for Change*. Jason Aronson, New York.

Zaidi, Z. F. (2010) 'Gender differences in human brain: a review', *The Open Anatomy Journal*, 2: 37–55.

Zaraska, M. (2 April 2012) 'Too much happiness can make you unhappy studies show', *The Washington Post*.

Zimbardo, P. G. (1971) 'The power and pathology of imprisonment', *Congressional Record* (Serial No. 15, 25 October 1971). Hearings before Subcommittee No. 3, of the Committee on the Judiciary, House of Representatives, Ninety-Second Congress, *First Session on Corrections, Part II, Prisons, Prison Reform and Prisoners' Rights: California*. Government Printing Office, Washington, DC: US.